The Form and Function of the Tricolon
in the Psalms of Ascents

The Form and Function of the Tricolon in the Psalms of Ascents

Introducing a New Paradigm for
Hebrew Poetic Line-Form

SIMON P. STOCKS

Foreword by David G. Firth

PICKWICK *Publications* · Eugene, Oregon

THE FORM AND FUNCTION OF THE TRICOLON
IN THE PSALMS OF ASCENTS
Introducing a New Paradigm for Hebrew Poetic Line-Form

Pickwick Publications
An Imprint of Wipf and Stock Publishers
199 W. 8th Av.e, Suite 3
Eugene, OR 97401

www.wipfandstock.com

ISBN 13: 978-1-61097-808-8

Cataloging-in-Publication data:

Stocks, Simon P.

    The Form and Function of the Tricolon in the Psalms of Ascents: Introducing a New Paradigm for Hebrew Poetic Line-Form / Simon P. Stocks, with a foreword by David G. Firth.

    xvi + 274 p. ; 23 cm. Includes bibliographical references and index.

    ISBN 13: 978-1-61097-808-8

    1. Hebrew poetry, Biblical. 2. Hebrew poetry, Biblical—History and criticism. 3. Hebrew language, Biblical. 4. Bible. O.T. Psalms—Criticism, interpretation, etc. I. Firth, David G. II. Title.

BS1430.52 S777 2012

Manufactured in the U.S.A.

לְאָבִי

Norman Stocks

1925–2005

Contents

Tables

Foreword

THE MEANS BY WHICH we interpret the Old Testament's poetry continues to be a lively debate. This is true of both the aesthetic level at which poetry works and also, of particular importance here, the formal processes by which it produces meaning. Although introductory textbooks sometimes give the impression that the issues of parallelism and the structure of the colon are largely resolved, this is actually a field where there is considerable discussion. Lowth did not, after all, say all that was needed about this important topic, and neither have some of the more recent comprehensive studies. In particular, although scholars routinely discuss a "bicolon" or "tricolon"—and sometimes even a "monocolon"— clear definition of these remains elusive. This is particularly true of the tricolon, something that quickly becomes apparent from a comparison of a few commentaries or translations of the Psalms where poetic lines are actually represented in a variety of forms. We use the terminology, but clear processes for identifying a tricolon have remained elusive.

In light of this discussion I am pleased to commend this careful work to you. Simon Stocks here brings methodological rigour and clarity to this complex area as he provides us with a means of understanding the tricolon while at the same time opening up new vistas on how the poetic line can be formed and function. Of course, such a study can remain simply at the level of theory, but a real strength of Simon Stocks' work is the way he integrates his analysis with the Songs of the Ascents. This means that both his critique of those who have gone before him and also the developing of his own positive contribution to the field can be seen in the light of these sample psalms. We are thus able to see the weaknesses of previous analyses as they apply to specific texts and also how closer attention to the poetic forms provides us with fresh insights into these poems. There is more work to be done, but this clear and insightful study provides us with a way forward in understanding this important area of biblical poetics.

David G. Firth
St John's College, Nottingham, UK

Acknowledgments

THIS BOOK CONSISTS OF my PhD thesis, the research for which was carried out through Cliff College between 2007 and 2010. I was superbly guided and supported in that process by David Firth: he was an excellent supervisor.

I am very grateful to Nick Lunn, and a significant number of other biblical scholars, many met only briefly at conferences, who offered encouragement, inspiration, and practical assistance along the way.

My doctoral studies were funded by the Arts and Humanities Research Council doctoral programme. I am also grateful to several other individuals and institutions who supplemented that support.

I hope that this work will make a significant, if modest, contribution to the field of Biblical Hebrew poetics.

Simon P. Stocks

Abbreviations

PUBLICATIONS, SERIES, MANUSCRIPTS AND GENERAL

4QPs^b	Psalms scroll from Qumran Cave 4, represented in DJD XVI
4QPs^e	Psalms scroll from Qumran Cave 4, represented in DJD XVI
11QPs^a	Psalms scroll from Qumran Cave 11, represented in DJD IV
AB	Anchor Bible
AER	*American Ecclesiastical Review*
AJSL	*The American Journal of Semitic Languages and Literatures*
AOAT	Alter Orient und altes Testament
ASV	American Standard Version
ArOr	*Archiv orientální*
AV	Authorised Version
BCOT	Baker Commentary on the Old Testament
BDB	Francis Brown, S. R. Driver, and Charles A. Briggs. *Hebrew and English Lexicon of the Old Testament.* Oxford: Clarendon, 1907
BBR	*Bulletin for Biblical Research*
BHS	*Biblia Hebraica Stuttgartensia*
Bib	*Biblica*
BN	*Biblische Notizen*
BThSt	Biblisch-Theologische Studien
BZAW	Beihefte zur Zeitschrift für die alttestamentliche Wissenschaft
CBQ	*Catholic Biblical Quarterly*

CBQMS	Catholic Biblical Quarterly Monograph Series
CE	Common Era
cf.	*confer*, compare with
CV	*Communio viatorum*
DJD	Discoveries in the Judaean Desert
EBC	The Expositor's Bible Commentary
ET	*Expository Times*
ETL	*Ephemerides theologicae lovanienses*
fn	footnote
FOTL	Forms of the Old Testament Literature
HB	Hebrew Bible
HS	*Hebrew Studies*
HThKAT	Herders Theologischer Kommentar zum Alten Testament
HvTSt	*Hervormde teologiese studies*
ICC	International Critical Commentary
Int	*Interpretation*
JBL	*Journal of Biblical Literature*
JETS	*Journal of the Evangelical Theological Society*
JJS	*Journal of Jewish Studies*
JNSL	*Journal of Northwest Semitic Languages*
JQRSup	Jewish Quarterly Review Supplement
JSOT	*Journal for the Study of the Old Testament*
JSOTSup	Journal for the Study of the Old Testament Supplement Series
JSS	*Journal of Semitic Studies*
JTS	*Journal of Theological Studies*
JTT	*Journal of Translation and Textlinguistics*
LXX	Septuagint as represented by Göttingen edition
LXX^A	Codex Alexandrinus
LXX^א	Codex Sinaiticus
ms(s)	manuscript(s)
MT	Masoretic text as represented by BHS
MA	Aleppo Codex
ML	Codex Leningradensis

NASB	New American Standard Bible
NCB	New Century Bible
NEB	New English Bible
NIV	New International Version
NRSV	New Revised Standard Version
OBO	Orbis biblicus et orientalis
OTE	*Old Testament Essays*
PTMS	Pittsburgh Theological Monograph Series
RSV	Revised Standard Version
SBLDS	Society of Biblical Literature Disseration Series
SBLMasS	Society of Biblical Literature Masoretic Studies
SBLMS	Society of Biblical Literature Monograph Series
SBS	Stuttgarter Bibelstudien
Sem	*Semitica*
SIL	Summer Institute of Linguistics (Wycliffe Bible Translators)
STDJ	Studies on the Texts of the Desert of Judah
TZ	*Theologische Zeitschrift*
v.	verse
vv.	verses
VT	*Vetus Testamentum*
VTSup	Vetus Testamentum Supplement Series
WBC	Word Biblical Commentary
WUNT	Wissenschaftliche Untersuchungen zum Neuen Testament
YCS	Yale Classical Studies
ZAW	*Zeitschrift für die alttestamentliche Wissenschaft*

GRAMMATICAL NOMENCLATURE

1	first person
2	second person
3	third person
A	definite article
Aj	adjective
c.	common gender

CC	copulative clause
Cj	conjunction
Cp	copula
D	adverb
DP	adverbial phrase
do	direct object
f.	feminine
io	indirect object
m.	masculine
N	noun
Ng	negative particle
NP	noun phrase
p.	plural
P	particle (including prepositions)
Pn	pronoun
R	relative pronoun
s.	singular
S	sentence
S^i	incomplete sentence
su	subject
V	verb
V-o	verb with pronominal object suffix
VC	verbal clause
(...)	in the phrase structure diagrams, elided constituents are bracketed; where the subject of a clause is elided and its person, number and gender are indicated by the verb inflection, the term V(su) or Cp(su) is used.

1

Introduction

Background

A S SOON AS BIBLICAL Hebrew poetry is encountered, certain characteristics are apparent: words are used sparingly, creating a terse and
semantically dense text; the text is divided into short cola, each typically
a three-word phrase; and these cola interrelate, both syntactically and
semantically.[1] The cola normally appear in matching pairs, and Robert
Lowth used the term "parallelism" to describe this phenomenon. His
insight was not a new one, as the colometry of the psalms, and other
poetic texts, was clearly attested in the presentation of many ancient
manuscripts.[2] The recognition of "parallelism" gives rise to a number of
questions about its nature: What governs the formation of cola? Exactly
how do the cola relate to each other? What governs the arrangement of
cola? Is there absolute regularity in the structure or is it flexible? And
upon what principle is regularity based: metre, syntax, or a non-linguis-
tic feature? The answers to these questions are varied, and considerable
effort has been expended on developing theories of poetic structure and
in particular of "parallelism."

To the uninitiated reader, it soon becomes apparent that the poetry does not exhibit absolute regularity. The majority of lines of the text

1. Variant terminology is a pitfall of the field; see Cloete, "Colometry," 15–17. A
consistent terminology has been established for the current study and this is defined in
the Glossary. The definitions incorporate reference to variant terms used by some theorists in order to help to correlate between them. Terms will be used as they are defined
in the Glossary, except in the case of direct quotations from other works, wherein the
original terminology of that work will be reproduced.

2. See the overview in Kugel, *Idea*, 119–27; see further the section "Source manuscripts" on pp. 11–17.

consist of two short cola, but there are exceptions. Some lines seem to be significantly longer than others, consisting of three cola and designated tricola. Such lines include three phrases and two caesurae, and stand out from the common line-form of two cola separated by a single caesura (a bicolon).[3] Such exceptional lines could be regarded as aberrations, if it is assumed that the poetry should be regular.[4] If not aberrations, they might simply represent a fluidity of style that allows for irregularity but which has no rhetorical or structural function. On the other hand, it is possible that the variation in style is deliberate and serves a particular purpose in the way the structure of poetry functions. These views are variously represented within the spectrum of theories of Hebrew poetry.

Despite the general acknowledgement of the existence of tricola, and the considerable scholarly enterprise that has gone into expounding the nature of Hebrew poetry, remarkably little work has been carried out specific to the tricolon. In reasonably extensive treatments of "parallelism," Berlin makes no reference to tricola at all, and Kugel is expressly dismissive of the tricolon having any significance: "We have treated the question of ternary lines somewhat casually because the difference between binary and ternary lines *is not crucial*."[5]

A less dismissive but particularly unimaginative perspective on tricola was offered by Kissane: "Sometimes, because the thought cannot be adequately expressed in the normal verse of two clauses, or merely for the sake of variety, the poet adds a third member to form a triplet, or verse of three clauses."[6]

A more nuanced assessment is given by Alter who not only identifies tricola but also hypothesises their function. In reference to Ps 18 he comments, "In some of the relatively long poems, like this one, triadic lines appear to have been used with purposeful selectiveness to mark some special emphasis or to indicate the beginning or conclusion of a segment within the poem."[7] However, this hypothesis is not tested sys-

---

3. Short lines consisting of only a single colon, designated monocola, also occur.

4. Seybold, "Anmerkungen," 111, dismisses many tricola as secondary accretions and not a genuine poetic form.

5. Kugel, *Idea*, 52, emphasis original. Similarly Ryken, *Words*, 181 makes only a passing reference; Petersen and Richards, *Interpreting*, 23–24, are concerned to validate the existence of tricola but ascribe no particular significance to them.

6. Kissane, *Book of Psalms*, xxxviii–ix.

7. Alter, *Art*, 35.

tematically, nor carried through and applied in other instances. Similarly, Watson has more recently commented, "Since the couplet is the norm, the presence of a tricolon most probably acts as a marker of some kind. In fact it seems to function largely as a transition marker, to open and/ or close units of verse."[8]

In his original guide to the techniques of Hebrew poetry, Watson gave reasonable attention to tricola and postulated their functions as opening, closing, climax, and merismus.[9] However, this was little more than an observation of the location or semantic content of some tricola. The means by which a tricolon achieves opening or closing was not addressed, and he noted that many other tricola do not fall within any of these categories. Similarly he did not address the questions of how or why the particular line-form of a tricolon should interact with the semantic function of merismus.[10]

Notwithstanding these unsubstantiated and minimalizing explanations, a few specific studies of tricola have been undertaken, of which more extensive appraisal is required.

Previous Tricolon Studies

Whilst tricola have been incorporated within previous theories of poetic structure, they have received little detailed attention; only one major work, by Mowinckel, has focussed on the phenomenon of the tricolon, and that was as long ago as 1957.[11] A little over twenty years later, Willis commented that, "generally speaking, scholars do not seem to have considered it sufficiently important or fruitful to examine this phenomenon at length in Old Testament poetry."[12] Indeed, most recent theorists have had other concerns, and their treatment of tricola has generally sought to incorporate them within a wider theory of poetic structure.

Mowinckel's detailed analysis of tricola in the Psalms is based very largely on his proposition that Hebrew poetry is characterized by an iambic metre.[13] His scansion of the text involves introducing additional

8. Watson, "Hebrew Poetry," 262.

9. Watson, *Classical*, 177–85.

10. Ibid., 183–85.

11. Mowinckel, *Real and Apparent*.

12. Willis, "Juxtaposition," 465.

13. As detailed in his earlier work, Mowinckel, *Psalms*, 159–75, 261–66 (translated from original 1951).

accents on every alternate syllable in a word going back from the tonal syllable. He does not distinguish between these additional accents and the tonal accent, resulting in very unusual vocalisation. For example, a conjunction at the beginning of a word may receive an accent equal in value to the tonal accent of that word.

Mowinckel seems to have followed the nineteenth-century scholars who sought to impose a rigid metre on the text in a classical style, without embracing the work of Grimme who demonstrated that this could only give a satisfactory result if variations in syllable length were accounted for.[14]

Mowinckel's metrical proposal forms the basis of his colometry and he scans lines according to his iambic metre so that they almost always appear as bicola. However, the consequence of this rigidity is that lines may be split in a way that disregards the syntax. For instance, in Ps 1:1 a verb and its negative modifier are separated between cola.[15]

Thus the rigidity of Mowinckel's metrical scheme fails to cohere with either pronunciation or syntax. His desire to find regularity in psalm poetry is evidenced in his thesis that tricola occur only throughout a psalm or distinct section of a psalm, never in isolation. His analysis of "real" and "apparent" tricola is substantiated on the basis of his metrical theory in order to demonstrate this point. But it seems clear that his theses are taking priority over the actual evidence of the text. In considering textual variants, he adds to the MT an extra colon where this produces two bicola instead of a tricolon, but is equally content to delete a colon from MT if it is omitted in any other witnesses. Some exegetical arguments are offered, but it is generally apparent that any assessment of variant texts is skewed heavily in favor of those that support his proposal, and so the adoption of such variants cannot reasonably be said to validate his thesis.[16]

Does Mowinckel have anything to say about the character of true tricola? According to him they should demonstrate "more or less exact parallelism" between the three cola.[17] Although not explicit, it seems that

14. See Leatherman, "Four Current Theories," 39–41, for a critical summary of Grimme's thesis. A rare endorsement of Mowinckel's proposal came from Segert, "Hebräischen Metrik," 514–16.

15. Mowinckel, *Real and Apparent*, 8–10.

16. See Mowinckel, *Real and Apparent*, 32–35. For a similar critique, see for example T. H. Robinson, Review of *Real and Apparent*.

17. Mowinckel, *Real and Apparent*, 17.

Mowinckel's use of the term "parallelism" is limited to semantic parallelism. Yet even Mowinckel's few examples of "real" tricola fail to hit the mark, as he admits in respect of 138:8, "all three cola only have a logical connection between each other, without building any thought rhyme at all."[18] Perhaps his most reliable comment comes from the conclusion of this discussion: "The 3rd (or the 2nd) colon can add a new element of the picture or idea, but never a quite new idea or thought."[19] Here is an axiom worth taking forward, that a tricolon should exhibit a clear connection between its members, for otherwise it is hard to explain or justify its identity as such.

More recent studies of tricola by Willis and Yaron have focussed on the internal structure of the line, without any regard for its place within a poem. Willis, without specifically justifying his identification of tricola, cited a range of tricola that exhibit a partly synonymous and partly chiastic structure. By chiastic is meant in this context a chiastic arrangement of word order, i.e., a surface-level syntactical chiasm. In passing, Willis criticizes Mowinckel's analysis of tricola, suggesting that he is too insistent on regular metre, and noting that he imposes pre-conceived ideas about poetic structure onto the texts he analyzes, rather than addressing the texts on their own terms.[20] The tricola identified by Willis are all broadly synonymous, in that they convey the same basic thought in each colon but without verbatim repetition. He notes that some of these are "fully synonymous," some have synonymous A and B cola with chiastic B and C cola, whilst others have chiastic A and B cola with synonymous B and C cola. The weakness of this analysis is that "synonymous" and "chiastic" are not mutually exclusive categories. The former is a semantic term, the latter (as Willis uses it) a syntactic term. In actual fact, Willis is simply highlighting the technique of poetic defamiliarisation: a change in word order in order to introduce variety and interest. He does offer some comments as to the function of the tricola: "emphatic, climactic effect" (Ps 6:9b–10), "climax in a progression of thought" (Ps 143:5), and "progression of thought leading to a climax" (Ps 7:6).[21] However, he does not explicate how these effects are related to the use of chiasm, i.e., to the variation in word order. Willis also offers some comments on

18. Ibid., 21.
19. Ibid.
20. Willis, "Juxtaposition," 466–67.
21. Ibid., 473–75.

the potential purposes of tricola: to convey something that could not be accommodated in a bicolon; as a variation in the scansion to reflect a variation in mood, scene or voice; as an aid to teaching and memory in the cult; and to create a climax.[22]

A similar type of analysis to Willis' is mentioned in passing by Meynet in the process of expounding his overall theory of poetic structure (discussed fully in "Rhetorico-Structural Approaches" on pp. 61–65). He finds examples of tricola having semantic structures ABC, AA'B, ABB', and ABA'. Where there is no symmetry apparent—the ABC structure—he notes that there is usually some form of progression, be it numerical, logical, or chronological. Meynet also notes that in these lines the syntactic relationships between cola do not necessarily match the semantic relationships.[23]

Yaron also made a study of the internal structure of tricola, reading tricola from Proverbs and observing that the final colon is usually "climactic."[24] However, his "tricola" are lines, or groups of lines, that would not normally be read as tricola. Prov 6:27–29 would normally be regarded as three bicola, and lines such as Prov 25:3 as a bicolon with "internal parallelism" (or possibly a merism) in the first colon.[25] Therefore Yaron's work offers no real insight into the identity of a tricolon. However, his analysis of a rhetorical form that takes two similar thoughts and modifies them with a third one could be a device that operates at various structural levels, including the tricolon.

Van Grol made a study of pairs of lines of the form bicolon plus tricolon (or vice versa) where the central colon links the two lines by relating to both the preceding pair of cola and the following pair of cola. As such the central colon does double-duty, either semantically or syntactically, in order to form what Van Grol terms "paired tricola."[26] Whether the central colon of the pair acts as an intermediate phrase in a narrative sequence, as a pivot, or as a climax, the key aspect is that it

---

22. Ibid., 480.

23. Meynet, *Rhetorical Analysis*, 224–29.

24. Yaron, "Climactic," 153.

25. Ibid., 153–54. For "internal parallelism" see Watson, "Half-line Parallelism" and the section "The Problem of Four-Word Cola" on pp. 44–46.

26. Van Grol, "Paired Tricola," 55–57. The basis for the underlying colometry that allows identification of such lines is explicitly stated as following "the delimitation of the cola in BHS."

stands distinct in some way from the adjoining cola whilst cohering the two lines into a unit. Some form of matching between the initial two cola and the final two cola is also preferred in identifying such "paired" lines.[27] Van Grol investigated the place of such "paired tricola" within their broader structural context. Employing the strophic analysis of Van der Lugt (see the section "Strophic approaches" on pp. 56–60), he found that paired tricola often form an entire strophe; that where there are other lines in the strophe, the paired tricola usually come at the end of the strophe; and that such strophes are usually found at the beginning or end of a higher textual unit.[28] He therefore determined their function as either an "impressive, solemn or festive introduction" or an "expanded conclusion."[29] Alternatively, a strophe of paired tricola occasionally was found as the middle strophe of a poem and functions "as a core."[30]

Bringing all these studies together, a contrast is apparent between Mowinckel's insistence on "exact parallelism" between the three cola of a tricolon, and the consistent observation amongst others of the variety of relationships between the three cola. Willis, Van Grol and Yaron each observed that two of the cola are more closely connected and that one, usually the third, whilst still being connected also carries a distinction. Alter made the same observation in relation to Ps 39:1–3, commenting on the "element of imbalance in the semantic parallelism," whereby he identified that, "in each of these three lines the third verset stands in some relation of tension to the two preceding versets, retrospectively casting a new light on them."[31] However, there is no consensus or uniformity about this: both Willis and Watson identify tricola that exhibit synonymy between all three cola.[32]

Much more recently, Van der Lugt has addressed the question of the function of the tricolon within psalms, following a reasonably rigorous methodology. His study is based on strophic analysis of the psalms that divides the texts into units within a hierarchy of levels. The division is determined by the identification of "transition markers" and the pat-

27. Ibid., 59.
28. Ibid., 66–67.
29. Ibid., 67–68.
30. Ibid., 69.
31. Alter, *Art*, 69.
32. Willis, "Juxtaposition," 467; Watson, *Classical*, 178–79.

tern of verbal repetitions within the psalm.[33] Based on his analysis of the entire Psalter, he tested the hypothesis that tricola function as transition markers, indicating either the closing of a strophe or the opening of a higher rhetorical unit.[34] The result of his analysis, that the data do not fit his hypothesis, leads him to the conclusion that no general statement can be made about the transition marking function of tricola. Whilst this is apparent, it remains the case that a tricolon *may* act as a transition marker in some instances, but the presence of tricola with other functions obscures the data.

In the light of these previous studies of tricola and their possible functions, a clear scope can be established for a study that identifies tricola on a consistent basis and seeks to assess their function both in terms of their internal structure and their location in the broader context of poetic structure.

Purpose of the Study

The purpose of this study is to identify and analyze on a consistent basis certain exceptional lines of Hebrew poetry—initially identified as tricola—and to explore their function.

While much study has been made of the form, structure and functioning of Hebrew poetry, and these studies have incorporated the tricolon, very little has been asked of the significance of this variation in line-form. The review of previous studies above ("Previous Tricolon Studies" on pp. 3–8) reveals that where there has been an effort to examine the specific function of the tricolon, this has been hampered by at least four factors. First, the basis for the colometry of the source text has been undefined, inconsistent or based upon specific theories that have obvious weaknesses. Therefore the identification of tricola has been misleading or contingent upon other, sometimes unidentified, theories. Secondly, studies have tended to highlight selected texts that fitted the author's thesis, rather than a systematic appraisal of a well-defined corpus. Thirdly, some studies have examined either the internal structure of a tricolon or its place within its poetic context, but not both. Fourthly, the function of a tricolon has not been disambiguated from other poetic

---

33. See the section "Strophic Approaches" on pp. 56–60 for a more detailed exposition of the method.

34. Van der Lugt, *Cantos and Strophes*, 522–35.

features that contribute to the same function.[35] It may also be noted that, with the exception of Van der Lugt, almost no contribution has been made to the topic in over twenty years.

Therefore a systematic and detailed study of the tricolon is a valuable contribution to the field of Hebrew poetics, especially in the context of the theories of poetic structure of the last twenty years or so. A synthesis of the most reliable aspects of metrical, syntactical, stylistic and semantic theories of Hebrew poetic line-form will facilitate a consistent means of colometry and therefore identification of tricola. By setting out an explicit rationale for this process, the results can be appraised objectively, and their sensitivity to underlying assumptions will be apparent for any who wish to adopt variant colometry. A syntactic and semantic analysis of the internal structure of each tricolon thus identified will contribute to an understanding of the defining features of tricola and characterization of the variation they offer. Engagement with a variety of theories of broader poetic structure will then allow the purpose of the placement of the tricolon within that structure to be postulated.

The initial assumptions for the study are minimal. It is taken as given that the dominant line-form in Hebrew poetry is a bicolon and that variations from this norm do occur. In focusing on the specific variation that presents as a tricolon and questioning its function, at the outset of the study there is no presumption that the tricolon has a consistent function, only that it does indeed have an identifiable function of some sort in each particular instance.

The key questions therefore that this study seeks to answer are:

- What specific function does each tricolon achieve?

- Can such lines be characterized in terms of their internal structure?

- Why did the conclusions of previous studies disagree on these points?

The results of the study should inform and nuance other extant theories of Hebrew poetic structure. The internal structure of tricola will add an additional dimension to studies of "parallelism" and the nature of syntactic and semantic relationships between cola. The place of tricola

---

35. For example, see the comments on Watson in the section "Background" on pp. 1–3.

within rhetorical and prosodic structures of a poem may reinforce or highlight the way in which a rhetorical skeleton is realized in poetic form. In both of these ways, the study seeks to generate an enhanced appreciation of this particular aspect of Hebrew poetry and therefore a more nuanced and better-substantiated literary reading of the text.

With these aims in mind, the study begins with a clearly stated and objectively defined methodology.

Methodology

Corpus

The study has confined itself to the Psalms of Ascents (Pss 120–34) as a textual corpus in order to provide a manageable scope. The Psalms of Ascents are an identifiable collection within the Psalter by means of their common superscription.[36] Theories of the meaning of the superscription abound, mostly reading a reference to a particular context for composition or use, occasionally to a description of a certain poetic form.[37] Such theories do not influence this study's approach to the text, but it is worth noting that a number of readers have recognised a relatively high degree of "terrace-pattern parallelism" in the collection, i.e., words at the end of one colon being repeated at the beginning of the next.[38]

Along with all of the psalms, the Psalms of Ascents are clearly identifiable as poetry, and they are quite discrete, with no ambiguity over their beginnings or endings. As such they provide a useful sample of well-defined poems as a basis for analysis. They are mostly quite short which has the advantage that considerations of their macro-structures are likely to be less complicated than longer psalms. Grossberg has classified them all as having "centripetal" structures, by which is meant that the emphasis in each psalm is on the unity of the psalm as a whole rather than on the distinction of the individual parts. They have clear themes and strong structure markers.[39] They are thus well suited to analysis of

36. With a minor variation in Ps 121.

37. For surveys of interpretations of the superscription see Crow, *Songs of Ascents*, 1–27; Hossfeld and Zenger, *Psalmen*, 392–400; Keet, *Psalms of Ascents*, 1–17; Vesco, *Psautier de David*, 1161–67.

38. Delitzsch, *Commentary*, 259; Hunter, *Psalms*, 182–91. On "terrace-pattern" or anadiplosis, see Watson, *Classical*, 208.

39. Grossberg, *Centripetal*, 5–7 and 19–47; see also Viviers, "Trust and Lament" and Viviers, "Coherence."

their structure. Wilson also finds significant thematic coherence in the collection, commenting that they "join in an almost unbroken song of reliance on YHWH alone."[40]

The dating and provenance of the Psalms of Ascents cannot be verified conclusively, but they are likely to be exilic or post-exilic.[41] Their original life-setting may be as pilgrim songs or in the return from exile.[42] Crow believes them to have an agricultural northern Israelite provenance, with a Zionist redactional layer.[43] However, this study is not concerned with the history of the text but adopts a canonical approach, taking as its starting point the final form of the text.

Source Manuscripts

The analysis will be based principally on the Masoretic text presented in BHS, taking note of variant readings where these are apparent. Some theories of poetic structure make appeal to an earlier form of the text, with reconstructed vocalisation and removal of material identified as redactional. That approach is not adopted in this study, for two reasons. First, the reconstruction of an original text can only be speculative and would, in the case of ambiguous colometry, generally serve only to substantiate a particular theory, thus creating a circular argument. The identification and removal of redactional material is usually done in support of a theory that is being substantiated, and so actually demonstrates very little. Secondly, it is the canonical form of the text that would have been used during the second temple period (and subsequently) and which therefore was identified and used as a poetic text.[44] Therefore this study seeks to understand the way the canonical text functioned at that

40. Wilson, *Editing*, 224. On the structure of, and thematic development within, the collection see also Barker, "Voices"; Hunter, *Psalms*, 229–48; Mannati, "Psaumes Graduels"; Prinsloo, "Role of Space."

41. Hunter, *Psalms*, 181–82; Viviers, "Why?," 804.

42. Exemplified in Seybold, *Die Wallfahrtspsalmen* and Goulder, *Psalms of Return* respectively. Deurloo "Gedächtnis" suggests that they were deliberately developed with both settings in view.

43. Crow, *Songs of Ascents*, 159–81. See also Seybold, "Redaktion" and Willi, "Zion" on the significance of Zion in the collection.

44. According to Flint, *Dead Sea Scrolls*, 238–39, Book V of the Psalter stabilised relatively late, and so strictly we should speak of a proto-Masoretic text being in use at that time. See also the section "Masoretic accentuation in a canonical approach" on pp. 16–17.

time, whilst noting indications of the redactional history of the text in order to qualify any conclusions as appropriate. Dependent upon the outcomes of the present analysis, a future study could potentially consider the extent to which its conclusions are still valid when applied to a reconstructed original text.

The relationship between the text of BHS and the original Masoretic manuscripts is made apparent in the BHS apparatus, but the relationship between the presentations of the text in each case is not. The editors of BHS have made decisions regarding colometry and presented the text accordingly, but no basis or explanation of this is provided. Therefore, a worthwhile exercise is a review of the manner of presentation of poetic texts in some of the principal Masoretic, Qumran and Septuagint[45] manuscripts.

ALEPPO CODEX (M[A])

Poetic sections of the text, including Psalms, are set out in two columns per page rather than three, in order to better facilitate the presentation of a full poetic line on each page-line. As far as possible the presentation of the text follows the Masoretic accentuation. Each verse is written on a single page-line, with a gap after the mid-verse accent. In the case of slightly longer verses the text runs right through without a mid-verse gap due to lack of space on the page.[46]

Where a verse is too long to be written on a single page-line, the usual solution is that the verse fills one page-line, with or without a gap, and continues on the next page-line without any apparent attention paid to the point at which the text is split between page-lines. Even words joined by a *maqqeph* may be split between page-lines (so 120:5). The text then continues with a pair of full cola per page-line, separated by a gap, as normal. If a verse has taken up one and a half page-lines, the consequence is that subsequent page-lines consist of the second colon of one verse and the initial colon of the next verse.

In a few cases, a long verse is spread over two page-lines, with the introduction of an additional gap. When this happens, the division of the verse into four cola matches its syntactic structure (thus 125:5; 126:2, 6; 127:1, 2; 128:3; 129:8; 131:1).

---

45. Note that Codex Vaticanus does not include texts studied here.

46. See also the comments of Sanders, P., "Colometric," 246–48.

In the Psalms of Ascents, the only exception to these principles are in 126:3 and 128:4, where the mid-verse gap does not follow the mid-verse accent (*rebia* in both cases); and in 127:1 where the final word of the first (poetic) line (וֹבּ) has carried over to the next page-line.

Codex Leningradensis (M^L)

The layout of the text appears to follow similar principles to those described for M^A. However, the physical width of the column is less, resulting in more page-lines that do not exhibit a gap in the text. Additionally, the scribe of M^L seems to have been more concerned about using the space on the page efficiently, and so often commenced a verse at the end of a page-line, even if only the first word of the verse, rather than add/increase a gap in that page-line and commence the next verse on the next page-line. Consequently, there is less correlation between verses and page-lines when compared with M^A. Once the page-lineation has departed from the verse division, due to a long verse, the correlation of subsequent page-line divisions with verse or mid-verse divisions is much less consistent than in M^A.[47]

In a few instances a gap is not introduced into the text at the mid-verse accent but is introduced elsewhere. Some of these are at syntactic pauses: 120:1, 127:2 (at a *paseq*), 130:2 (indicating a bicolon with v. 1), 130:5 (after the tetragrammaton) and 133:2a (as reflected in BHS). Others are not at syntactic pauses: 122:1 (after the tetragrammaton), 128:5, and 133:2c (as reflected in layout of BHS).

Qumran Scrolls

The main psalms scroll, 11QPs^a, has almost no evidence of colometric presentation. Each psalm begins on a new page-line, but thereafter the text is generally continuous, written in a single column without gapping. Occasional gaps do occur, but not necessarily coincident with the mid-verse pauses of MT. The lineation of the acrostic Ps 119 is respected (col. VI) but again without evidence of any division of the line into cola.

Similarly, 4QPs^e, which contains portions of Pss 120, 125, 126, 129, and 130, has no evidence of colometric presentation, but in contrast, 4QPs^b does. For example, Ps 94 is presented with one colon per page-line of the scroll, in a single column. The cola definitions match the ac-

---

47. See also the comments of Norton, "Diplomatic," 198.

cents of MT.[48] In some instances there is a clear division of a poetic line into three cola: 102:27 and 103:20.[49] Unfortunately, this scroll does not contain any portions of the Psalms of Ascents.

CODEX SINAITICUS (LXX[ℵ])

The poetry of the Psalter is recognised by the arrangement of the text into two columns per leaf, rather than the four columns of the narrative books. Even so, these wider columns still do not accommodate a full poetic line, and the text is carried over as indicated by indentation of the text on the following page-line. Thus a new poetic line is indicated by its lack of indentation.

Throughout the Psalms of Ascents, a new page-line is used for either a new verse or for a new colon within a verse. The approach is not consistent, and the reason for the variation not apparent. For example, Ps 120[50] is presented with a new page-line for each verse, and there is no division of the verses into cola; whereas Pss 127 and 130 have each colon presented on a new page-line. Other psalms are presented in a mixture of the two styles. Where verses are divided into cola, the division strongly correlates with the Masoretic accentuation. The exceptional cases generally coincide with verses of ambiguous colometry and/or variant translation e.g. 120:6–7, 122:4.

In some instances a verse is divided into three cola: 123:4, 124:7, 125:5, 133:2.

CODEX ALEXANDRINUS (LXX[A])

The psalms are presented in two columns per leaf, but this is no different to the presentation of the narrative books. The basic style of presentation is the same as LXX[ℵ] in that text that does not fit within the width of the column is continued on the next page-line but indented. There are no gaps in the text; the beginning of a poetic line/colon is indicated only by its beginning on a new page-line without indentation.

The verses of the psalms are more often divided into cola than in LXX[ℵ], but still not universally so. For instance, in LXX[ℵ] 120:1–2 are presented as a single piece of text per verse; in LXX[A] 120:1 is the same but

---

48. See Ulrich et al., *Cave 4*, 31.

49. See ibid., 39 and 42.

50. That is LXX Ps119; psalm numbering here follows the MT for consistency.

120:2 is presented as two separate pieces of text (i.e., cola).[51] As with LXX[ℵ], the division of a verse into cola correlates strongly with the Masoretic accentuation.

SUMMARY OF EVIDENCE OF MANUSCRIPT COLOMETRY

The impression given by the Masoretic manuscripts is that the scribes did not have any view of colometry other than that indicated by the accentuation or occasionally adduced from syntactic structure. It is also evident that the presentation of the text on the page was influenced at least as much by sparing use of the parchment as by any colometric considerations, particularly in the case of M[L].

Although it is not possible to make specific comments about the Psalms of Ascents in the Qumran scrolls, the evidence of 4QPs[b] is that an understanding of the division of the text into cola was extant in the second temple period, and that this matched, at least in some instances, the later Masoretic accentuation of the text. This understanding clearly embraced the phenomenon of lines characterized as tricola, as distinct from bicola.

The evidence of Septuagint manuscripts is inconsistent and perhaps reflects the struggles involved in presenting a translation of poetry. Nevertheless, division into cola is apparent, and this was clearly influenced by a tradition that closely matched that of the accentuation later added by the Masoretes. It seems to be the case that issues of translation and issues of presentation of poetic form were independent of one another.[52]

It is possible to hypothesise a history of the poetic form of the text that recognises that poetic conventions could have been implicit rather than explicit in the text. Whilst these could have been obvious to a reader in the post-exilic period, understanding of these conventions would have waned in the inter-testamental period, resulting in an inconsistent approach to them in presenting a translated text, and the occasional desire to make them explicit. As Tov comments in relation to the Qumran scrolls, "The stichographic arrangements of poetical texts

51. An exceptional reversal of this generality is 126:5, which is two cola in LXX[ℵ] but a single colon in LXX[A].

52. Ulrich, "Dead Sea Scrolls," 331–36, suggests that the original Old Greek was lost and that the LXX represents a later recension towards MT. If correct as regards translation, it may also shed light on the presentation of the poetic form.

reflect a certain understanding of the poetical structure of the text, but it is unclear to what extent these layouts reflect the original intention of the poets behind the texts."[53]

By the time of the late Masoretic scribes, a particular interpretation of the poetic form would have been settled and perpetuated in the accentuation. Given the conspicuous role of the Masoretic accentuation in this review of the original manuscripts, a framework for interacting with the accentuation must be established.

Masoretic Accentuation in a Canonical Approach

The general approach to the text in this study is Childs' "canonical" approach. This incorporates consideration of the entire process that led to the final form of the text, and particularly with the religious tradition that gave rise to the text.[54] The significance of that tradition is to ascribe greater importance to the final form of the text than any supposed earlier or "original" form. An understanding of the literary development of the text may then serve to elucidate the theological motives behind the development that led to the final stabilized form of the text. One particular implication of this approach for poetic texts is that the theological literary development of the text may have resulted in an original poetic form being lost or corrupted. The canonical approach seeks to "understand the nature of the theological shape of the text rather than to recover an original literary or aesthetic unity."[55] Therefore the final form of the text, which was regarded and used as poetry, provides the fundamental basis for any enquiry; but with the recognition that the text is founded on poetic forms that might have been obscured by subsequent theological literary developments.

Childs supports the view that prior to the time of stabilization of the final form of the text (*circa* first century CE), a plurality of traditions was in existence, evidenced in plural textual traditions.[56] The evidence of readings that vary from the Masoretic text (such as LXX) should therefore be taken as alternative textual traditions that came to be regarded as less authoritative, rather than necessarily as an earlier and more accurate

---

53. Tov, "Special Layout," 116.

54. Childs, *Introduction*, 17 and 58–60.

55. Ibid., 74, 104.

56. Ibid., 100–102. On the relationship between MT and Qumran scrolls see Wilson, *Editing*, 91–92.

witness to the "original" text. This is not to disregard the important task of textual criticism, since textual corruption certainly occurred both before and after the time of stabilization of the canonical text. Rather it is to allow textual criticism to distinguish between errors of transmission, and theological literary development.[57] The possibility of errors of transmission means that the MT need not be bound to be accepted as the canonical text, and there may be good reasons for recovering alternative readings.

Within this schema the significance of the Masoretic vocalisation and accentuation of the text is that it witnesses to a particular oral tradition of the community that transmitted the text from around the time of its stabilisation and beyond.[58] Therefore it can be regarded as having particular value in relation to the theological interpretation of text, less so in relation to indications of the original poetic structure from which the final form of the text is derived. Therefore it is appropriate to take cognisance of the accentuation as a starting point for poetic analysis, whilst also being open to underlying poetic structure that it has obscured.

In this way, Childs' principle of using the MT as a vehicle to recover the canonical text can be applied by seeking to identify aspects of poetic form that have been corrupted in the post-stabilisation transmission of the text. It may also be possible to consider whether there are instances of poetic forms being corrupted by the pre-stabilisation theological development of the text. However, this would require a very well-defined theory of acceptable poetic form as its starting point, and is beyond the scope of the present study.

Preliminary Questions

Having identified a corpus of text in which to conduct the study, and established a framework for relating to the textual variants and accentuation of the source manuscripts, a few further issues must be addressed. Before an analysis of the function of the tricolon within the structure of a psalm can be carried out, there are two preliminary questions: how is a tricolon to be identified, and how is the overall structure of a poem to be understood?

57. Childs, *Introduction*, 104.
58. Ibid., 98.

The answers to these questions form the framework within which an analysis of the function of the tricolon can be carried out. In actual fact, it is seeking to provide a coherent answer to these two "preliminary" questions that form the bulk of the challenge, rather than the consequent appraisal of the tricola themselves. Both questions are contingent upon a consistent approach towards the colometry of the text. How is the reader to decide upon the appropriate division of the text into cola? The question is fundamental to achieving a realistic appreciation of the poetry, since the colometry "controls the reader's or listener's temporal experience of the poem."[59]

The use of theories of poetic structure to deduce colometry creates the possibility of circular arguments. Some theorists propose textual emendations and revised colometry, such that the texts no longer substantiate the theory but rather are subject to it.[60] In a similar manner, there is a risk in this study that deductions about the function of a tricolon may be contingent upon an earlier assumption about the structure of the poetry that forms part of the identification of the tricolon. Some degree of circularity of argument is perhaps inevitable. The important matter is to identify it, and to explicate any conclusions that are conditional.

The process therefore involves critically reviewing a selection of extant theories of colometry and poetic structure in order to provide a consistent basis for subsequent analysis.

Theoretical Base

The literature on the subject of Hebrew poetics is so vast that all of it could not reasonably be taken into account. Hobbins' "Annotated Bibliography" runs to fifty-four pages despite commenting that "studies published more than 50 years ago are under-represented"![61] Therefore some selectivity is needed.

Theories that rely on comparison with other ANE poetry, such as Ugaritic, have been excluded. This study is an analysis of Biblical Hebrew poetry in its own right. Within theories of Hebrew poetic structure, it is useful to distinguish theories based upon the structural level at which they operate. Most metrical theories are focussed on the formation of

---

59. Cloete, "Colometry," 20.

60. A practice that Kraft, "Further Observations," 68–69, argues strongly against.

61. Hobbins, "Bibliography."

individual cola. Studies concerned with the relationships between cola and the juxtaposition of cola to form a line are those commonly identified with "parallelism." Beyond the level of the line, structural theorists have looked at the aggregation of lines to form strophes and stanzas. These broad areas of study based around a hierarchy of structural levels of the text—colon, line, strophe/stanza/poem—form appropriate groupings for a review of relevant literature. However, the boundaries are fuzzy since, for example, the strophic analysis of structure proposed by Van der Lugt also concerns itself with colometry, the formation of cola. Nevertheless these areas allow categorisation of theories for ready comparison, with overlaps of area referred to where necessary.

These areas of study also set limits to the scope of the analysis. Theory that concerns itself with levels of hierarchy below the colon—words, syllables, morae—are engaged with only in so far as they contribute to an understanding and definition of the colon. At the other end of the scale, the limit of analysis is set at the overall structure of an individual psalm. Considerations of connections between psalms, and of deliberate editing of the Psalter in light of those connections, are excluded from this study.[62]

Within these categories of theory, works have been selected based on either the extent of their acceptance and use by others or by their being relatively recent. Preference has also been given to those that exhibit a clear methodology that allows consistent application. In this way it is hoped that the best scholarship of the past can be integrated with the latest insights. The critical review of these theories (chapter 2 "Theories of Poetic Structure") provides a solid theoretical framework within which a systematic analysis of the Psalms of Ascents can be undertaken.

Analysis

Each of the Psalms of Ascents will be analyzed in order to determine its colometry and its overall structure (chapter 3 "Colometric and Structural Analysis of the Psalms of Ascents"). Such analysis will be complemented by consultation of a range of commentaries, focusing on those that concern themselves with poetic structure. The identification of tricola results directly from the colometric analysis. These particular

---

62. Vesco, *Psautier de David*, 1167–69, notes that he has identified at least eight separate theories regarding the structure of the Psalms of Ascents collection, all of which are based on interpretation of themes, not any formal aspect.

lines will be subject to closer scrutiny in order to reveal their internal structure from both a syntactic and semantic point of view (chapter 4 "Internal Analysis of Tricola and Para-tricola"). This will lead to conclusions about the character of each individual tricolon. The analysis of the structure of each psalm will identify the place of each tricolon within it. It will then also be possible to investigate the interaction between the internal structure of the tricolon and the place of the tricolon within the structure of the psalm. Such manifold analysis will provide all the necessary data for an assessment of the function of each tricolon (chapter 5 "Functions of Tricola and Para-tricola").

Identification of Specific Functions

The identification of the function of each tricolon requires first that the meaning of "function" be explored. A range of functions is possible for the tricolon, corresponding to the various approaches to poetic structure. On the basis of the previous tricola studies cited above, and a general appreciation of theories of Hebrew poetics, the following possible functions may be postulated at this stage:

- Prosodic: a means of fitting rhythmically variant text into a prosodic system, or facilitating a deliberate variation in rhythm.

- Syntactic: creating a particular pattern of syntactic relationships between cola.

- Structural: marking a significant node in the structure of the psalm, such as opening, closure, center, or pivot.

- Aesthetic: variation from the normal line-form as an adornment to add interest or to introduce speech that follows the normal bicolic line-form.

- Rhetorical: expressing emphasis or climax, either of the tricolon within the psalm or of a particular colon within the tricolon; or presenting summary.

It should be apparent that the list is not exhaustive and that these concepts are not mutually exclusive; for example, a variation in rhythm may go hand-in-glove with the expression of climax. Therefore the identification of function is not a one-dimensional exercise, but involves an examination of the interaction between the various aspects.

Nevertheless, some degree of clarity must be maintained between the different aspects. A failure to maintain such clarity has been one of the failings of some previous assessments of function, as noted above ("Previous Tricolon Studies" on pp. 3–8). Axiomatic to this present study is the principle that the form of a tricolon, once discerned, should not be conflated with its function.

Characterization of Tricola

The results of the identification and analyses of individual lines will be brought together to form conclusions regarding the structure and function of tricola in general (chapter 6 "Conclusions"). These conclusions will be contingent upon the theories used for the analysis and will be provisional, given the limited textual corpus. However, they should shed some light onto the questions posed above (in section "Purpose of the Study" on pp. 8–10) regarding the character of tricola and the reasons for inconsistent indications from previous studies.

2

Theories of Poetic Structure

Theories Concerning the Form of a Colon

General

A WIDE VARIETY OF theories have been developed in the attempt to establish a definitive basis for the colometry of Biblical Hebrew poetry. Often driven by a comparison with ancient Greek and Latin poetry, a number of attempts have been made to discern a metre in Hebrew poetry. These have in common the principle of regularity of a phonic feature of the text, the actual feature chosen varying between words, stresses/accents, syllables and smaller time-units that aggregate to form syllables of varying lengths.

The multiplicity of approaches to metrical analysis, and their failure to provide a clear or consistent demonstration of metre, has lead others to suggest that colometry is not metrically-based at all but lies in other spheres. The distinction between metrical theories of colometry and non-metrical theories provides a structure to the discussion of various theories that follows. Non-metrical theories of colometry include syntactic constraints, numerical approaches and reliance on Masoretic accentuation or pausal forms.

Most of these various approaches depend to some degree on the implied colometry of the Masoretic accentuation, at least as a starting point for any analysis. This reliance is made explicit in some analyses, but not all.

Metrical Approaches

ACCENTUAL METRE

In his review and critique of various metricists of the nineteenth century, Cobb highlights the work of Ley, Bickell, and Sievers as the most important. The consensus of these authors is that the metre of Hebrew poetry is not quantitative, in the way of classical Greek or Latin verse, but is primarily accentual. Whilst differing in the detail of the basic form of the Hebrew poetic foot, they each develop a system of analysis that demonstrates a more-or-less regular form of accentual rhythm.[1]

Ley's system designated one stressed syllable to each significant word (the tone syllable) and paid little or no regard to the number of unstressed syllables. Allowing some flexibility for the treatment of particles, he sought to demonstrate a general pattern of balanced cola (i.e., having an equal number of stresses) in a line.[2] While being a reasonably simple and consistent approach, it fails to yield the consistent results that are claimed for it and is thus better considered as a means of describing a line of poetry rather than defining its correct form.

Bickell's system took account of both stressed and unstressed syllables, denoting every colon as either iambic or trochaic.[3] Like Ley, Bickell was concerned to demonstrate that lines are formed of symmetrical cola, that is having the same number of syllables and hence of stresses.[4] However, in contrast to Ley, Bickell ignored *shewas* and helping vowels. The weaknesses of Bickell's system were the extensive use that it made of comparative Syriac linguistics, thereby excluding any distinctive characteristic of the Hebrew language, and the very significant amount of textual emendation that was necessary to produce the desired result.[5]

Sievers developed the work of Ley by additionally taking account of unstressed syllables. The background and detail of Sievers' system is presented here in more detail, representing as it does the apex of nineteenth century German scholarship.

---

1. Cobb, *Criticism*, 185–86.

2. The principles of Ley's analysis are listed by ibid., 89–94.

3. Depending on whether the number of syllables in the colon is odd or even, so that the final syllable in the line is always unstressed. Ibid., 113–14.

4. Ibid., 122.

5. Ibid., 127 and 187–88.

Sievers found that the dominant stress pattern in Hebrew poetry was anapaestic, and developed a theory that all Hebrew poetry was metrical based on anapaestic feet.[6] His expansive theory therefore required considerable detailed work to deal with texts that are not naturally anapaestic.

Sievers' system denotes every syllable, including *shewas*, as stressed or unstressed. The natural stress pattern of Hebrew thereby results in a series of stresses, one for each word, on the final or penultimate syllable of the word. Sievers then proposes subtle changes to the rhythm of vocalisation to account for the varying numbers of unstressed syllables in each word. So words with excessively longs chains of unstressed syllables (three or more) are allocated a secondary stress, preferably on the second syllable.[7] Short words (monosyllables) are either left unstressed or are treated as being stretched so that a single vowel sound becomes a disyllable.

Some aspects of Sievers' system result in a departure from the natural vocalisation of Hebrew. The addition of secondary stress is one example. Another is the allocation of a full stress to words in the construct state. Sievers acknowledges that words in the construct state do not normally take any stress, but allows for them to take a stress or not depending upon their length and relation to the following word.[8] Segholate forms present a particular problem for Sievers' system, as they tend to result in adjacent stressed syllables. He overcomes this by quite radical revocalisation, both moving the segholate's stress onto the final syllable, and throwing back the stress in the preceding word.[9] This highlights the weakness of Sievers' thesis, which is that he has unnecessarily tried to force all the text into an anapaestic form. Indeed, Cobb notes that other basic foot forms are equally plausible, and that Sievers' use of only the most regular sample texts prejudiced his supposedly universal conclusions.[10]

6. Sievers, *Metrische Studien*, 99. The personal background to Sievers' work is described by Cobb, *Criticism*, 169–70.

7. Sievers, *Metrische Studien*, 177–78.

8. Thus for example a monosyllable word in the construct state can remain unstressed when followed by one or two unstressed syllables, whereas a disyllable word in the construct state cannot. Ibid., 199–202. Similar principles apply to particles and nouns in apposition, see ibid., 188–99.

9. Ibid., 226.

10. Cobb, *Criticism*, 182.

Sievers' detailed work on the distribution of stress facilitates the scansion of each colon of Hebrew poetry as a number of anapaestic feet.[11] He identifies the most common lines as 3+3 or 4+4 bicola, whilst also recognizing the existence of a wide range of other possibilities (e.g., 3+2, 4+3).[12] He notes that lines with 3+4 feet are unusual and stand out as being irregular.[13] In many instances Sievers prefers to downplay pauses between (potential) cola, and instead presents many lines as monocola of 4, 5, or 6 feet, although he does indicate some degree of medial pause within such monocola. So, for example, Sievers will characterize a line as "4" and present it as a monocolon, whilst also indicating a medial pause. To avoid confusion of terminology, such a presentation is denoted here as 2–2, in order to distinguish it from a 2+2 bicolon. As a result there is fluidity in Sievers' approach between presenting a line as a monocolon, albeit with minor medial pause, and presenting it as a bicolon. This ambivalence over colometry is particularly evident when considering lines that are possible tricola.

Sievers' analysis of six-stress lines is particularly worthy of attention. He notes that a six feet line may be read as 2+4, 4+2, 3+3, or 2–2–2.[14] Because he was concerned more with rhythm than with parallelism he considered all these options to be equivalent. Therefore, a line without any strong caesura and characterized by a rhythm of 2–2–2 is interchangeable with the more common class of six-stress line, the 3+3 bicolon. His key point is that a 2–2–2 "monocolon" and a 3+3 bicolon are rhythmically equivalent: "Der Doppeldreier wechselt zumal in Sprechtexten ... derart mit dem (trichotomischen) Sechser, dass man sie als rhythmisch gleichwertig betrachten muss."[15]

As an example he cites Ps 1:1, which he presents as:

---

11. Sievers' colometry is based on the Masoretic verse division, with each verse divided into lines and cola on metrical grounds.

12. Sievers, *Metrische Studien*, 100–102. The annotation of the rhythm of a line here follows the practice of Kraus, Watson, Allen et al. using "3+3" where Sievers used "3 : 3." A development of this convention to accommodate the nuance of Sievers' analysis is described in the following discussion.

13. Ibid., 112–15.

14. Using the adapted conventional annotation. The 2–2–2 line was annotated by Sievers simply as "6."

15. Ibid., 103.

אַשְׁרֵי־הָאִישׁ   אֲשֶׁר לֹא הָלַךְ   בַּעֲצַת רְשָׁעִים

וּבְדֶרֶךְ חַטָּאִים לֹא עָמָד   וּבְמוֹשַׁב לֵצִים לֹא יָשָׁב:

In this example, the *maqqeph* in v. 1a is ignored and each instance of the negative particle is unstressed.[16] Thus the proposed rhythm of the two lines is 2–2–2 / 3+3 (although Sievers denotes it simply as "6" and "3:3"). The two lines match each other as variant manifestations of a six-stress unit, the one being tripartite with minor pauses and the other bipartite with a stronger caesura. To make a musical analogy, as Sievers himself was wont to do, the 2–2–2 line is rhythmically equivalent to the 3+3 line in like manner to how a triplet is a group of three notes performed in the time of two.[17]

Sievers did not consider in detail the length of pauses within lines or the difference between a full caesura in a bicolon and a minor caesura in a line of the type 2–2–2. In seeking to appreciate the rhythmical equivalence that he proposed, it is helpful to hypothesise rhythmical lengths for these pauses: equivalent to an anapaestic foot for a major caesura and equivalent to a single stressed syllable for a minor caesura. In this way a major caesura is approximately equivalent to two minor caesurae, and the total rhythmical lengths of a 3+3 bicolon and a 2–2–2 line are the same.

Amongst those who have adopted rhythmical analysis following the theory of Sievers (see below) it has been common to present 2–2–2 lines as 2+2+2 tricola. For example, Watson does so, but noticing the brevity of such lines compared to "full" tricola, he labels them as "staccato" tricola.[18] However, careful analysis of this type of line leads to the conclusion that a more nuanced approach to the classification of lines may be required. The polar assessment of bicolon or tricolon does not adequately accommodate the type of line encountered here. The presentation of a 2–2–2 line as a tricolon implies a significant distinction from a 3+3 bicolon, whereas in rhythmical terms it has more in common with a 3+3 bicolon, or even a 4+2 bicolon, than with a tricolon. Therefore,

---

16. Ibid., 103. Sievers ignores the *maqqeph* of the MT and allocates a full stress to אַשְׁרֵי to follow his rules regarding the accentuation of construct forms (see above).

17. With gratitude to Doug Ingram for this insight.

18. Allen and Kraus tend consistently to present such lines as full tricola, presumably taking the analysis of Sievers to imply this approach. The label "staccato" is taken from Watson, *Classical*, 178.

while the line cannot readily be presented as a bicolon, it would not be truly reflective of its character to present it as a tricolon, as if it were completely distinct from adjacent bicola.[19]

In order to take account of Sievers' analysis and to fully implement his system of rhythmical description, a new designation is needed to describe a six-stress line that is tripartite and yet rhythmically equivalent to a couplet. The designation proposed is the term "para-tricolon," taken to suggest a line that looks like a tricolon but is not. A working definition of this feature is proposed as follows:

> Para-tricolon: A line comprising three phrases, each having two stresses. The rhythmical length of the line is measured as six stresses and two minor caesurae, being rhythmically equivalent to a bicolon of six stresses and one major caesura.

Note that this definition is concerned solely with the *rhythmical* character of a line; it presupposes nothing of the syntactic or semantic structure of such a line. In the colometric analysis of the Psalms of Ascents, this definition will provide the criteria for the identification of para-tricola, which, alongside full tricola, will be examined further to assess their function.

As far as full tricola are concerned, Sievers presents them as bicolon plus monocolon, arguing that the break in sense between bicolon and colon is necessarily stronger than the caesura within the bicolon.[20] For example, Ps 2:2 is presented as 3+3 and 3:

וְרוֹזְנִים נוֹסְדוּ־יָחַד   יִתְיַצְּבוּ מַלְכֵי־אֶרֶץ
עַל־יְהוָה וְעַל־מְשִׁיחוֹ׃

Sievers appears to offer this colometry based on his assessment of the relative strengths of the pauses in the verse, not on any text critical considerations.[21] Thus Sievers never presents a line as a tricolon. His disinclination to do so is curious when set alongside his willingness to present a para-tricolon in the form of a monocolon with minor pauses. This is probably indicative of his strong emphasis on rhythmical considerations

---

19. Note, for example, that in the example of Ps 1:1, the 2–2–2 line is actually shorter than the 3+3 bicolon, in terms of both syllables and space on the page.

20. Sievers, *Metrische Studien*, 123–26.

21. Ibid., 501. The BHS apparatus suggests that the third colon is a gloss. Other examples include Ps 4:2 and Ps 7:6; Ibid., 503–05.

and his relatively lesser interest in semantics and wider structural considerations. His worked examples do not include any of the Psalms of Ascents and so direct comparison of his approach with other analyses is not possible for those texts.

Several modern commentators, in adopting an accentual analysis of poetry, refer to the work of Gray and Robinson, who had developed Sievers' proposals.[22] However, their approaches are less rigorous and combine metrical and semantic aspects in an undefined manner. Gray supported Sievers' anapaestic analysis with flexibility of vocalisation. However he did not believe that the rhythm should follow any specific or regular scheme. Indeed he was critical of those, presumably including Sievers, who amend the text in order to fit a regular rhythm.[23] The consequence of his flexibility of approach is that he does not offer any guidance to assist in determining ambiguous cases.[24] Gray had a preference for breaking the text into the shortest possible cola, typically presenting a four-word clause as a 2+2 bicolon in order to highlight any parallelism and allow significant medial pause.[25]

Robinson's approach to Hebrew poetry was at the interface between semantics and rhythm, with the emphasis on semantics. He was concerned with the "thought-rhythm" of the poetry, and described "parallelism" in these terms: "Every verse must consist of at least two 'members,' the second of which must, more or less completely, satisfy the expectation raised by the first."[26] This definition is too restrictive, since is precludes both monocola and enjambment within bicola, features which are clearly evident. Robinson considers the rhythm of Hebrew poetry to be an accentual rhythm and refers in broad terms to the work of Gray. However, he proposed that there be no specific rules regarding the proportions of stressed and unstressed syllables, because for him the sound of the poetry is subordinate to its sense.[27] He therefore described the rhythm in terms of "thought units," although this was clearly intended

22. Gray's work was first published in 1915, Robinson's in 1947.

23. Gray, *Forms*, 226–27.

24. See his treatment of particles, ibid., 147–50. His approach allows, for example, the word כֹּל to be an unstressed monosyllable, a stressed monosyllable or a stressed disyllable, but he does not discuss how to determine any specific instance.

25. Ibid., 161–63.

26. T. H. Robinson, *Poetry*, 21.

27. Ibid., *Poetry*, 24–25.

to match the stresses of Gray's analysis.[28] Robinson did not explain his allocation of "thought units," but it may be rooted in his preference (unlike Gray) for finding regularity of rhythm. Indeed he suggested that an irregular rhythm, say a 3+3 line in a poem that is otherwise 2+2 or 3+2, is adequate cause to question the integrity of the text.[29] Robinson did allow some exceptions to his ideally regular rhythm; he was open to the inclusion of an anacrusis, as a device deliberately intended to create a pause and thereby draw extra attention to the following line.[30] He followed Gray in a preference for breaking the text into shorter cola; thus commentators who refer to Gray and Robinson (such as Kraus and Allen) tend to take lines analyzed according to Sievers' system as 2–2–2 and present them as 2+2+2 tricola. As has been demonstrated above, this is a departure from Sievers' own understanding of such lines.

Amongst those who have adopted an accentual analysis of Hebrew poetry, a consistent desire is expressed to find "balanced" cola, by which is meant an equal number of stresses in each colon of a line. It is evident that such an expectation is rooted more in the work of Gray and Robinson than of Sievers.

Syllabic Metre

An early attempt at syllabic appraisal was made by Ewald.[31] Dahood's appraisal of poetic texts strongly favored matching syllable counts for each colon in a line, but without proposing a comprehensive framework for analysis or colometry.[32] A detailed proposal for syllabic metre was developed by Stuart who built on the earlier work of Freedman. Proposals for the original, pre-Masoretic vocalisation of Hebrew had been used by Freedman to count the number of original syllables per line of poetry. His purpose was to comment on the range and distribution of number of syllables per line and per stanza and to propose that stanza lengths were balanced out in order to meet a constraint on the overall length of a poem.[33] He was not concerned with the formation of individual cola

---

28. Ibid., 32.

29. Ibid., 39.

30. Ibid., 36.

31. See Cobb, *Criticism*, 62–82, or Leatherman, "Four Current Theories," 29, for a description and critique.

32. Dahood, "New Metrical Pattern," and *Psalms*, XXVI–XXVII.

33. Freedman, *Pottery*, 58–61 and 69–71. The value of his observations is limited by

within a line, although he did hint at a preference for balanced cola, i.e., having the same number of syllables.[34] Stuart went considerably further, and claimed that in early Hebrew poetry, each colon within a line had the same number of syllables. However, he did not discern any consistency in the length of whole lines, so that again, his scheme could not really be called metre in the classical sense.[35] His demonstration was limited to early poetry, and even that required various emendations to forms of constructs, suffixes and prepositions. Since these emendations were made *metri causa*, there is a good chance that Stuart was offering a circular argument.[36] Syllable counting has more recently been resurrected by Fokkelman, not to suggest a form of metre, but to suggest significance in the average number of syllables per colon across a complete poem.[37]

These theories have not produced consistent results and of themselves do not define the colometry of poetry, although again the theme of "balanced" cola within a line is apparent.

Syntactic Approaches

The syntactic definition of the colon was most comprehensively attempted by O'Connor.[38] He rightly refuted the idea that a colon should necessarily be a single clause, noting that this is clearly not always the case.[39] Instead, he proposed a series of syntactic constraints—on the numbers and combinations of word-units[40], "constituents"[41], and predicators—that are allowable in a colon. This system describes the range of cola found in Hebrew poetry, but seems to be an unnecessarily com-

---

their being based only on a corpus of acrostic poems. His arguments are recapitulated in Freedman, "Another Look," 18–20.

34. See Freedman's analysis of Ps 113; Freedman, *Pottery*, 9.

35. So for example, a typical analysis of a line by Stuart would be 8+8 syllables. The following line might be 10+10 syllables, or indeed any other number.

36. Stuart, *Studies*, 27–28.

37. Fokkelman, *Major Poems II*, 10–11. This proposal is considered of very little significance since the average number of syllables per colon has no cognitive or aesthetic function and the basis of the analysis is questionable; a full critique is not relevant here.

38. Syntactic analysis has also been carried out by Collins, *Line-forms*, but only to describe the varied style of different poets, not to define or describe the fundamental form of the poetry.

39. O'Connor, *Verse Structure*, 73.

40. A verb or noun together with its dependent particles.

41. A verb or nominal phrase together with its dependent particles.

plicated way of explaining them. His constraint of a maximum of five "word units" will almost entirely account for the poetic corpus, without recourse to his additional syntactic constraints.

A specific flaw in O'Connor's analysis is evident when applied to a typically difficult issue of colometry: the division of two verbs each governing a single word-unit nominal phrase. According to O'Connor's constraints, these would always have to be divided into two cola, since a single colon with two predicators each governing a nominal phrase is not admissible. So, for example O'Connor divides Ps 107:26 thus:

יַעֲלוּ שָׁמַיִם
יֵרְדוּ תְהוֹמוֹת
נַפְשָׁם בְּרָעָה תִתְמוֹגָג׃

No other division is possible within his constraints. However, an alternative understanding of the first two clauses is that they combine to form a single thought—they went up-and-down—that exhibits "internal parallelism" as identified by Watson.[42] O'Connor's system cannot explain why it precludes such a reading. This unnecessary rigidity is even more apparent in 107:43a where O'Connor divides מִי־חָכָם וְיִשְׁמָר־אֵלֶּה into two cola, when a four-word colon expressing a single thought is surely more appropriate.[43] Holladay defended O'Connor's theory by labeling such a pair of short cola as "conjoint" and suggesting that together they parallel a single longer colon.[44] But by introducing a hierarchy of structural relationships between cola, he effectively undermines the claimed universality of O'Connor's definition of the colon.

The emphasis on syntactic features to the exclusion of semantic considerations does not reflect the way readers/hearers interact with poetry. If cola with identical syntactic structures, but potentially divergent meanings, are said to "match," why should the same not apply to cola with similar meanings but different syntax?[45] Cloete sought to develop O'Connor's theory by additionally taking account of stresses and adding

42. See Watson, "Half-line Parallelism," and the section "The problem of four-word cola" on pp. 44–46.

43. See Kugel, *Idea*, 317–19, for a similar critique. Kugel also notes that O'Connor's constraints are satisfied by much prose as well as poetry, and therefore questions their validity as a "definition" of poetry.

44. Holladay, "Conjoint Cola," 404–5.

45. See a similar critique in Kugel, *Idea*, 321–22.

a constraint of one to four stresses per colon.[46] However, he still found it necessary to take account of other, non-syntactic, factors in delimiting cola.[47] Similarly, Holladay, in seeking to clarify the definition of a "word-unit," found it necessary to count combinations of monosyllabic particles that would not count individually, and to take account of the semantic function of the interrogative pronoun מַה.[48] A system of syntactic constraints alone therefore does not determine correct colometry.

Other Approaches

Other approaches to colometry include those that are based on counting either consonants or words and colometry that is derived solely from traditional accentuation or vocalisation.

A theory based on counting consonants was proposed by Loretz and Kottsieper. Their premise is that each line consists of balanced cola, i.e., cola having the same number of consonants. However, the examples they cite do not substantiate their theory with any consistency. For example, their analysis of Ps 21:3–5 yields the syllable counts ten/fifteen, twelve/thirteen, thirteen/twelve.[49]

Kosmala proposed a theory of poetic structure based on matching the number of "word-units" in adjacent lines. By considering the number of "word-units" per whole line, he downplays the significance of the division of each line into cola, and has almost nothing to say about that feature.[50] Whilst this fails to do justice to the most basic aspect of the structure of Hebrew poetry, it is interesting that in his system, a 2-2-2 line is presented as being equivalent to a 3+3 line, in much the same way as Sievers demonstrated these to be metrically equivalent.[51]

Hobbins has recently proposed a "new descriptive model" for Biblical Hebrew poetry that is set "within the framework of the prosodic

---

46. Cloete, *Versification*, 200–07.

47. Ibid., 215.

48. Holladay, "Which Words?," 26–27, 30. The consequent similarity to an accentual analysis is striking.

49. Loretz and Kottsieper, *Colometry*, 48. Since their work drew heavily on comparisons with Ugaritic and Canaanite texts, it would in any case strictly not contribute according to the remit of the present study.

50. Kosmala, "Form and Structure," 424–26.

51. Ibid., 433.

structure hypothesis of contemporary linguistic theory."[52] His starting point is the accentual analysis of Sievers as subsequently interpreted and applied by Alter: that a colon contains two to four stresses and a line two to four cola.[53] He then constrains this description by proposing that all four-stress cola can be, and should be, understood as pairs of two-stress phrases. Thus a line traditionally denoted as 4+3, in Hobbins' model becomes (2:2):3 with both a minor caesura and a major caesura. Thus such "bipartite lines are better understood as tripartite lines." This principle is generalised into a rule that any colon may contain only either two or three stresses.[54] Therefore he interprets lines of poetry as having any possible combination of two-stress and three-stress cola, provided always that in a "tripartite line" there is both a minor caesura and a major caesura. Hobbins also extrapolates such an approach and suggests a hierarchy of structural levels of the text—cola, lines, strophes, stanzas, sections—each of which consists of two or three of the next level down.[55] Defined according to this model, each level of the hierarchy is then explored in terms of its correspondence to a level of the "prosodic structure hypothesis formulated by E. Selkirk and other linguists."[56]

A number of difficulties present themselves in relation to Hobbins' proposal. He does not justify the division of the text into such short cola other than to observe that it is possible to do so: "what 4s, 5s, and 6s have in common is that they are all expressible in terms of 2s and 3s."[57] Such a simplistic arithmetic observation appears to neglect any broader consideration of rhythmical, rhetorical, or aesthetic concerns. Nor does Hobbins suggest that there is any significant difference—rhetorical, metrical, or otherwise—between a bipartite line and a tripartite line (using his terminology). His comparisons with prosodic theory are of interest, but do not of themselves substantiate his proposal. A colon is

---

52. Hobbins, "Regularities," 583.

53. Ibid., 565.

54. Ibid., 567.

55. Ibid., 567–68. As such it is very similar to the strophic analysis of the Kampen school and almost identical to Fokkelman's proposal except for the much tighter constraint on colon length; see the section "Strophic Approaches" on pp. 56–60.

56. Ibid., 568.

57. Hobbins, "Regularities," 570. The quotation actually reads, "what 4's, 5's and 6's have in common is that they are all expressible in terms of 2's and 3's."

equated with a "phonological phrase" and the matching appears good.[58] However, a limit on the length of the colon to three prosodic words (equating to the stresses of rhythmical analysis) is not necessary for the correspondence to be maintained. A colon of four prosodic words would work just as well. Therefore, Hobbins' thesis is not considered a useful contribution to the development of a consistent theory of colometry that can account for the fundamental structural difference between a bicolon and a tricolon.

Fokkelman has proposed quite simply that a colon normally contains two to four stresses, with one or five stresses very occasionally occurring.[59] By stress is meant the accent of normal vocalisation. This idea is elegant in its simplicity, and can be used to define any colon. Its major weakness is its ambiguity when applied to a four- or five-word phrase: should this be a single colon or two? Clearly the decision rests on wider structural or semantic considerations, and so this approach of itself cannot be prescriptive. Fokkelman's proposal is in fact part of a wider theory of the macrostructure of Biblical Hebrew poetry, and is one strand of the strophic approach of the Kampen school (see the section "Strophic approaches" on pp. 56–60). Other proponents of that school offer a more detailed consideration of colometry.

Korpel and de Moor's approach to colometry is based primarily upon the Masoretic accentuation of the text, with account taken of semantic structures, parallelism and rhythmical balance.[60] No systematic method for determining colometry is proposed; rather the balance of probabilities is weighed. The colometry is then described in terms of "feet," with a foot always having one stressed syllable and therefore usually being coincident with a single word. No limits are applied to the number of feet per colon and it is asserted that Hebrew poetry has "free-rhythm," such that there is no value in looking for any form of metre or in counting syllables. Nevertheless, the poetry is said to have a tendency towards a regular number of feet per colon, with two to five being the common range.[61]

58. Ibid.

59. Fokkelman, *Major Poems II*, 41; see also Fokkelman, *Reading*, 37.

60. Korpel and de Moor, "Fundamentals," 5–6. Their use of the Masoretic accentuation has been criticised by de Hoop for its inconsistency. He argues that only the four major disjunctive accents can mark the end of a colon, and that their position in the line must be taken into account. De Hoop, "Colometry," 61–62, 68.

61. Korpel and de Moor, "Fundamentals," 2–4.

The linking of cola to make a line[62] is done on the basis of parallelism between cola and comparison with parallel passages. This results in much greater variation in line length than is suggested by most other models. The lack of semantic parallelism in lines that Lowth would identify as "synthetic" results in these often being presented as two monocola.[63] Conversely, a repeated element or syntactic construction in four or more cola, results in these being linked as a multi-cola line.[64]

By contrast, Van der Lugt asserts that, at least in the Psalter, there are no monocola (with the possible exception of 128:5) and there is no line longer than a tricolon.[65] However, the basis of this assertion is not fully worked out. Van der Lugt does clearly specify the role of Masoretic accentuation in the identification of tricola, stating that the first colon normally concludes with either *rᵉbîaᵃ gādôl* or *ᵓôleh wᵉyôrēd* and the second colon concludes with *ᵓatnach*.[66] This is a helpful proposition, but leaves questions of how to identify tricola that do not follow this pattern (such as 125:2) and how to deal with verses that follow this pattern but are not tricola (such as 126:2,6; 127:2). It is probably the case that Van der Lugt has other criteria in mind, such as colon length and syntax, but these are not made explicit. This unfortunately limits the usefulness of his analysis as regards colometry.

The colometric analysis of Korpel and de Moor grossly underplays rhythmical considerations. Whilst the view that the text is not metrical is probably valid, it is not helpful to ignore the intonational rhythm created by a succession of short phrases, that is, cola. The cadence of a regular succession of short and long pauses at the ends of cola and lines has some rhythmical quality that should not be ignored.[67] It is slightly strange that this aspect is neglected, given the assertion that "all ancient Oriental poetry was meant to be sung or recited to the accompaniment of music."[68] The experience of poetry as an aural phenomenon must influence the understanding of its structure.

62. "Verse" in their terminology.

63. See comments on the "Kurzvers" in Korpel and de Moor, "Fundamentals," 21. Note that the appraisal of parallel texts takes precedence in their analysis over considerations of the wider structural context of any one line.

64. See Korpel and de Moor, "Fundamentals," 24–29 for examples.

65. Van der Lugt, *Cantos and Strophes*, 523–24.

66. Ibid., 524.

67. Cf. Kugel, *Idea*, 1–2, 70–75.

68. Korpel and de Moor, "Fundamentals," 2.

This point is reinforced by the definition provided for a colon: "it is likely that the colon is the unit that could be recited or sung in one breath."[69] This is a useful concept, and it is a pity that no similar defining characteristic is identified for the line. How the line is experienced by the hearer/reader of the poetry is a question that receives no attention. This has particular implications for determination of colometry. In poetry that consists mainly of bicolic lines, there must be some significance in variations from that norm. And so the conclusion that "there is no reason whatsoever why we should not write a 'synthetical' bicolon as two independent unicola"[70] is entirely wrong. Were it not, the entire enterprise of distinguishing between cola and lines would be needless. In view of these points, the system of Korpel and de Moor is relatively weak in the area of colometry.[71] It is stronger in the area of the analysis of strophes and higher structural units, discussed below (see the section "Strophic Approaches" on pp. 56–60).

A final approach to colometry, distinct from any of the categories above, is to rely entirely on the pausal forms indicated in the Masoretic vocalisation. Revell proposed that these provide the key to colometry. Since they are independent of accentuation (they are the same in all three accentuation traditions), he asserts that they were fixed relatively early on in the transmission of the text and reflect a well-established reading tradition.[72] Revell focuses on those lines of poetry where the two cola (indicated by pausal forms) are sub-divided into two smaller units. Typically these smaller units are each a single clause, and may exhibit parallelism within the pair.[73] However, he asserts that the pausal forms indicate the priority of the larger units (cola) over against the sub-units, i.e., the cola should not be sub-divided but should remain intact, resulting in internal parallelism. One implication of this is that a colon may therefore contain two distinct grammatical units, and hence the

69. Ibid., 4.

70. Ibid., 23.

71. As is also that of Van der Lugt, *Cantos and Strophes*, 73, who espouses a "top-down" approach, whereby colometry is considered in the light of macrostructure. However he can only analyze macrostructure on the basis of an assumed colometry, and provides no evidence of reviewing that colometry in the light of macrostructure. It is therefore doubtful that his claims about his method can be sustained.

72. Revell, "Pausal Forms and Structure," 187–88; Revell, "Accents: Hierarchy," 88–89; P. Sanders, "Pausal Forms," 264–66.

73. Revell, "Pausal Forms and Structure," 189–90; cf. Stuart, *Studies*, 216.

grammatical structure of a colon is a matter of style, and is not fixed by poetic structure (*contra* O'Connor, as dicussed in the section "Syntactic Approaches" on pp. 30–32). Revell then goes on to consider "unbalanced" lines, in which one colon contains two sub-units and the other colon does not. The first colon may be the longer (e.g., Ps 120:3) or the second colon may be the longer (e.g., Ps 121:5).[74] Revell notes that these lines are usually presented as tricola, or are divided differently in order to create balance, or are emended according to some theory of poetic structure. He argues that they should remain as unbalanced bicola, as indicated by the pausal forms. He cites examples from the Qumran scrolls and from Akkadian texts in support of such a form.[75] Although not explicit, Revell would appear to allow a tricolon only where indicated by three pausal forms (Ps 5:9, 28:9 and 86:11).[76] Whilst Revell's theory can readily and consistently be applied to the text, it has the obvious weakness that pausal forms cannot always be distinguished and therefore has to rely also on the Masoretic accentuation. This becomes particularly problematic when dealing with long verses that, by any other reckoning, would be regarded as two lines rather than one (e.g., 127:1).

Sanders has adopted Revell's approach and sought to address the anomalies that it throws up, concluding, "It is as good as impossible to answer the question why in [Psalm 5:9] each colon ends with a pausal form, whereas in cases such as Psalm 2:2 there is a non-pausal form at the end of one of the cola. Is it a matter of syntax, of carelessness or of mere chance?"[77] Perhaps an answer might lie in the fact that Ps 5:9 is a full tricolon, with stress pattern 3+2+3, whereas Ps 2:2 has six stresses and fits the line-form identified as a para-tricolon.[78] Here is an indication that tricola and para-tricola merit distinction.

Reviews and Summary

At the end of the twentieth century, two critical reviews of poetic theories were produced. Vance carried out a systematic evaluation of all the

74. Revell, "Pausal Forms and Structure," 191. Ps 130:7 also has a long second colon, but marked only by contextual forms, not pausal forms.

75. Ibid., 194–95.

76. Ibid., 189.

77. P. Sanders, "Pausal Forms," 269.

78. Ibid., 273–74, addresses further "inconsistencies" in lines that are all (potentially) six-stress lines.

metrical theories considered above; Leatherman's doctoral dissertation offered a critical review and application of those theories, and of others, under four headings: minimal unit counting (incorporating various metrical approaches and some other numerical-based approaches); Collins' line-form analysis; O'Connor's syntactic constraints; and the semantic strophic analysis of the Kampen school.

Leatherman applied each theory to four texts, one of which was Ps 126. He concluded that no single system of minimal-unit counting yields a consistent verse structure, but that the counting systems are useful for a descriptive approach to the text.[79] Vance applied the various metrical theories to a wider corpus of texts, and found that, whilst none produced a genuinely metrical result, an accentual measure gave the highest regularity.[80]

The application of the theories to specific texts illustrated the deficiencies identified in the review above. Moreover, an issue of methodology highlights the complexity of the topic. Leatherman applied the various theories to the texts in their "traditional" colometry, without defining or defending the term "traditional."[81] Since even the most ancient manuscripts and versions differ in their colometry, any notion of a "traditional" colometry must involve some theoretical interpretive evaluation, but the nature of this is completely ignored. For example, Leatherman presents 126:2 as a double bicolon and 126:6 as a single bicolon[82], whereas MA presents both as double bicola, and ML is ambiguous. In the application of minimal unit counting, Leatherman fails to take account of the fact that various metricists have proposed changes to colometry and accentuation in support of their theories. So having identified the fact that 126:6 violates O'Connor's constraint on "constituents," he is silent on whether this represents cause to question O'Connor's theory or cause to question the "traditional" colometry.[83]

---

79. Leatherman, "Four Current Theories," 52. Similarly Raabe, *Psalm Structures*, 158 concluded that while no psalm has a regular stress pattern, most have a dominant pattern.

80. Vance, *Question of Meter*, 494–95.

81. Similarly, Vance based his evaluation of the colometry of BHS.

82. Leatherman, "Four Current Theories," 191.

83. Other than to highlight the inadequacy of Loretz and Kottsieper's proposal for colometric theory. Leatherman, "Four Current Theories," 311.

In summary, there is no convincing evidence, amongst all the various theories, for consistent regularity in the formation of cola. Fokkelman's five-stress limit for a colon seems to be the simplest and best substantiated starting point for assessing colometry of a text, incorporating as it does the most favorable aspects of O'Connor's analysis, having synergy with a number of other approaches and providing a good basis for accentual analysis.[84] However, of itself it does not deal with ambiguities in the allocation of stresses, nor answer the question of how to decide when four and five word cola should remain intact and when they should be split. This topic is specifically addressed below in the section "The Problem of Four-Word Cola" on pp. 44–46. Sievers' system remains the most well defined method for describing the rhythm of a line, particularly in dealing with the detailed allocation of stresses to words in such a manner that facilitates phonic regularity without too radically departing from normal vocalisation.[85] The attempts at demonstrating syllabic metre do not produce consistent results and have been criticised for not taking account of variation of syllable length.[86] However, the general trend amongst syllable counters to look for cola of matching lengths does give cause to question lines comprising cola of widely divergent syllable counts. Similarly, it has been noted that many who adopt accentual rhythm as an analytic tool favor balanced cola.

Theories concerning Relationships between Cola

The Problem with "Parallelism"

Turning to the relationships between cola, attention needs first to be given to the terminology employed. The term "parallelism" is often used in reference to Hebrew poetry, but is used to refer to different features by different authors. Lowth's original coining of the term *"parallelismus membrorum"* was in fact a reference to the predominant structural characteristic of the poetry as being written in couplets. This is evidenced by the fact that he included within his definition his so-called "synthetic" parallelism in instances where there is nothing parallel between the

---

84. Further substantiation comes from work on psalm structures by Raabe, *Psalm Structures*, 190.

85. As endorsed by Vance, *Question of Meter*, 173.

86. See Cobb, *Criticism*, 185–90, for a discussion of the work of Grimme on time measurement and the potential for that approach to be combined with Sievers'.

two cola at all. Robinson recognised this, and suggested such lines be described as "formal parallelism."[87] Many others have made the same criticism of Lowth, including Kugel.[88] But Kugel, whilst both elucidating the way in which one colon "seconds" another, and explaining various devices that can generate equivalence between cola, fails to clarify that these two features need not necessarily coincide. Similarly, Alter identifies both the dynamic development of cola and the devices that bind them together, without distinguishing these two functions. He, like most authors, tends to use the term "parallelism" to refer to any form of connection between cola, and therefore as a fundamental characteristic of all Hebrew poetry. The need to make the distinction is evidenced by the observation by Miller of pairs of cola that are partly parallel and partly sequential.[89]

In the work of Korpel and de Moor, cola that do not exhibit clear semantic or syntactic parallelism are split between lines, assuming that where no parallelism exists, no structural juxtaposition should be permitted.[90] This results in the fundamental structural form of the poetry being corrupted. They also provide considerable analysis of sentences that run through several cola and present this as evidence for the existence of lines of more than three cola. But at a more basic level, the non-alignment of colon and clause, or line and clause, or line and sentence, can be taken as clear evidence that the poetry has an underlying structural form that is not directly dependent on semantic or syntactic considerations. The undue precedence given to semantics over structural form, and the misunderstanding of parallelism come together in their appraisal of "synthetic" parallelism leading to the view that "Masoretic tradition recognized the 'synthesis' as a legitimate form of parallelism."[91] On the contrary, it is the case that Masoretic tradition recognized the norm of a structural form of bicolon, whether or not parallelism existed between the cola.

---

87. T. H. Robinson, *Poetry*, 23; see also Gray, *Forms*, 50–51.

88. Kugel, *Idea*, 15.

89. P. D. Miller, "Synonymous-Sequential."

90. Similarly Fohrer, "Kurzvers," 199–200, and 224, while rightly arguing for the existence of monocola ("Kurzvers"), presents Isa 62:10 as a set of monocola due to their lack of "parallelism."

91. Korpel and de Moor, "Fundamentals," 23 n. 41.

Dobbs-Allsopp has addressed the question of the nature of the non-parallel bicolon and found in his study of Lamentations that most such lines exhibit enjambment, that is they have an integral syntactic structure that is disrupted by the caesura. The incomplete syntax at the caesura creates a forward impulse that links the cola together, in a manner that he likens to the matching of parallel cola and so he discerns "two dominant strategies for linking the component lines of a couplet—parallelism and enjambment—which exist on a continuum."[92] This insight implies that a study of the internal division of a line of Hebrew poetry, that is its "line-form," must encompass investigation of its syntactic structure and consequent enjambment as well as any parallelism that arises from matching between its component cola.

The clearest distinction between the bicolon as a dominant structural form and parallelism that only sometimes is apparent in a bicolon, has been made by Clines in observing: "What is predictable about Hebrew poetry generally is its structure as couplets (or triplets, i.e., extended couplets). What is unpredictable is how the lines of that couplet (or triplet) will turn out to relate to one another. Will they be synonymously parallel, will they exhibit . . . some other parallelistic relation—or no parallelism at all?"[93]

More recently, Dobbs-Allsopp has commented that "to continue labelling lines as parallel even when they do not exhibit any recognizable form of parallelism simply renders the whole notion of parallelism meaningless."[94] Lunn has similarly stood against the tendency to overuse the term "parallelism" and reserved it for those instances where there is a significant semantic matching (i.e., synonymy) between cola.[95] Wendland has countered that this definition of parallelism is too narrow and should not exclude "obviously related lines."[96] Nevertheless, the potential range of connections between cola is vast (as Wendland acknowledges: "virtually any other type of meaningful connection"[97])

---

92. Dobbs-Allsopp, "Enjambing Line (Part 1)," 237–38. He uses "line" to mean "colon."

93. Clines, "Greater Precision," 94.

94. Dobbs-Allsopp, "Enjambing Line (Part 1)," 221.

95. Lunn, *Word-order*, 15–25, esp. 25 n. 60. This reflects a perspective advocated very much earlier by Kaddari, "Semantic Approach," 168–71.

96. Wendland, "Aspects," 108.

97. Ibid., 108.

and a narrower use of the term parallelism is the one that is preferable, although it need not be so narrow as to exclude non-semantic forms of matching between cola.

Therefore in the present study the term is used in single quotes— "parallelism"—when referring to the structural juxtaposition of cola without any regard for identifiable matching or equivalence between them. Where parallelism does occur, it may comprise semantic, syntactic, or phonological equivalence, as discussed below.

The Nature of "Parallelism"

Having noted that the juxtaposition of cola to form a bicolon does not necessarily involve parallelism between the two cola, the question remains as to the nature of the relationship between the cola, be it some form of parallelism or otherwise. Theories concerning the relationships between cola cannot readily be categorised, and so each significant author is considered separately.[98]

For Kugel, the consistent relationship between cola in a line is that of "seconding," which he characterizes as "A, and what's more, B." The impact of a line lies in the synthesis of the cola, the following colon connecting with and expanding the meaning of the preceding.[99] This theory works well for most texts, and rightly emphasises that no cola are truly synonymous, nor do they simply aggregate to generate meaning.[100] Rather meaning is found in the interaction between cola. However, Kugel's work is too simplistic, not explicating how that interaction works.[101] His theory also fails to describe appropriately those lines of poetry that display narrative development.

Alter produced a more nuanced work than Kugel, examining ways in which cola can interrelate from a mainly aesthetic point of view, exploring the function of the semantic aspect of "parallelism." He identifies a number line forms in which "dynamic development" is evident in the

98. In addition to those reviewed, the wide range of poetic devices that inform inter-colon relations are expounded by Watson, *Classical*, and Seybold, *Poetik*.

99. Kugel, *Idea*, 8–12.

100. Tsumura, "Vertical Grammar" has propounded the view that, at least syntactically, the cola of a synonymous bicolon do simply aggregate to form a single sentence. This approach appears to downplay the complexity and richness of interaction between cola that is inherent in parallelism.

101. Berlin, *Dynamics*, 64–65, hints at this.

progression between cola. These include moving from a standard term to a literary one, generating an original metaphor, and incremental repetition.[102] The development effect of such forms may serve to emphasise, to intensify, to focus, to specify, or to dramatise.[103] Alter's work was also particularly helpful in identifying interlinear features within the poetry, both parallelisms and narrative development.[104] Whilst providing the means to a deeper appreciation of a poem's message, Alter's work is of limited value in defining an underlying structure, particularly in the areas of difficult colometry.[105]

Berlin produced a wide-ranging analysis of the ways in which cola interrelate: the "dynamics of parallelism." Her work is explicitly linguistic, rather than aesthetic, and categorizes relationships of grammatical, semantic, and phonological aspects.[106] Berlin identifies the various ways in which cola can display equivalence, such as morphological pairing, syntactic matching, word pairs, and sound pairs. The principles are thorough and well-illustrated. These categories assist in the identification and understanding of parallelism.[107] They possibly go too far, particularly in the grammatical category, and suggest equivalence where there is none. For example, Berlin cites pairings of words with contrasting morphology (of person, number or gender) as contributory to their cola's equivalence. However, had words with the same morphology been used instead, the effect would still be the same. So then it cannot be the morphology that creates the equivalence. Similarly, in asserting that parallelism is created by equivalent deep structures of syntax, Berlin identifies parallelism in a wide range of divergent surface structures.[108] Given that most of the examples cited also exhibit semantic equivalence,

---

102. Alter, *Art*, 14–18.

103. Ibid., 18–25.

104. Ibid., 27–29.

105. Watson, *Classical*, 150–59, has similarly explored aesthetic devices that generate a relationship between cola, using terms such as "staircase parallelism" and "terrace-pattern parallelism."

106. Berlin, *Dynamics*; Watson, *Classical*, 114–49, explores the same topics, but in less depth.

107. Although the wide range of categories, and the lack of an over-arching scheme, give no assistance in deciding which aspect should take precedence in cases of ambiguous colometry. A similar criticism applies to O'Connor, *Verse Structure* and Watson, *Classical*. Watson, "Problems and Solutions," 374, acknowledges this point.

108. Berlin, *Dynamics*, 53–62.

it is difficult to be convinced that the deep syntactic parallelism is as significant as is claimed.[109]

In summary, the wide range of potential relationships between cola evident in this brief survey means that these theories are only of secondary benefit in determining colometry and the aggregation of cola to make lines. Nevertheless, a good understanding of the workings of "parallelism" do allow a description of the nature of lines of poetry, and identification of more likely or less likely combinations of cola.

The Problem of Four-Word Cola

In considering the formation of cola, the ambiguities presented by potential four- and five-word cola was noted (see the section "Other Approaches" on pp. 32–37). The full nature of this issue can now be explored in the context of the nature of relationships between cola.

Watson has highlighted the phenomenon of what he terms "half-line parallelism" or "internal parallelism," which is the parallelism of two grammatical sub-units that together make up a colon. He cited many examples almost all of which are four word cola, and noted that these mainly occurred as the first colon in a bicolon.[110] It was noted above that Revell views such cola as indivisible, strictly adhering to pausal forms as the only evidence for a caesura (in the section "Other Approaches" on pp. 32–37). But Watson's approach is more flexible, as he comments: "Such couplets could also be considered tricola—with the equivalent of three lines packed into two—or they may be the forerunners of true tricola with three full lines."[111] However, treatment of such a four-word unit as a single colon with internal parallelism stands at odds with certain other scholars.

Gray specifically addressed the phenomenon of a four-word colon, suggesting a preference for presentation as a 2+2 bicolon in order to highlight any parallelism and allow significant medial pause.[112] Robinson similarly expressed a preference to divide four and five "thought-units" into twos and threes.[113] Drawing on Gray and Robinson, Kraus and

109. Cf. the critique of Greenstein in the section "Syntactic relationships" on pp. 46–52.

110. Watson, "Half-line Parallelism," 59.

111. Ibid., 60. Watson uses "lines" to mean "cola."

112. Gray, *Forms*, 161–63.

113. T. H. Robinson, *Poetry*, 30.

Allen therefore are more likely to present a line as a 2+2+3 or 3+2+2 tricolon than a 4+3 or 3+4 bicolon.[114] Recently, Hobbins has proposed the same approach, although for quite different reasons which have not been fully substantiated.[115]

Despite the arguments to the contrary, Watson's approach offers the more realistic assessment. Just as true parallelism sometimes exists between cola and sometimes not, so it may be reasoned that Hebrew poets sometimes used parallelism within the formation of a colon but not always. If four-word cola are regarded as admissible, then the presence of parallelism within such a colon need not necessarily imply that it should be divided. After all, it would not be divided were parallelism not present, and the identification of parallelism is a subjective exercise. Therefore, the identification of parallelism within a colon cannot be an aspect of a coherent method for determining colometry.

However, it has already been proposed that para-tricola of the form 2–2–2 exist, and it may similarly be hypothesised that tricola of the form 2+2+3 could be valid. The question remains how are these line-forms to be distinguished from 4+2 and 4+3 bicola respectively.[116] Two criteria are proposed: an objective one, the counting of syllables, and a subjective one, the appropriate strength of pause.

Fokkelman proposed that the normal range of syllables for a colon is six to nine, with four to twelve being the absolute limit. These statistics are closely related to his assertion that a colon has no more than five stresses.[117] Culley assessed colometry more subjectively, based on "parallelism" and syntactic boundaries, and found the common range to be six to ten syllables, with some cola in the range five to fifteen.[118] Whereas Culley counted every Masoretic syllable, Fokkelman counted "pre-Masoretic" syllables, based upon a complex set of criteria for recovering the "original" vocalisation of the text.[119] Fokkelman's approach to colometry is the preferable of the two, but in order to accord with Sievers' approach of counting every syllable of the MT in allocating stresses, every syllable of the MT will be counted in assessing colon length. The result does not

114. E.g., Ps 120:2–3, Kraus, *Psalms 60–150*, 422; Allen, *Psalms 101–50*, 197.

115. Hobbins, "Regularities," 567; see the section "Other Approaches" on pp. 32–37.

116. Similar principles will apply to 2+4 and 3+4 bicola.

117. Fokkelman, *Major Poems I*, 8.

118. Culley, "Metrical Analysis," 18–24.

119. Fokkelman, *Major Poems II*, 15–16.

therefore comply exactly with Fokkelman's approach, generally yielding slightly higher values, but nevertheless offers a phonologically-relevant quantitative assessment of colon length. Adopting this concept provides a criterion for assessing a potential four- or five-word colon: that it be divided into two cola if it would exceed twelve syllables, and that its validity be tested carefully if it has eleven or twelve syllables. The presence of nine or ten syllables does not warrant a split, since any four- or five-word colon would inevitably be at the upper end of the syllable range and otherwise the assessment would be heavily weighted in favor of splitting.

A secondary criterion will be the extent to which a caesura (in the case of a potential tricolon) or minor caesura (in the case of a potential para-tricolon) is appropriate at the potential division point in light of the semantic and syntactic structure of the line. This will necessarily be a subjective judgement, but can be informed by a measure of the degree of enjambment that would be created by the introduction of a caesura and by an assessment of the phrase structure of the line being predominantly bipartite or tripartite. Such assessments will require a theoretical framework for the syntactic and semantic analyses of a poetic line, to which attention now turns.

Syntactic and Semantic Relationships

It has been noted that an investigation into the relationships between the cola that constitute a poetic line must encompass parallelism, which may manifest in semantic, syntactic, phonological, and rhythmical domains, and enjambment, which arises from the interaction between colometry and syntax. Therefore, in order to appreciate fully the character of tricola, and to explore their structural and rhetorical significance, a consistent and substantiated basis for describing the syntactic and semantic relationships between cola is required.

SYNTACTIC RELATIONSHIPS

An analysis of the syntax of lines of poetry requires a theoretical framework to provide consistent labelling and diagramming of the lines' syntactic structures. The transformational generative grammar of Chomsky has been adopted by a number of scholars concerned with syntax,[120] and

---

120. See Berlin, *Dynamics*, 18–26, for an overview of the key contributors.

is particularly well suited for exploring not only syntax but also the relationship between syntax and semantics.[121]

In generative grammar, a sentence is generated by the division of the sentence into its constituent components and illustrating these in a hierarchical tree.[122] So an English sentence typically consists of a noun phrase and a verb phrase, the verb phrase consisting of a main verb and a noun phrase. This would be represented in a phrase structure diagram as follows:

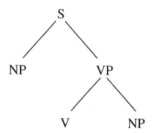

The rules that govern the substitution of one level of the tree for the level above are known as Phrase Structure rules and the resultant diagram is a Phrase Marker. The substitution of more detailed constituents continues until a simple sentence has been fully generated and the resultant phrase marker is known as a "base phrase marker."[123] At this point, the actual words represented by the constituents in the phrase marker can be substituted in order to form the phonological representation of the sentence.

The transformational aspect of the grammar is a device that accommodates the complexity and (supposed) infinite variety of allowable sentence forms without requiring unduly complex, or infinite, Phrase Structure rules. Phrase Structure rules are limited so that they are able to generate only single clause, declarative, active, present tense sentences. Obligatory transformations are applied to base phrase markers—for example, to ensure agreement of person, number, and gender of nouns and

---

121. For example, Price, *Theory*, bases a holistic theory of Bible translation around transformational generative grammar.

122. Chomsky's original presentation of the theory can be found in Chomsky, *Syntactic Structures*, 26–46; more readable recapitulations are found in Grinder and Elgin *Guide*, 56–71, and Ruwet, *Introduction*, 83–106.

123. Chomsky, *Topics*, 51–53.

verbs—in order to produce "kernel sentences."[124] The diagram above could be a base phrase marker, representing the generation of a kernel sentence such as "The boy eats an apple."

A series of optional transformations may be applied to kernel sentences in order to modify the tense, voice, and mood of the sentence and to combine with other sentences in order to embed and allow subordinate clauses. Such transformations may be applied iteratively in order to generate the theoretically infinite possibilities of actual language. Transformations are also used to produce sentences with alternative word order or elided elements. The application of all necessary and optional transformations results in a Final Derived Phrase Marker, the constituents of which can be substituted by actual words in order to produce the surface structure of a sentence.[125] So for example the kernel sentence above might undergo transformations for past tense and passive voice in order to generate a surface structure "An apple was eaten by the boy."

It should be apparent that a single kernel sentence can produce a variety of different surface structures depending on the transformations applied to it. Conversely, and less obviously, apparently similar surface structures may in fact be derived from different kernel sentence structures that have undergone different transformations. For example, the exclamation "Got it" has an elided subject and an ambiguous time reference. It may be derived from, amongst other sentences, both "I got it yesterday" and "You have got it now."

The two-stage process of generating a sentence—first the application of phrase structure rules, then the application of transformations—leads to a distinction between the deep structure of a sentence, represented by the kernel sentence(s), and the surface structure of a sentence. Exploration of the implications of this distinction has lead to the conclusion that whilst the surface structure alone contains all the information necessary for the phonetic representation of the sentence, the deep structure alone contains the information necessary for the semantic representation of the sentence.[126]

---

124. Chomsky, *Syntactic Structure*, 46–47; Grinder and Elgin *Guide*, 71.

125. Ibid., 61–84.

126. Ibid., 92–105, presents the argument that syntax and semantics are distinct, and in Chomsky, *Topics*, 55–59, asserts that phonology and semantics derive from surface structure only and deep structure only respectively.

The transformational generative grammar thus described is a theoretical tool for producing all possible grammatical sentences whilst not producing ungrammatical sentences. It also paves the way for a study of the derivation of meaning from a sentence's deep structure. However, the task in the present study is to analyze the syntactic (and semantic) structure of a given piece of text, and the process is therefore the converse. Rather than beginning with the abstract notion of a sentence and generating a valid phonetic representation for it, the task begins with a given phonetic representation, the structural nature of which requires determination. So what then will be of interest: the surface structure, the deep structure or both? As far as syntax is concerned, evidence for the priority of surface structure comes from two sources—observations of surface features peculiar to poetry and explorations of syntactic parallelism.

Distinctive surface features of poetic texts reflect the nature of poetry as a literary medium that elevates the significance of the phonetic component of speech and therefore its surface structure. Grinder and Elgin have explored some additional optional transformations that generate surface features considered acceptable in poetic text that would be unacceptable in prose. For example, they explore the phenomenon of a word or phrase appearing to do "double-duty" as a constituent of both a preceding clause and a subsequent clause. This arises because one of a pair of juxtaposed, lexically identical items has been deleted, by a transformation they term "overlap deletion."[127] As an example, they cite e. e. cummings: "... the ocean wanders the streets are so ancient ..." In this text "the streets" is a constituent of two clauses, albeit having different grammatical functions in the two. They observe that such transformations operate on the actual words of the text, not the phrase markers, implying that a representation of the text as its deep structure would not accurately convey an important characteristic of the text.

Therefore, a syntactic analysis of poetic lines must focus on the surface structure of the text, in order to avoid confusion with the semantic analysis (which will depend on deep structures) and in order to account for the way in which the text is most immediately experienced and processed in its phonological representation.

---

127. This technique is identified by Watson as "Janus parallelism"; Watson, *Classical*, 159.

A similar conclusion may be adduced from a critique of a work of Greenstein. In his exploration of the syntactic aspect of "parallelism," Greenstein concerned himself mainly with deep structures, arguing that cola with matching deep structures are parallel even though they might exhibit different surface structures.[128] A principal example cited by him is Ps 105:17:

> He sent a man ahead of them / Joseph was sold as a slave.

If passivization and word-order transformations are reversed, these two cola can be seen to have the same deep structure.[129] A significant problem with this approach is that since the deep structure is the basis of the semantic interpretation of a sentence, there is a very subtle distinction between parallel deep structures and parallel semantic content. All the examples cited by Greenstein exhibit some aspect of semantic parallelism, so it is not at all apparent that the similarity of deep structure is as significant as is implied. Indeed, it is hard to conceive of a bicolon that exhibits dissimilar surface structures and no semantic parallelism and yet can be interpreted as "parallel" due to similar deep structures. Therefore, it seems more plausible to suggest that if syntactic parallelism is an identifiable feature in a text, it will be at the level of surface structure, as Greenstein himself recognises can be the case.[130] At this level there can be no confusion with other semantic aspects of the text.

Having established that syntactic analysis should be focused primarily on surface structure, a particular area of interest is the relationship between that structure and the colometric division of the text. The non-coincidence of clause boundary and colon boundary is the phenomenon known as enjambment. Cloete has reviewed various views on whether Hebrew poetry exhibits enjambment or not.[131] In his own analysis he found virtually no enjambment, but was apparently only considering non-alignment of sentence boundary and line.[132] A more thorough assessment will additionally encompass clause and colon boundaries and will inevitably discern more instances of enjambment.[133] Kirk made a

---

128. Greenstein, "How?," 46–49.
129. Ibid., 48.
130. Ibid., 48 n. 20.
131. Cloete, "Colometry," 18.
132. Cloete, *Versification*, 216.
133. Dobbs-Allsopp, "Enjambing Line (Part 1)," 221–22.

detailed study of enjambment in the work of Homer, and has described categories of enjambment that helpfully distinguish varying degrees of non-alignment of clause and colon.[134] Where a sentence and colon co-incide, there is no enjambment, evidenced by a full stop in the syntax at the end of the colon. Where a colon could represent a complete sentence but the following colon continues the sentence with additional material, the enjambment is identified as "progressive," evidenced by a comma at the end of the colon in place of a possible full stop. Where a colon comprises an incomplete sentence that must be carried on, there are two possibilities. If the colon break coincides with a comma in the syntax, typically between a subordinate clause and a following main clause, the enjambment is termed "periodic." If however there is no stop or pause at all in the syntax at the colon break, then the enjambment is termed "integral." These four types, therefore, represent increasing degrees of enjambment based on decreasing degrees of syntactic stop at the end of the colon.[135] They are summarised thus:[136]

Degree	Term	Typical punctuation in English translation
0	(none)	Full stop.
1	Progressive	Comma, but full stop possible.
2	Periodic	Comma.
3	Integral	None.

These measures of degrees of enjambment will allow a quantitative assessment of the role of enjambment in the structure of tripartite lines of Hebrew poetry.[137]

134. Kirk was concerned with hexametric lines of poetry; the same concepts are here applied to cola.

135. Kirk, "Studies," 106–7. The theory of Kirk is cited by Watson, *Classical*, 334, in his appraisal of enjambment, but Watson erroneously references a different paper by Kirk from the same volume of YCS.

136. Adapted from Kirk, "Studies," 108. Punctuation marks colon and semicolon do not feature in this assessment, probably since the degree of syntactic pause that they represent is always the same as either a full stop or a comma. What distinguishes them is an indication of logical relationship between the two clauses they separate, which is a semantic rather than syntactic function.

137. Dobbs-Allsopp, "Enjambing Line (Part 1)," 224–38, produces a more nuanced taxonomy of enjambment, which he relates to Kirk's more readily quantifiable categories.

In assessing the functions of enjambment, Dobbs-Allsopp has not-ed that it has a role in controlling audience attention.[138] This observation may be related to insights garnered by Greenstein regarding the relation-ship between deep syntactic structure and surface syntactic structure. He discusses the fact that, "clauses that entail transformations have been found to demand more 'effort,' or 'audience participation,' than clauses in which the surface sequence more clearly reflects its deep structure."[139] He is particularly concerned here with sentences that have undergone transformations that produce significant changes in word order or dele-tions. Drawing on the work of others, he adopts the terms "hot" clauses, to describe those that have a surface structure close to the deep struc-ture, and "cool" clauses, to describe those that have a surface structure significantly transformed from its deep structure. His significant obser-vation is that "hot" clauses are readily interpreted and therefore tend to disengage the reader/listener, whereas "cool" clauses are more difficult and so tend to engage the reader/listener.[140] He postulates that a succes-sion of "cool" clauses within a line holds the attention and may lead to a climax. Conversely, a "hot" line at the end of a sequence of "cool" lines creates a closure as the reader/listener disengages.[141]

SEMANTIC RELATIONSHIPS

It was noted above that whilst the surface structure of a text provides the most appropriate basis for an analysis of the syntax of a poetic line, the semantic structure of the text is located in its deep structure, as rep-resented by "kernel sentences." According to Price, in the field of Bible translation at least two frameworks have been developed for analyzing the semantic structure of a text. Nida developed "dynamic equivalence theory" based on analyzing "kernel structures," which are essentially the same as Chomsky's "kernel sentences." Beekman, Callow, and Larson developed "meaning-based" translation, which is very similar but refers

---

138. Dobbs-Allsopp, "Enjambing Line (Part 2)," 375–76.

139. Greenstein, "How?," 54.

140. Ibid., 54–58. Greenstein actually uses the terms "hot parallelism" and "cool parallelism" but he is not referring to any relationships between the cola of a line, merely to the syntactic structure of each clause within it.

141. Ibid., 55–58.

to "propositions" rather than "kernel structures."[142] The latter theory will be adopted here.

Analysis of semantic structure of texts is achieved by breaking down the semantic content of the text into its component propositions, and determining the relations between these propositions.[143] Each proposition is a minimal semantic unit communicating an event or a state.[144] The illocutionary force of the proposition may be a statement, a question, or a command.[145] As already discussed, propositions embody the semantic content of the text and do not necessarily match the surface structure of the text, i.e., the particular terms used, the order of the words and the syntactic constructions. Thus a semantic proposition may be coincident with a grammatical clause, but often is not.[146] The recognition of "skewing" between semantic structure and syntactic structure therefore provides valuable insights into the function of the text.[147]

The meaning of a text is located not only in its component propositions but also in the relations between them. Propositions may be of equal prominence, with neither more important than the other. In this case, they would be related by "addition," corresponding to the grammatical relation of coordination. Other pairs of propositions may be of unequal importance, with one providing associated information for the other. In this case the proposition of lesser prominence will have a "support" relation to the other, corresponding to the grammatical relation of subordination.[148] Within these two broad categories are many different possible types of relation. A selection of those most pertinent to the evaluation of tricola in the Psalms of Ascents is given below.[149] In this presentation, capitalised descriptions are used to denote propositions of greater prominence; where such a proposition has no significant defining characteristic, it is denoted by the generic term "HEAD."

142. Price, *Theory*, 3–5.

143. See Beekman and Callow, *Translating*, 267–326 and Larson, *Translation*, 187–346. Wendland, *Analyzing*, 61–95, adopts the same technique.

144. Beekman and Callow, *Translating*, 273; Larson, *Translation*, 189.

145. Larson, *Translation*, 196.

146. Ibid., 189.

147. See ibid., 224–33.

148. Ibid., 275.

149. For a fuller list and explanation see Larson, *Translation*, 271–321, or Beekman and Callow, *Translating*, 284–312.

Propositions of equal prominence, related by addition, are pairs of head propositions and are denoted HEAD^1, HEAD^2.

Circumstance-HEAD	One proposition describes or defines the location, time, or other circumstance of the head proposition.
Orienter-CONTENT	One proposition introduces the content of speech, thought, sense, volition, or evaluation (relation characterized by "that").
HEAD-Equivalent	Head proposition is restated by an equivalent proposition.
HEAD-Amplification	Head proposition is restated with additional information.
GENERIC-Specifics	A broad proposition is clarified by more specific information.
HEAD-Manner	Head proposition is clarified by a proposition stating the manner in which the head proposition takes place.
HEAD-Comparison	An aspect of the thing or event that is the topic is compared to a corresponding aspect of a different thing or event (relation characterized by "as" or "like").
HEAD-Contrast	An aspect of the thing or event that is the topic is contrasted with an aspect of another thing or event that has some similarity (relation characterized by "but" or "except").
Reason-RESULT	One proposition gives a reason why the other is the case (relation characterized by "because" or "therefore").
Means-RESULT	One proposition explains the means by which the other proposition came about (relation characterized by "by" or "through").
MEANS-purpose	One proposition describes what action was undertaken to achieve an intended result (relation characterized by "in order to" or "so that").
Condition-CONSEQUENCE	One proposition describes a possible cause, and the other describes the consequent effect (relation characterized by "if").
HEAD-identification or HEAD-description	One proposition identifies or describes a particular concept in the head proposition, rather than relating to the head proposition as a whole.

Each of these relations can exist at different levels in a text, so whilst a pair of propositions might be related to each other in a certain way, as a pair they may relate to other propositions in a different way. When applied to poetry, the simplest analysis occurs when each colon in a line embodies a single proposition and these can readily be related. However, cola frequently embody either only part of a proposition or more than one proposition. The latter situation occurs, for example, whenever a colon incorporates a genitive phrase. A genitive phrase in itself embodies at least one, and possibly more than one, proposition.[150] For example, the phrase "his word," which is signified as a single word in Hebrew, may embody, among others, any of the following propositions:

- "He will speak a word."

- "He revealed a word."

- "Someone spoke a word about him."

- "He made a promise."

Even a single abstract noun typically embodies an event proposition.[151] Therefore the analysis of even short texts has the potential to be very complex. The application of this analysis to poetic lines can provide an insight into how they function semantically.

Theories of Poetic Macrostructure

General

Having considered the theoretical basis of the division of poetic text into cola and the way in which cola inter-relate in the formation of lines, attention now turns to the consideration of larger scale poetic structure. An intuitive response to almost any poetry but the shortest suggests that it is not merely a long succession of lines, but that lines are grouped and that these sets of lines have prosodic, structural, or rhetorical significance. The analysis and interpretation of such structuring can be carried out in a variety of ways, three broad types of which are considered here.

The most immediate sense of structure in a psalm is its division into sections according to their thematic content. This approach under-

---

150. Larson, *Translation*, 228–31.

151. Ibid., 226–27.

pins the form-critical approach to the psalms developed by Gunkel.[152] However, whilst the different functional components of a psalm might indicate a structure, the identification of its overall *Gattung* and *Sitz im Leben* do not add anything further and are not directly relevant to the present study.

A strophic analysis of poetic structure looks for patterns in the lengths of lines and groups of lines. It is concerned with the interface between prosody and semantics. It may be informed by the rhetorical impact of the words in so far as this influences the intonational division of the text. Rhythmical considerations naturally come within the orbit of this type of analysis, but a specific or regular rhythm is not an essential aspect of it. Where rhythm is a consideration, it can interpreted broadly, encompassing "thought rhythm" (cf. Robinson's analysis discussed in the section "Accentual metre" on pp. 23–29) as well as more formal phonic unit counting.

An alternative approach to structural analysis takes the principles of parallelism and applies them on a larger scale. Patterns of symmetry can be identified within the formal features of the poetry, such as word repetitions, matching or opposing grammatical forms and rhyme. This approach is identified here as "rhetorico-structural" for reasons discussed below (see the section "Rhetorico-Structural Approaches" on pp. 61–65).

Strophic and rhetorico-structural theories warrant a detailed exposition, in order to apply them appropriately to the Psalms of Ascents.

Strophic Approaches

A range of scholars adopt some form of strophic analysis of poetic texts, with widely varying degrees of methodology. Terrien's commentary subtitled "Strophic Structure," gives the most meagre indication of how he has arrived at his division into strophes.[153] It is probable that in fact his basis is something akin to what Kissane makes explicit: that each strophe is a group of verses expressing "a certain phase of the poet's thought" such that there is "a definite break in the sense between one strophe and

---

152. Gunkel, *Psalms*; for a simple introduction to the concepts see Gillingham, *Poems and Psalms*, 177–80.

153. Terrien, *Strophic Structure*, 39–40; he is similarly critiqued by Wendland, "Aspects," 115 n. 21.

another."[154] The subjective nature of this type of approach is immediately apparent.

A much more thorough, and ostensibly objective, methodology was developed by Van der Lugt in his dissertation on strophic structures in Biblical Hebrew poetry at Kampen in 1980.[155] Since then other scholars associated with the Kampen School of Theology have developed a method of formal analysis of Hebrew poetry based on Van der Lugt's work.[156] There are important differences between Van der Lugt's and others' approach to Hebrew poetry, but their common origin and substantial overlap justify a combined discussion.

The systems proposed by these scholars combine some semantic aspects—particularly examining how certain lexemes mark openings and closures—with prosodic concerns. The systems encompass analysis of poetic structure at every level, from cola up to complete poems. As noted above (in the section "Other approaches" on pp. 32–37), they are relatively weak in the area of colometry. They are stronger in the area of the analysis of strophes and higher structural units. Here the systematic identification of semantic and formal markers has much to commend it, and the identification of a strophe as essentially a semantic unit carries much more validity. Indeed, it is precisely because the colon and line do not necessarily coincide with semantic units, that a division into semantic units at a higher level is necessary and reflective of the experience of the hearer/reader of the poetry.

Beyond the level of the line, a hierarchy of structural levels of poetry can be defined, the immediate aggregation of lines commonly being referred to as strophes. Van der Lugt provides a thorough historical survey of the many theories of strophic structures.[157] The identification of strophes has most commonly been proposed on the basis of their content. Some theorists have characterized strophes as chiastic, such as Lund;[158] others as marked out by deictic particles, by syntax and by

---

154. Kissane, *Book of Psalms*, xxxix–xl.

155. Recently re-presented and applied to the Psalter in Van der Lugt, *Cantos and Strophes*.

156. See particularly Van der Meer and de Moor, *Structural Analysis*; the work of Fokkelman is also rooted in the same school of thought.

157. Van der Lugt, *Cantos and Strophes*, 2–68.

158. Lund, "Chiasmus in the Psalms," 287–312; Van der Lugt, *Cantos and Strophes*, 31–33.

variation of line length to indicate conclusion, such as Kraft.[159] Common to almost all theorists is the view that some poems have equal strophes, others have unequal strophes.

For Korpel and de Moor, the aggregation of lines into higher levels, and the demarcation of these levels, is based on the identification of parallelism between lines and of transition markers.[160] The markers are primarily semantic, "securing the renewed interest of the audience, for example deictic particles, imperatives, vocatives, tautological parallelism, extra long verses, and so on."[161] According to such analysis, a strophe is found to consist of one to four lines. Similarly groupings of strophes into higher-level units is also undertaken. A "canticle" is said to consist of one to five strophes, and a "canto" of one to four canticles, although the delimitation of these structural units is somewhat less clear than is the case for strophes.[162] Van der Lugt employs a slightly different use of the terminology, suggesting that strophes and cantos are the common divisions, and that the canticle is an intermediate level found only in longer poems. He does not specify any limits for these structural units; he suggests that a strophe usually consists of two or three lines and discerns strophes of one to three lines and cantos of one to five strophes.[163]

A similarity is evident here with the proposal of Fokkelman. His numerical basis of structural analysis is as follows: each colon has two to four stresses (although one or five can occur), each line has two or three cola, each strophe has two or three lines, and each stanza has two or three strophes.[164] The derivation of this system is based on Fokkelman's own reading and observation of poetic texts. The evidence he presents for such groupings varies widely, including anaphora, chiasms, key words, rhyme, change, in speaker or genre, and quotation formula. The range of evidence is so wide that the choice of determining factor, and hence the

159. Kraft, "Further Observations," 64–65; Van der Lugt, *Cantos and Strophes*, 35 and 49.

160. Korpel and de Moor use the term "separation marker"; Van der Lugt uses "transition marker"; Van der Lugt's term is used here for consistency.

161. Korpel and de Moor, "Fundamentals," 33. Contrast the most evident grouping of lines in acrostic poems by means of a lexical feature. By "tautological parallelism" seems to be meant verbatim repetition of a word or suffix. It is quite ambiguous how this functions as a transition marker.

162. Korpel and de Moor, "Fundamentals," 38–53.

163. Van der Lugt, *Cantos and Strophes*, 71–72, 420–26.

164. Fokkelman, *Major Poems II*, 41; see also Fokkelman, *Reading*, 37.

demarcation of strophes, is rather subjective, as he acknowledges: "How does the strophe manifest and distinguish itself? . . . there is no simple recipe and I'm not going to look for it."[165]

In Korpel and de Moor's work, the identification of transition markers does not distinguish between "upwards" separation and "downwards" separation; the same markers are said to fulfil either function. Since many strophes consist of only two lines, this means that separation markers are identified in every line. Such prevalence tends to diminish their weight as functional elements and calls into question how they communicate to the hearer/reader whether they demark the beginning or end of a strophe.

Van der Lugt notes this criticism of Korpel and de Moor's work and clearly distinguishes between opening and closing transition markers.[166] He also refines the understanding of transition markers by suggesting that an *opening* marker can also be found at the *end* of a higher rhetorical unit; and that a *closure* marker can also be found at the *beginning* of a higher unit. Some of Van der Lugt's proposed markers are self-evident: vocatives, interrogatives and imperatives marking opening; references to eternity marking closure.[167] However, others are not: some "emphatic" particles mark opening whilst others mark closure; some demonstratives and pronouns mark opening whilst others mark closure. The distinction is based on the incidence of each particular word at the beginning or at the end of a strophe or higher rhetorical unit. However, the counts are based on strophic analyses, which, in turn, are said to be based (in part) upon the identification of transition markers. It therefore seems that a circular argument has been created, and Van der Lugt's conclusions must be taken cautiously.[168] For example, there can be no semantic or syntactic reason why אֲנִי is an opening marker and אָנֹכִי is a closing marker. It is difficult to believe that this was a poetic convention that would be recognised by the users of the psalms; rather it may simply

---

165. Fokkelman, *Major Poems I*, 9.

166. Van der Lugt, *Cantos and Strophes*, 78–80. He also cites Fokkelman's criticism of there being too many transition markers and refutes this: Van der Lugt, *Cantos and Strophes*, 58fn83.

167. Cf. Wyckoff, "Closure," 84–85, on עוֹלָם as a marker of closure.

168. See Van der Lugt, *Cantos and Strophes*, 537–64, for the full analysis of occurrences of each marker.

be that these words happen to have different distributions amongst the lines of the Psalter.[169]

Korpel and de Moor identify a line that is a tricolon (or longer) as a transition marker. At the end of a strophe this makes good sense: the, possibly unexpectedly, longer line marking the end of a structural semantic unit and a pause in the flow of thought. However, at the beginning of a strophe, the transition marker would need to be at the beginning of the line, in order to "secure the renewed interest of the audience,"[170] whereas the identification of a tricolon comes only at the end of a line. It is difficult to conceive how the tricolon, when heard/read, could indicate a division that was supposed to have occurred prior to it.

Van der Lugt's more detailed, and inconclusive, assessment of the transition marking function of tricola has been discussed above (see the section "Previous Tricolon Studies" on pp. 3–8).[171]

In addition to his identification of transition markers, Van der Lugt has also provided a detailed analysis of "verbal repetitions"[172] within a poem. These he distinguishes between "responsions" that provide linear development within a poem and typically bind lines within a strophe, "concatenations" that provide continuity between strophes, and "inclusios" that frame a poem or section of a poem at its beginning and end.[173] However, whilst an inclusion can mark closure, the functions of responsion and concatenation are quite distinct from transition marking.

In general, Van der Lugt's analysis of transition markers is more thorough and plausible than that of Korpel and de Moor. However, his analysis must be tempered by recognition of its partly self-substantiating nature and conclusions drawn on weak statistical grounds, as discussed above. Provided these specific issues are taken into account, the identification of transition markers, and analysis of repetitions, offer a good means of analyzing the strophic structures of Hebrew poetry.

169. Since the most common strophe length is two lines, most occurrences of a given word will fall in either the opening or closing line of a strophe. Similar comments apply to זאת (opening) and זה (closing).

170. Korpel and de Moor, "Fundamentals," 33.

171. Van der Lugt, *Cantos and Strophes*, 522–35.

172. The expression "verbal repetition" is used by Van der Lugt to mean "verbatim repetition"; it is not limited to verbs or verbal forms.

173. Ibid., 82–83 and 462–87. On *concatenatio* see also Van Dyke Parunak, "Transitional Techniques," 526–28.

Rhetorico-Structural Approaches

A body of literature has developed around the premise that the symmetrical features of Hebrew poetry manifested as "parallelism" at the level of the line are also operative on a much larger scale. That is to say, structures of symmetry can be discerned within a text (be it poetry or narrative), wherein a sequence (of words, forms or themes) is either repeated identically or repeated in an inverted order. An identical repeated sequence creates a parallel structure, whilst a sequence repeated in inverted form creates a chiastic structure. Instances of chiastic structures having an additional unique central element are labelled as concentric structures.[174] Since such structures are regarded as integral to the rhetorical function of the text, the process of their identification is variously referred to as "structural analysis" (Francophone scholars' "analyse structurelle") or "rhetorical analysis." Unfortunately these terms are ambiguous, the former, when rendered thus in English, potentially referring to a number of approaches to a text, and the latter prone to confusion with "rhetorical criticism," which is the analysis of texts in relation to classical rhetoric. In light of the potential confusion, Lunn has coined the term "rhetorico-structural analysis" to refer specifically to the analysis of structures of symmetry within a text that inform its rhetorical function.[175]

174. Meynet, *Rhetorical Analysis*, 199.

175. Lunn, *Word-Order*, 161–62. A fuller discussion of the terminology is in Meynet, *Rhetorical Analysis*, 37–40. Whether the approach comes under the umbrella of Structuralism is a matter of ambiguity. Girard, *Psaumes 1:1–50*, 28–29, believes that it does not, since it deals with the "surface structure" of the text rather than the "deep structures" of Chomskyan generative grammar. However, Girard is possibly failing to discriminate between the origins of Structuralism and its application to literature. Those authors who have examined the application of Structuralism to the study of literature, highlight the very same type of structures that form the basis of rhetorico-structural analysis. Sturrock, *Structuralism*, 103–28, explains that Structuralist analysis of texts is concerned with uncovering the rules that govern their composition, in order to show how texts "work" and therefore enrich them semantically. He cites an understanding of parallelism as a particular instance of such an analysis. Similarly, Culler, *Structuralist Poetics*, 58–63, refers to Jakobson's Structuralist analysis of poetry, which includes a demonstration of "how symmetrical distribution of grammatical items organizes the stanzas into various groupings." The similarity to rhetorico-structural analysis is most apparent. Indeed, Culler goes on to make the criticism that Jakobson's overall method "permits one to find in a poem any type of organization which one looks for," the very same criticism of the more liberal rhetorico-structural analyses which follows below. Scholes, *Structuralism*, 157–58, attempts to bridge between the approaches by distinguishing "high structuralism" and "low structuralism," whereby "poetics is . . . low structuralism. At its worst it degenerates into mere taxonomy."

Two authors have provided a detailed background to, and methodology for, rhetorico-structural analysis: Meynet, who applies the method to both narrative and poetic texts, and Girard, who has applied the method in detail to the psalms.[176] Meynet's introduction to the method of rhetorico-structural analysis ("rhetorical analysis" in his terminology), traces its origins in the nineteenth century in the work of Jebb and Boys, through Lund's detailed theories about chiastic structures, to an outline of the method at the present time. Jebb and Boys each adopted the principles of parallelism, as identified by Lowth, in order to analyze the interlinear structures of texts. They found instances of both alternating parallelism, denoted typically ABA'B', and what they termed "introverted parallelism," denoted ABB'A'.

The latter, of course, came to be known more commonly as chiasmus. The correspondences they identified ranged across semantic, lexical, syntactic, and morphological domains.[177]

An appreciation of chiastic structures was greatly enhanced by the work of Lund.[178] In analyzing specific texts, he observed that textual units could exhibit a mixture of chiastic and alternating structures.[179] In the second half of the twentieth century a wide range of authors have offered analysis of specific texts, although not always backed up with a clear methodology.[180]

Meynet has expounded his own set of principles for a rhetorico-structural analysis of a text. The linguistic domains of the text with which he engages are lexemes, morphemes, syntactical function, rhythm, and discourse function. He seeks to identify relationships of "identity" or

---

Notwithstanding these comments, the rhetorico-structural approach is probably best not identified definitively with Structuralism, both because of the objection of some of its practitioners (e.g., Girard) and because it does not necessarily embrace the fundamental assumptions about the nature of language that are embodied in Structuralism. This is best expressed by Bovon "Structuralism and Exegesis," 7, who made a clear distinction between the method of Structuralism and its ideology, commenting that "it is as a method . . . that this movement will be of service to theologians."

176. Probably the most prolific exponent of the method, Auffret, offers no methodology of his own but refers to Girard. Auffret, *Etude Structurelle*, v.

177. Meynet, *Rhetorical Analysis*, 69–126. See also the historical overview of Van Dyke Parunak, "Transitional Techniques," 525–26.

178. Lund, "Chiasmus in the Psalms" and *Chiasmus in New Testament*. Alden "Chiastic Psalms" and "Chiastic Psalms (III)" enthusiastically adopts his approach.

179. Lund, "Chiasmus in the Psalms," 283–84; Meynet, *Rhetorical Analysis*, 144.

180. See Girard, *Psaumes 1:1–50*, 19–23, for a survey of published psalms analyses.

"opposition" between textual elements in each of these domains.[181] Note that the first three domains in this list correspond to the aspects of parallelism studied by Berlin; that the domain of rhythm reflects engagement with the same concern as the metricists; and the final domain indicates a concern for syntactical analysis. Therefore the range of potential relationships being considered is very great indeed.[182]

Girard has a similar approach, which is both narrower and more carefully defined. The relationships identified by Girard are repetition, synonymy, synthesis, and antithesis, but he is careful to place greater weight on the significance of the (objectively-determined) repetitions than the more subjective semantic relationships.[183] The domain for such relationships is limited almost entirely by Girard to lexemes/words and cola. He does not concern himself with morphemes or rhythm, but focuses on the formal aspects of the text. He does make use of corresponding syntactical functions in practice, although this is not highlighted in the exposition of his methodology.

Meynet and Girard each suggest a hierarchy of structural levels of text. Whilst employing their own idiosyncratic terminology, their levels are virtually identical to those of the strophic analysts.[184] At each of these levels they then seek to identify structures of symmetry, be they parallel (having identical sequencing) or chiastic (inverted sequencing).

The relationships identified by Meynet over a range of linguistic domains are treated as all having equal value. In contrast, Girard is very careful to establish a hierarchy of validity of the types of correspondences that may be identified: word repetitions take precedence over semantic connections; priority is given to rarer words, repetition of common words being taken as structural indicators only with caution; and synonymous connections should not be assumed at higher levels unless they are well-attested at lower levels.[185] Similarly, Girard is clearer

181. Meynet, *Rhetorical Analysis*, 182–98.

182. The range could be expanded further: Levine, "Vertical Poetics" has explored "interlinear phonological parallelism."

183. Girard, *Psaumes 1:1–50*, 34, 99–100.

184. Meynet, *Rhetorical Analysis*, uses "member" for colon, "segment" for line, "piece" for strophe, "part" for stanza/canto; his method and terminology are intended for use with narrative as well as poetic texts. Girard, *Psaumes 1:1–50* does not make much use of explicit labelling, but his analysis operates at the level of words, cola and "larger units."

185. Girard, *Psaumes 1:1–50*, 111–14.

in his method with regard to use of different indicators at different levels. Whilst he analyzes the line level in the normal categories of parallelism, he identifies the higher textual units through features such as inclusio (delimiting a section of text), concatenation (linking separate sections of text), and other "signposting" such as anaphora, refrains, and acrostics.[186]

Whilst the results of such analyses are instructive and illuminating, a number of caveats must be raised in connection with his approach. These concern the extent to which the method should be limited in its quest for structures of symmetry. Meynet appears to suggest that there are no limits to the appropriate dissection of the text. "Texts which resist explanation will eventually yield the secret of their composition, *no matter what it takes*."[187] Such an assertion betrays an over-confidence in his particular theory of Hebrew rhetorical structure as the universal paradigm for analyzing the texts. His quest for structures of symmetry results in highly complex analyses, but little sense of an evaluation of the validity or benefit of these analyses. Girard does offer guidelines on how to assess the multiplicity of possible structural indicators, noting that more than one structure may be discerned but that not all apparent "structures" have equal value.[188] Indeed, he makes specific criticism of Auffret's analyses precisely because they tend to produce multiple results without any discrimination.[189]

Meynet's actual practice is to keep cola intact (except in instances of lexical correspondence between each individual term in adjacent cola), implying a perspective on the colon as the basic building block of the text, and thus allowing the identification of structures of symmetry that are commensurate with the way in which the text is experienced when read or heard. Girard adopts a similar approach, although he does on occasions split a colon between different structural sections. This appears to be valid, at least in some instances, when it is based on word repetitions that form a symmetrical structure. This would appear to indicate that there is an interplay between the rhetorico-structural shape

---

186. Ibid., 70–75, 89–91.

187. Meynet, *Rhetorical Analysis*, 172, emphasis not original.

188. Girard, *Psaumes 1:1–50*, 99–100, 111–14.

189. Ibid., 25–26, 94–95. Auffret, *Etude Structurelle*, has a much more liberal attitude towards the dissection of the text. His analysis of structures regularly involves the breaking down of cola, and even words into individual lexemes, with symmetries that might match an entire colon or line with a single preposition. His work has been rightly criticised by Girard for such uninhibited manipulation of the text.

of a text and the rhythmical pattern of its colometry which is not one of exact correspondence. A simple example would be a colon that forms the centre of a concentric structure. Within the rhetorical structure it would stand alone, but if set within a bicolic text, it would require a counterpart.

In summary, the method of rhetorico-structural analysis is a valuable tool in discerning the rhetorical and stylistic mechanisms upon which a text is built. Three specific caveats must regulate its appropriation: chiastic arrangements should not be overemphasised to the neglect of linear/sequential development; structures analyzed need to be reasonably commensurate with the more immediately experienced rhythmical (colometric) structure of the text; and the lexical and semantic correspondences that form the basis of the structure ought to be all the more apparent the further apart in the text they occur.[190]

Numerological Approaches

A substantial body of work has grown around the idea of numerological organisation of texts in general, and applied to specific psalms.[191] This involves counting words, cola and lines on the premises that instances of seven, eleven, seventeen and twenty six (and their multiples) convey significance and that the numerically central feature(s) of a psalm represents its focus. Notwithstanding any discussion regarding the validity of such an approach, it will not be engaged with in the present study since it does not provide a coherent framework for establishing colometry, but requires an assumed colometry as its starting point.[192]

---

190. The latter point is particularly emphasized in the study of inclusion as a marker of closure by Wyckoff, "Closure," 35.

191. See Christiansen, "Logoprosodic Analysis"; Labuschagne, "Logotechnical Analysis" and "Compositional Techniques"; and the substantial resources available through their websites.

192. In practice, its advocates tend to prioritise the Masoretic accentuation and the strophic analysis of the Kampen school, described in the section "Strophic Approaches" on pp. 56–60.

3

Colometric and Structural Analysis
of the Psalms of Ascents

Basis of Analysis

Colometry

THE MT OF THE Psalms of Ascents has been analyzed in the light of the review of theories of colometry described above (chapter 2 "Theories of Poetic Structure"). The starting point for determining colometry is taken as the lineation and accentuation of the MT. This provides an unambiguous datum for the analysis. Textual variants are noted and assessed from the point of view of their rhythmical implications and any evidence they might provide of errors of transmission or corruption of the poetic form of the text. Relationships between cola are assessed in order to identify any structural and aesthetic features that influence the colometry.

Each verse of the MT is initially assumed to represent a poetic line, with the locations of caesurae indicated by the major disjunctive accents. In instances where a verse of MT is plainly twice as long as most other verses in the psalm, or longer, it is read as two or more poetic lines. This initial colometry is reviewed in the light of Fokkelman's proposed limit of two to five word-units per colon with the allocation of stresses and rhythmical description of the text following Sievers' system.[1] Whilst *maqqephim* are included in the reproduction of the MT, along with some of the principal accents, the allocation of stresses following Sievers' theory may not necessarily result in reading words joined by a *maqqeph* as

---

1. Comparison with O'Connor's constraints is also made in some instances, but the flaws identified in O'Connor's system mean that it is not regarded as determinative.

a single-stress unit. Where this review and rhythmical appraisal throws up conflicts or ambiguities, the alternative solutions are appraised, taking into account the following criteria (without any particular order of precedence):

- A caesura should normally coincide with a disjunctive accent, or in other words, word-units connected by a conjunctive accent should not normally be split between cola. The major disjunctive accent in a line should coincide with a caesura.

- The assessment of potentially long cola incorporates comparison with Fokkelman's proposed limit of twelve syllables per colon as a normal maximum.

- In the case of a possible four word-unit colon, it is preferably not split into two cola for the reasons discussed in the section "The Problem of Four-Word Cola" on pp. 44–46, unless there are broader rhythmical or structural reasons for doing so. The identification of the line as a para-tricolon is one such reason.

- The case of a possible five word-unit colon is regarded as exceptional and is preferably split unless all other criteria can be satisfied.

- If patterns of rhythmical regularity are discernible in a psalm, colometry that matches this is preferable.

- Enjambment is preferably minimized, such that rhythmical pauses coincide with syntactic pauses where possible.

The layout of the MT at the head of each section represents the colometry that is concluded from this process. Reference to individual cola, using the labels a, b, c, etc., is based upon this colometry, not upon that indicated in BHS nor that implied by any other author. In labelling the cola of each first verse, the superscription has been ignored, such that v. 1a refers to the first colon after the superscription.

Psalm Structure

The overall structure of each psalm is analyzed from three perspectives. First, a brief comment on the thematic content of the psalm is offered. This is based mainly on the work of form critics who tend to analyze and relate the content to possible liturgical contexts.

Secondly, the strophic analysis proposed by Van der Lugt is implemented. The text of each psalm is reproduced in such a way as to illustrate the method: words identified as transition markers are boxed and words/lexemes that are repeated are circled. The overall structure of the psalm is indicated according to Van der Lugt's nomenclature, with the number of lines per strophe listed, a dot separating strophes within a canto and a vertical bar separating cantos.[2] The characteristics of each strophe and areas of ambiguity are discussed, and comparison to strophic analyses by other scholars is made.

Thirdly, the rhetorico-structural method is adopted in order to determine the rhetorical structure of each psalm. The principles established by Girard form the basis of this approach, focusing on the lexical repetitions that are annotated in the strophic analysis sub-section. The work of Auffret, and other analysts, is also noted for comparison where relevant.

Psalm 120

Colometric Analysis

1 שִׁיר הַמַּעֲלוֹת

אֶל־יְהוָה בַּצָּרָתָה לִּי   קָרָאתִי וַיַּעֲנֵנִי׃

2 יְהוָה הַצִּילָה נַפְשִׁי   מִשְּׂפַת־שֶׁקֶר מִלָּשׁוֹן רְמִיָּה׃

3 מַה־יִּתֵּן לְךָ וּמַה־יֹּסִיף לָךְ   לָשׁוֹן רְמִיָּה׃

4 חִצֵּי גִבּוֹר שְׁנוּנִים   עִם גַּחֲלֵי רְתָמִים׃

5 אוֹיָה־לִי כִּי־גַרְתִּי מֶשֶׁךְ   שָׁכַנְתִּי עִם־אָהֳלֵי קֵדָר׃

6 רַבַּת שָׁכְנָה־לָּהּ נַפְשִׁי   עִם שׂוֹנֵא שָׁלוֹם׃

7 אֲנִי־שָׁלוֹם וְכִי אֲדַבֵּר   הֵמָּה לַמִּלְחָמָה׃

Verse 1 consists of an opening bicolon. A minor curiosity here is that M[L] presents the mid-line gap after קָרָאתִי despite the imbalanced rhythm this generates (4+1) and the accentuation indicating the caesura at לִּי. Perhaps the scribe considered the first colon incomplete without its verb. Indeed the splitting of a verbal clause in this way generates an integral enjambment (caesura at a place of no syntactic pause), which is very

---

2. Although in the present study the term "stanza" is preferred, Van der Lugt's use of "canto" is retained in citations and discussions of his strophic analysis. The two terms may be regarded as synonyms.

unusual and would normally be regarded as an indication of potentially corrupt colometry. So, for example, in the light of this and of the unusual word order, Lunn reads the line as a monocolon.[3] However, it is also possible to recognize in the line a poetic device that creates ambiguity and forward impetus[4] and which creates a syntactic discomfort illustrating the distress that the line describes. The resolution of the ambiguity in the second colon ties the line together. The line is therefore read according to the accentuation as a 3+2 bicolon.

Verse 2 opens with a vocative phrase of three words, the conjunctive accent on the imperative verb indicating that the words should not be divided. This leaves three more word-units in the line (both according to the *maqqeph* and according to Sievers' theory) and these are formed of two phrases.[5] Three options for the distribution of stresses between cola are immediately apparent.[6] One option is to read a bicolon, following the accentuation that divides the line at שֶׁקֶר thus creating an imbalanced 4+2 rhythm but also a degree of synonymy between cola.[7] This is similar to the type of "unbalanced bicolon" proposed by Revell, except that the two synonymous phrases are split between cola whereas Revell was concerned with lines exhibiting internal parallelism in the longer colon. A second option is to read the line as a 3+2+2 tricolon, ignoring the *maqqeph* and ascribing two stresses to מִשְּׂפַת־שֶׁקֶר. Following Gray's, and Robinson's, preference for equating two-word phrases with cola (see the sections "Accentual Metre" on pp. 23–29 and "The Problem of Four-Word Cola" on pp. 44–46), this approach is adopted by several translators.[8] However, this approach is rooted in reading the line according to

3. Lunn, *Word-order*, 191.

4. Dobbs-Allsopp, "Enjambing Line (Part 1)," 226–27 and "Enjambing Line (Part 2)," 371.

5. The disyllable construct is unstressed before the stressed syllable of a segholate. Sievers, *Metrische Studien*, 200. This approach is matched by the vocalization implied by the *maqqeph* joining the words.

6. Assuming that the text is kept intact. Jacquet, *Les Psaumes*, 408, deletes נַפְשִׁי, along with other emendations, in order to maintain a consistent 3+2 rhythm for every line. Such an approach is purely speculative and gives undue weight to metrical theory against all the textual evidence.

7. Lunn, *Word-order*, 18fn43, follows the accentuation and reads the line as a parallel bicolon with double ellipsis (of the verb and the object).

8. NRSV, Weiser, *The Psalms*, 741, and Allen, *Psalms 101–50*, 197 (citing Kraus, *Psalms 60–150*, 422), all present this line as a tricolon, suggesting that it thus "matches" verse 3.

Sievers' 2–2–2 pattern, which is not compatible with assigning a total of seven stresses to the line rather than six. A third option is to divide the line at נַפְשִׁי to give a balanced rhythm and generate internal parallelism within the following colon.[9] All three options satisfy O'Connor's and Fokkelman's numerical constraints. The syllable count for the three phrases, 7/4/6, does not suggest any means of achieving "balanced" cola. There is not sufficient evidence to regard the line as a full tricolon, nor does it fit the 2–2–2 pattern. It is therefore regarded as a bicolon, with some residual ambiguity over the division of the line.

A further possibility arises if a modification of the Masoretic lineation can be countenanced. Briggs and Briggs indicate that the divine name at the head of v. 2 actually belongs at the end of v. 1, but without giving a reason.[10] As such it would not be a vocative but the subject of the preceding verb. Were this the case, the first line would then be a balanced bicolon, 3+3, and the second line would be read either as a 3+2 bicolon or with an extra stress as a 2–2–2, albeit departing from Sievers' stress system in the allocation of the extra stress. The appeal of such an approach is that it potentially allows every line of the psalm to read as either 3+3 or 2–2–2. However, the necessary modification to lineation and stress allocation means that it is at best speculative, and cannot be a valid basis for determining the function and character of tripartite lines.

Verse 3 typifies a whole class of lines in Biblical Hebrew poetry. It consists of three two-word phrases, in this instance with a degree of parallelism between the first two.[11]

מַה־יִּתֵּן לְךָ   וּמַה־יֹּסִיף לָךְ   לָשׁוֹן רְמִיָּה׃

There are textual variants in each of the three phrases, but they concern re-pointing the verbs and possibly adding a preposition to the final noun phrase and so do not have a bearing on the division into cola. The two alternative ways of dividing the line are as an unbalanced bicolon (4+2), according to the Masoretic accentuation, or as a para-tricolon (2–2–2).[12]

9. Thus Fokkelman, *Major Poems II*, 294, without any explicit justification.

10. Briggs and Briggs, *Exegetical Commentary*, 444–45.

11. Cf. 121:4, 130:5; with parallelism between the second and third phrases: 122:5, 130:6; with no significant semantic parallelism: 124:6, 126:1.

12. Kraus, *Psalms 60–150*, 422–23 (translated from German edition of 1978) and Allen, *Psalms 101–50*, 197, present the line as a tricolon but curiously cite its rhythm as 3+2+2, the derivation of which is not apparent. Allen and Kraus tend consistently to present such lines as full tricola, presumably taking the analysis of Sievers to imply this approach. Kissane, *Book of Psalms*, 564, also reads a tricolon.

The ambiguity between the two options is evident when various theories are applied to them. Both options generally satisfy O'Connor's syntactic constraints and Fokkelman's numerical limits (including syllable counts).[13] Gray and Robinson would split the first two phrases into distinct cola in order to highlight their parallelism. On the other hand, Watson would leave the two phrases combined in a single colon and point out its "internal parallelism." In his review of such lines, Watson comments "such couplets could also be considered tricola—with the equivalent of three lines packed into two—or they may be the forerunners of true tricola with three full lines."[14] Similarly, Revell, who regards only pausal forms as definitive evidence for a caesura, would present the line as an unbalanced bicolon, also pointing out the internal parallelism within the first colon. Whichever perspective is adopted, it remains clear that the line comprises three distinct phrases, with little evidence for either of the pauses between them being stronger than the other. Therefore the line is classified, and will be explored further, as a para-tricolon.

Verses 4–6 are all bicola. Each colon has syntactical integrity, and each line has development between cola. The rhythm of each line is 3+3.[15] There are lexical difficulties in verses 5 and 6, but these would not influence the colometry.[16] Verse 5 expresses a complaint in two broadly synonymous cola, and v. 6 repeats it at greater length.

Verse 7 is puzzling, both in its syntax and its colometry.[17] The initial two words, joined by a *maqqeph*, either form a nominal clause or imply

13. The only exception being that the unbalanced bicolon option fails to comply with O'Connor's prohibition on two predicators each governing a nominal phrase in the first colon. However, this is further evidence of the weakness of O'Connor's theory rather than grounds to reject the line as a bicolon.

14. Watson, "Half-line Parallelism," 60. Watson uses "line" to mean "colon"; see Glossary.

15. It is also possible to read v. 6 as 3+2 by leaving עַם unstressed as it is followed by only one other unstressed syllable. Note, however, that reading the following participle as plural (with LXX) introduces an extra unstressed syllable and supports the retention of full stress on the preposition, maintaining the 3+3 rhythm. Allen, *Psalms 101–50*, 198, notes the textual evidence for a plural and suggests that the MT might represent a scribal abbreviation.

16. Whether מֶשֶׁךְ is read as a noun with a missing preposition or as a verb; the meaning of the unusual ethical dative construction in v. 6a; and whether the participle in v. 6b is read as singular (MT) or plural (LXX).

17. The variant colometry of LXX, reading v. 7a with v. 6, implies an excessively long line and loses the obvious contrast between שָׁלוֹם and מִלְחָמָה. It is not considered a reliable tradition. See Crow, *Songs of Ascents*, 31.

an elided element. Common interpretations of an elided element are a verb,[18] such as דבר, or the copula, assuming that the noun שָׁלוֹם is used adjectivally.[19] Alternatively, the first four words of the line may be read together as a single clause. Kraus does this by emending כִּי to כֵּן so that the two nouns stand in conjunction as the object of the verb, but there is no textual evidence for such a reading.[20] Allen originally read a single clause by regarding the unusual word order as a form of emphasis, but has since regarded וְכִי as the marker of a new clause.[21] In this he follows Cody who studied other instances of וְכִי and concluded that it represents a simple conjunction and the opening of a new clause.[22] The lack of evidence for a variant text and the lack of a convincing explanation for the presence of וְכִי in the middle of a single clause lead to the conclusion that the first four words represent two conjoined clauses. The final nominal clause of the line is joined paratactically, and its relationship to the other two must be inferred. Most translations and commentaries regard it as governing the medial clause, which is read as a subordinate clause of circumstance. However, these two clauses could equally well be regarded as independent.[23]

The accentuation indicates a division of the line as a 3+2 bicolon, shortening the pattern of 3+3 of the previous lines. However, Sievers believed that pronouns should almost always be stressed.[24] Allocation of a full stress to the 1c.s. pronoun that opens the line, therefore ignoring the *maqqeph*, results in a six stress line that naturally divides according to its syntactic structure into three cola of two stresses each i.e., reading the line as 2–2–2.[25] Fokkelman presents the line thus, commenting that "the

---

18. Although the clauses do not fit the criteria for typical verb ellipsis; see C. L. Miller, "Linguistic Approach," 262–65.

19. Cody, "Psalm 120," 61; Crow, *Songs of Ascents*, 31.

20. Kraus, *Psalms 60–150*, 422–23.

21. Allen, *Psalms 101–50*, 198; Briggs and Briggs, *Exegetical Commentary* state categorically "nor can [שלם] be obj. of אדבר, thrown before for emphasis."

22. Cody, "Psalm 120," 59–60.

23. Anderson, *Psalms: Volume 2*, 850.

24. Sievers, *Metrische Studien*, 198–99.

25. This would probably be Sievers' approach. The stress on הֵמָּה would be transferred to the final syllable; cf. his treatment of Ps 25:6, ibid., 519. Note also that the addition of a preposition to the noun, attested in two mss, would also result in the allocation of a full stress to the pronoun.

three predicators require a tricolon."[26] This comment is consonant with O'Connor's constraints: the bicolon fails his criteria because the initial colon would contain a predicator and a nominal phrase that is not dependent on it. As with v. 2, the syllable count offers little assistance: the three phrases having 4/5/6 syllables means that either a bicolon or para-tricolon would be acceptable. The ambiguity over the relationships of the medial clause supports reading a para-tricolon. If the medial clause is subordinate to the third clause, then a bicolon that separated these two clauses would unreasonably distort the structure of the line. Therefore since the tripartite structure of the line is very clear, it is identified as a para-tricolon.

Structural Analyses

Thematic Analysis

Gerstenberger reads the psalm as a complaint and does not detect any structure beyond the lineation.[27] Kraus discerns an extra level of structuring by grouping:

> vv. 1–2 as prayer,
>
> vv. 3–4 as "a cry for revenge,"
>
> and vv. 5–7 as a reference to the locus of the psalmist's distress.[28]

In fact Kraus prefers to read the psalm as a thanksgiving, such that v. 1 is thanksgiving and v. 2 a citation of past prayer; but this does not affect the structuring.

---

26. Fokkelman, *Major Poems II*, 294. Seybold, *Die Psalmen*, 476, also reads a tricolon.

27. Gerstenberger, *Psalms*, 317. Similarly Weiser, *The Psalms*, 742–44 links only vv. 5–6.

28. Kraus, *Psalms 60–150*, 423. So also Allen, *Psalms 101–50*, 198.

STROPHIC ANALYSIS

Structure: 2.2.3

Strophe 1 refers to, and voices, a cry of distress to Yahweh, and is dominated by first person singular forms. The vocative and imperative in v. 2 strictly are contra-indications of Van der Lugt's thesis, as they occur neither in the first line of the strophe nor in the last line of a higher rhetorical unit.[29] Nevertheless, the identity of the strophe is clear.

Strophe 2 is clearly marked by the interrogative at its opening, and comprises a question and answer. The repeated phrase from the end of v. 2 is a concatenation, providing continuity between strophes.

A plausible alternative structure would comprise a single line opening strophe (v. 1) followed by a three line strophe (vv. 2–4) marked by the vocative and imperative at the head of v. 2. This alternative would leave the questions in v. 3 as contra-indications, and would result in adjacent lines in second person address (vv. 2–3) being addressed to different parties. It is presumably for these reasons that Van der Lugt proposes the structure described above.

Strophe 3 is marked by an exclamation at its opening, and reverts to first person address. The lines of the strophe are linked by the repetitions of שׁכן and שָׁלוֹם. The pronouns in v. 7 are reckoned by Van der Lugt to function as transition markers for the beginning and end of a strophe respectively. However, clearly אֲנִי does not mark the beginning

---

29. It is interesting that this contra-indication is reduced if the divine name is relocated to the end of v. 1; see discussion in the section "Psalm 120: Colometric Analysis" on pp. 68–73.

of a structural unit. In fact, it is the two pronouns used together to create a contrast that forms a sense of closure to the psalm.

Other strophic analyses appear to depend on the interpretation of the relationship between v. 1 and the rest of the psalm and reflect the tension between the two alternatives mentioned above. Terrien links the recollection of past prayer and the immediate prayer as expressions of the same ongoing situation and proposes the same structure as Van der Lugt.[30] Kissane separates v. 1 from vv. 2–4, reading it as an introductory recollection, the past prayer and past lament being described in vv. 2–4 and vv. 5–7 respectively.[31] Note, however, that these approaches rely on interpretation of the text more than on prosodic considerations or assessment of formal features.

RHETORICO-STRUCTURAL ANALYSIS

Girard identifies connections between v. 1 and v. 5 (repetition of לִי and descriptions of adversity/woe), between v. 2 and v. 6 (repetition of נַפְשִׁי) and between vv. 3–4 and v. 7 (words relating to war: גִּבּוֹר and מִלְחָמָה). He therefore proposes a diptych structure with three sections of correspondence, the overall designation being ABC//ABC':[32]

v. 1	v. 5
v. 2	v. 6
v. 3–4	v. 7

The remaining repetitions within the psalm, Girard takes as concatenations between sections. Allen has commented on the development of thought revealed by this structure: "In each strophe an initial element is subsequently unpacked."[33] Whilst this development is clear within each of the two sides of the diptych, the lack of development between v. 4 and v. 5 confirms the break in the structure at that point. Allen has also suggested that the use of עִם followed by a plural construct in v. 4b and v. 5b forms a central pivot for the psalm. However, this is more com-

---

30. Terrien, *Strophic Structure*, 807–8; so also Fokkelman, *Psalms in Form*, 132, and Hunter, *Psalms*, 192. Jacquet, *Les Psaumes*, 406, separates v. 7 as a stand-alone conclusion to the psalm.

31. Kissane, *Book of Psalms*, 564.

32. Girard, *Psaumes 3: 101–150*, 288–89.

33. Allen, *Psalms 101–50*, 199.

mensurate with a chiastic structure for the psalm as a whole rather than the linear structure proposed by Girard.[34]

Girard suggests that the two sides of the diptych can also be identified by inclusios: vv. 1–4 by לִי /לְךָ and vv. 5–7 by כִּי. However, the use of such common lexemes to form an inclusio is very tenuous (not least as they do not even appear in the initial and final cola of the sides), and goes against Girard's own guidelines.[35]

Auffret divides the psalm into three sections: vv. 1–2, vv. 3–4, and vv. 5–7. This analysis is based on the distinction between descriptions of hardships and designations of a person/people; it is somewhat interpretive and does not yield a clear structure within each section. A more helpful observation is that the first and third sections concern the plight of the psalmist whereas the central section concerns the fate awaiting the psalmist's enemies.[36]

Summary

Rhythmically the psalm is fairly consistent throughout with cola of two or three stresses, except for v. 2a that might have four. Verses 3–6 each have six stresses, with v. 3 clearly having the form of a para-tricolon, and the others being 3+3 bicola. Verse 7 is syntactically and semantically ambiguous. It is accented with five stresses, as a 3+2 bicolon, but a strict application of Sievers' theory and consideration of its syntactic structure yields a six-stress line that should be read as a para-tricolon. The importance of making a distinction between tricola and para-tricola is illustrated by Hossfeld and Zenger's misleading comment on this line, "Dass der Psalm in v. 7 mit einem Trikolon abschließt, gibt diesem Vers ein besonderes Gewicht."[37] In actual fact what is important here is the rhythmical regularity of the psalm, and the final line, whilst tripartite, is no "weightier" than the others.

The psalm divides thematically into three sections. The strophic division matches this overall structure. The opening and closing lines are not quite as strongly connected to their strophes as are the medial lines. Rhetorically the first and second strophes together incorporate lexical and semantic elements that are matched in the third strophe.

---

34. Allen, *Psalms 101–50*, 199.

35. Cf. the comments of Wyckoff, "Closure," 35, 57.

36. Auffret, *Etude Structurelle*, 7–9.

37. Hossfeld and Zenger, *Psalmen*, 411.

Strophic structure	Thematic structure	Rhetorical structure
1a 1b 2a 2b	1–2	1 2
3a–3b–3c 4a 4b	3–4	3–4
5a 5b 6a 6b 7a–7b–7c	5–7	5 6 7

Psalm 121

Colometric Analysis

שִׁיר לַמַּעֲלוֹת 1

אֶשָּׂא עֵינַי אֶל־הֶהָרִים   מֵאַיִן יָבֹא עֶזְרִי׃

2 עֶזְרִי מֵעִם יְהוָה   עֹשֵׂה שָׁמַיִם וָאָרֶץ׃

3 אַל־יִתֵּן לַמּוֹט רַגְלֶךָ   אַל־יָנוּם שֹׁמְרֶךָ׃

4 הִנֵּה לֹא־יָנוּם וְלֹא יִישָׁן   שׁוֹמֵר יִשְׂרָאֵל׃

5 יְהוָה שֹׁמְרֶךָ   יְהוָה צִלְּךָ   עַל־יַד יְמִינֶךָ׃

6 יוֹמָם הַשֶּׁמֶשׁ לֹא־יַכֶּכָּה   וְיָרֵחַ בַּלָּיְלָה׃

7 יְהוָה יִשְׁמָרְךָ מִכָּל־רָע   יִשְׁמֹר אֶת־נַפְשֶׁךָ׃

8 יְהוָה יִשְׁמָר־   צֵאתְךָ וּבוֹאֶךָ   מֵעַתָּה וְעַד־עוֹלָם׃

The opening pair of lines (vv. 1–2) introduces the topic of the psalm, namely Yahweh as the source of the psalmist's security. The two lines are each a bicolon with a 3+3 rhythm. These lines are worded in the first person, but the remainder of the psalm is in the third person and addressed to a non-specific "you" (m.s.). In v. 4 Yahweh is referred to as the שׁוֹמֵר יִשְׂרָאֵל, and so the addressee may be assumed to be a representative Israelite. The change in grammatical person is often equated to a change in voice, but this need not necessarily be the case.[38]

In the remainder of the psalm, each line has a rhythm of either 3+2 or 2-2-2. The next two lines (vv. 3–4) expound this topic of security through Yahweh, with a series of four negative verbs. In v. 3 the verbs are

---

38. See, for example, Goldingay, *Psalms*, 455 and the section "Psalm 121: Thematic Analysis" on p. 83.

jussives and have a subject שֹׁמְרֶךָ; in v. 4 the verbs are imperfectives and have a subject שׁוֹמֵר יִשְׂרָאֵל. In the Masoretic accentuation, three of the negative particles are joined to the verb by a *maqqeph*; the fourth one (in v. 4) is not, and is also the only one to incorporate the conjunction. The rhythm of v. 3 is 3+2, both according to the accentuation and according to Sievers' system.

In v. 4 the rhythm has some ambiguity. The opening particle of this line, הִנֵּה can possibly be regarded as extra-metrical (anacrusis), in which case the line also appears as a bicolon with rhythm 3+2.[39] The same result could be achieved by allocating a full stress to הִנֵּה and merging וְלֹא יִישָׁן into a single word-unit, as if a *maqqeph* were present. Notwithstanding these possibilities, reading the line strictly according to its accentuation, which is also compatible with Sievers' system, the line has six stresses divided between three phrases.[40] Therefore it is possible to read v. 4 as an unbalanced bicolon or as a para-tricolon (2–2–2).[41] The structure of the line as three two-word phrases, with syntactic parallelism between the first two, is possibly attested by the lack of a *maqqeph* in the fourth negated verb, as distinct from the other three. Exactly the same considerations apply to the choice between the two options as did for 120:3 (see the section "Psalm 120: Colometric Analysis" on pp. 68–73). The ambiguity is again illustrated, in this case by Fokkelman's inconsistent treatment of such lines. His objection to presenting this particular line as a tricolon, is that the psalm is otherwise (in his view) "strictly bicolic."[42] However, Fokkelman does also present Ps 130:5–6 (which have the same characteristics) as tricola, in a psalm that he presents otherwise as entirely bicolic.[43] Perhaps this constitutes further evidence that an intermediate designation is required, to overcome the polar distinction between bicolon and tricolon. In this particular instance the conditions for a para-tricolon are met: there are three phrases, the first two being synonymous, and the third identifying the subject of each of the other two. The only possible contra-indication would be that the pause between

---

39. The Masoretic verse division in v. 4 is evidenced by a pausal form as well as an accent.

40. The treatment of וְלֹא יִישָׁן as two word-units matches his treatment of כִּי אִם־כַּמֹּץ in Ps 1:4; Sievers, *Metrische Studien*, 500–501.

41. Allen, *Psalms 101–50*, 203 presents a tricolon.

42. Fokkelman, *Major Poems III*, 272.

43. Ibid., 297.

the first and second phrases, being a break between clauses, merits a major caesura rather than a minor one. However, the two phrases are so closely connected as a kind of verbal hendiadys, that a minor caesura is considered adequate.[44] Therefore this line is classified as a para-tricolon.

Similar issues apply in verse 5 which could potentially be read as a para-tricolon (2–2–2), as evidenced by those who read a 2+2+2 tricolon.[45] The Masoretic text of the line comprises three phrases, the first two being nominal clauses with a degree of synonymy. The third phrase qualifies the second, and could be construed to qualify the first also, but this is not obvious. If the third phrase qualifies only the second, then the pause between the two nominal clauses perhaps ought to be stronger than that between the second and third phrases. The imbalance is evidenced by the Masoretic accentuation that splits the line after the first clause, thus creating an imbalanced 2+4 rhythm.[46] Perhaps this reflects an assumption that the third phrase relates only to the second, so that the first phrase stands apart from the other two. The result is a line that stands out both as an unusual line-form in Hebrew poetry in general and as distinct from the relatively regular rhythm of the other lines in this psalm.

It is perhaps not a coincidence that there are textual variants for this line. 11QPs[a] has:

בלילה יהוה שמרך צלכה על יד ימינך

This text has quite a different structure, and readily lends itself to a 3+3 rhythm with medial caesura. The difference is so great that it does not assist in resolving the ambiguities in MT. In the scroll the first two words of v. 5 match the last word of v. 6 and the first word of v. 7. It is not possible to hypothesise a simple process whereby one of the variants was

44. Watson, *Classical*, 326, cites an example of conjoined verbs in his exposition of hendiadys. Schmitt 1999, 60–63, regards the two verbs as a word pair operating in combination, but also with a sense of escalation of intensity; cf. Hossfeld and Zenger, *Psalmen*, 429–30, who read a description of a process of falling asleep.

45. Thus RSV and also Allen, *Psalms 101–50*, 203 but without specific explanation. Dahood, *Psalms*, 201, reads a tricolon based on reading עַל as a divine epithet paralleling the two tetragrammata.

46. Hossfeld and Zenger, *Psalmen*, 429, support a bicolon on the basis of the line consisting of two, not three, nominal clauses. But they are not consistent in this approach; see comments on 123:4 in the section "Psalm 123: Colometric Analysis" on pp. 96–99.

derived from the other, and therefore for the purposes of the present study, MT is retained as the preferred text.

LXX and Targum match MT except that they read an indicative verb form in the first phrase, matching v. 7, rather than a participle. It is apparent therefore that in the *Vorlage* of LXX v. 5 and v. 7 begin with the same two words. Whilst this might indicate a scribal error, on a textual basis alone it is not possible to determine which is the authentic reading. Considering the syntax of the line, an indicative verb form in the initial clause would mean that it could not be qualified by the final phrase. This rather exacerbates the difficulties with the rhythmical analysis of the text, reinforcing the strength of the caesura between the first two phrases of the line.

There is a temptation to mix and match the features of the various texts in order to produce an easier reading. For example, Weiser takes only the common elements of the MT and 11QPs[a], adding a conjunction in order to create a single clause line with 3+2 rhythm (עַל־יַד יְמִינָךְ   יְהוָה שֹׁמְרֶךָ וְצִלְּךָ). But he offers no substantiation for this text. Jacquet does the same, proposing that the copula was misread as *yod* and then reproduced by the scribes as the divine name. Such a proposal is purely speculative.[47]

There does not seem to be an adequate justification for accepting a variant text instead of MT. The analysis of the line could possibly also take into account its location within the structure of the psalm. Together with v. 4 it forms a pair of lines at the centre of the psalm, and so a variation in rhythm might reflect a function as a focus or pivot (see the discussion in section "Psalm 121: Structural Analyses" on pp. 83–86). Following the Masoretic accentuation strictly yields a rhythm for the two lines of 4+2 / 2+4, which is possibly suggestive of a pivot pattern. Equally, it is plausible that the two lines should be read as 2-2-2 para-tricola, as a distinct central focus in the context of lines that are otherwise 3+2.

The impact of the relationship between the form of the line and its place within the structure of the psalm is evident in others' analyses. Allen's reading of a tricolon seems to be driven by his overall structuring of the psalm (vv. 1–2 / 3–5 / 6–8) and a desire for "balanced strophes."[48] It appears that the identification of a tricolon is therefore dependent

---

47. Jacquet, *Les Psaumes*, 418; Weiser, *The Psalms*, 745.

48. Allen, *Psalms 101–50*, 203.

on the structuring of the psalm. In contrast Fokkelman structures the psalm vv. 1–2 / 3–4 // 5–6 / 7–8 and reads a bicolon.[49]

It does not seem possible to produce a definitive rhythmical analysis of v. 5 in light of the textual variants and conflicting theories. However, the possibility of its being a para-tricolon is sufficient for this possibility to be considered further, particularly with reference to its place within the structure of the psalm and its interaction with v. 4.

Verses 6 and 7 further extrapolate the theme of Yahweh's protection, each verse being a bicolon with 3+2 rhythm, although this is not always recognised. Watson cites vv. 6–7 as tricola but without any explanation or justification.[50] Dahood reads vv. 6–7 as tricola based on a desire for cola with syllable counts that are matching as closely as possible. However, the result is far from a match: v. 6 has 5/4/6 syllables, v. 7 has 6/3/6 syllables.[51] Allen reads v. 6 as a bicolon but v. 7 as a tricolon with rhythm 2+2+2. He, along with the others, fails to justify the allocation of two stresses to a "colon" of only three syllables (מִכָּל־רָע), which violently contradicts Sievers' system both in the treatment of the particles and in the creation of two adjacent stressed syllables. Even within the thinking of Robinson, on whom Allen more directly draws, this short phrase surely represents a single "thought-unit," not two. Allen's desire for "balanced strophes" does not justify such modification of the text's punctuation and rhythm and cannot be accepted.[52] The lines each consist of two phrases, not three. Some misconstruction may have arisen from the identification of a so-called "pivot pattern" in these two verses. As Goldingay comments, "a phrase at the centre . . . applies to both cola and thus binds the line together."[53] Whilst this is true in v. 6, it is an observation of syntax, and the rhythmical construction need not be identical with it. To read the line as a para-tricolon forces a full stress onto the negative particle, which would normally not be countenanced by Sievers, and suggests that the two caesurae are equal in strength whereas the second, at a clause boundary marked by the conjunction, is somewhat stronger than the hypothetical initial intra-clause caesura. In v. 7 it is not appropriate to infer the "pivot pattern" at all; rather the bicolon

49. Fokkelman, *Reading*, 217.

50. Watson, *Classical*, 182.

51. Dahood, *Psalms*, 202.

52. Allen, *Psalms 101–50*, 205; Kraus, *Psalms 60–150*, 427.

53. Goldingay, *Psalms*, 455–56.

comprises two clauses with a degree of synonymy, the second giving a specific instance of the more general statement in the first.

Verse 8 could follow the same pattern as vv. 6–7 as a 3+2 bicolon, or alternatively could be read as a para-tricolon by ignoring the *maqqeph* and allocating a full stress to יִשְׁמָר. Both options fulfil O'Connor's and Fokkelman's numerical constraints. The bicolon option works best if the initial tetragrammaton is deleted, following the BHS apparatus, in light of its omission from 11QPs[a]. However, it is still possible with the text as it stands. The para-tricolon option divides the line as it stands into three pairs of words.[54] These three phrases together make up a single clause and are of equal prominence, with only a minor syntactic pause occurring at each caesura. This reading generates a conflict with the Masoretic reading by the introduction of a caesura at the place of a *maqqeph*. However, since a *maqqeph* is essentially a rhythmical marker, not an accent, this represents an alternative rhythmical reading, not a disregard for the semantic structure of the line. This *maqqeph* is quite unusual in following a disyllabic verb. The common usage is after monosyllabic particles and conjunctions and within bound phrases.[55] Even in such contexts as those, its deletion to allow an alternative rhythmical reading of a line has already been found (120:7). This instance is not a bound phrase; the following infinitive construct has a closer semantic connection with the subsequent word, with which it forms a merism, than with the preceding verb.[56] Therefore the criteria for a para-tricolon are met; but since the line may equally plausibly be read as a 3+2 bicolon, matching the preceding lines, its identity as a para-tricolon is regarded as possible rather than definite.

---

54. Thus Allen, *Psalms 101–50*, 205, matching his treatment of v. 7; and Kraus, *Psalms 60–150*, 427.

55. See Scott, *Simplified Guide*, 6.

56. Alonso-Schökel, *Manual*, 91–93, refers to the pair as a "polarised expression" representing a particular form of merismus. Van der Lingen, "Military Term," 65, suggests that it originated as a military term and is used here with connotations of "success"; cf. Ceresko, "Psalm 121" regarding the psalm as a warrior's prayer.

Structural Analyses

THEMATIC ANALYSIS

Gunkel read this psalm as a form of liturgy with alternation of speaker between a petitioner and a worship official.[57] Gerstenberger concurs, reading vv. 1–2 as a supplicant's affirmation of confidence, vv. 3–4 as an official response and vv. 5–8 as words of assurance.[58] Kraus adopts the suggestion of Weiser and regards the whole of vv. 2–8 as a response to the initial question.[59]

STROPHIC ANALYSIS

Structure: Van der Lugt reads four strophes of two lines, 2.2|2.2, but this is not self-evident. The high number of repetitions of שמר, ךְ- , and יהוה make it possible to link the lines in several different combinations whilst still conveying a sense of structure. Only three transition markers are found in the psalm, the interrogative in v. 1 marking opening and the reference to eternity in v. 8 marking closure. The only other marker is the particle at the head of v. 4, and this might be thought to mark the

57. Gunkel and Begrich, *Introduction*, 314; cf. Creach, "Psalm 121," 48.

58. Gerstenberger, *Psalms*, 323–24; cf. Richter, "Von den Bergen."

59. Kraus, *Psalms 60–150*, 427–28; Weiser, *The Psalms*, 746. See Allen, *Psalms 101–50*, 204, for a survey of the views on the possible identities of the speakers in the dialogue.

beginning of a strophe. However, the change of person after v. 2 must be taken into account. The opening two lines are in the first person and have no addressee, but the remainder of the psalm is written in the third person, with Yahweh as the subject, and has an oft repeated "you" (m.s.) addressee. Therefore the exclamatory particle is not marking the beginning of a strophe but the end of a canto. This is reinforced by the fact that vv. 5–6 are linked thematically (references to shade and sun), as are vv. 7–8 (as an all-encompassing statement of protection). Therefore, the only reasonable alternative strophic division (based on transition markers) would be 3.3.2, but this would create a disjointed first strophe due to the change of person.

Thus strophe 1 identifies Yahweh as the source of the psalmist's help, and strophe 2 expounds Yahweh's constancy and reliability.

Strophe 3 describes Yahweh's protection in specific terms, acting as a shade and protecting from sun and moon. Strophe 4 develops this thought into a generalized statement of protection from all harm that continues for all time.

Several other analyses concur with Van der Lugt.[60] However, as mentioned above (in the section "Psalm 121: Colometric Analysis" on pp. 77–82), Allen reads a different structure, 2.3.3, but this is dependent upon his analysis of the rhythm of each line producing "balance strophes," which is not well substantiated. He also highlights the triple repetition in participial form of the key word שמר in vv. 3–5 in contrast to the triple repetition in imperfective form in vv. 6–8.[61] However, this is a rhetorico-structural approach rather than a strophic approach, and the observation is slightly misleading since the word does not occur at all in v. 6, so the lines could be split 3–6 / 7–8 and the same feature would still be apparent.

RHETORICO-STRUCTURAL ANALYSIS

Girard distinguishes vv. 1–2 from the remainder of the psalm based on the change of speaker, despite the fact that syntax is not a component of his analytical methodology. Nevertheless it seems reasonable to recognise vv. 1–2 as an autonomous section, formed of a question and its an-

---

60. Ceresko, "Psalm 121," 496–97; Fokkelman, *Psalms in Form*, 132; Hunter, *Psalms*, 195; Jacquet, *Les Psaumes*, 415; Kissane, *Book of Psalms*, 567; Terrien, *Strophic Structure*, 810.

61. Allen, *Psalms 101–50*, 203.

swer, since the two lines are linked by the repetition of עֶזְרִי and there are no contra-indications amongst other word repetitions. The remainder of the psalm expounds the idea developed in this opening part, the overall unity of the psalm indicated by the repetition of בוֹא in v. 1 and v. 8.[62]

Girard offers a structure for the remaining verses, but it is not the only possible option. The lines are dominated by the repetitions of שׁמר and יְהוָה, but these occur so often that no single structure is apparent. Girard distinguishes vv. 3–5 from vv. 7–8 based on the occurrence of participial and indicative verb forms of שׁמר respectively.[63] He notes also the matching number of occurrences of יְהוָה in these two sections and applauds the symmetry. He includes v. 6 with vv. 3–5, to create two sections vv. 3–6/vv. 7–8, but without explicit justification.[64] This seems odd given the alternatives: the text could just as well be divided vv. 3–5/vv. 6–8 and be even more symmetrical, in terms of equal numbers of lines; or v. 6 could stand as the central element of a concentric structure, vv. 3–5/v. 6/ vv. 7–8, which would seem fitting given the neat concentric structure of the verse itself: adverb-noun-(double-duty) verb-noun-adverb.

Allen favors the division vv. 3–5/vv. 6–8 and also comments on the pattern of verb negations through vv. 3–8, being negative-negative-positive / negative-positive-positive. Whilst the observation is valid that the general movement from negative to positive creates a sense of climax, the pattern does not clearly justify one division of the text over another. Indeed, if anything, the pattern favors the division into three strophes of two lines each, such that the three strophes represent negative/pivot/ positive, but this is the very structure that Allen is arguing against.[65]

Auffret analyzes the psalm and finds three distinct structures, with little discussion of the relationships between them.[66] In considering the keyword שׁמר he takes account of the cola that do not include it as well as those that do, and so suggests a structure for vv. 3–8 of 3–5a / 5b–6 / 7–8.[67] He also highlights the high incidence of merismus in the psalm:

62. Girard, *Psaumes 3: 101–150*, 295. Ceresko, "Psalm 121," 499, expands this and notes the repetition of the chain (וְ)מִ־בוֹא־(וְ)מִ in vv. 1–2 and vv. 7–8.

63. As also identified by Allen, *Psalms 101–50*, 205.

64. Girard, *Psaumes 3: 101–150*, 296–97. Note the comment in the section "Psalm 121: Strophic Analysis" on pp. 83–84 regarding the ambiguity over the place of v. 6 based on these criteria.

65. Allen, *Psalms 101–50*, 205.

66. Auffret, *Etude Structurelle*, 14–21.

67. Ibid., 16.

heaven/earth (v. 2), sun/moon (v. 6), day/night (v. 6), out/in (v. 8) and now/forever (v. 8). Taken together with the verbal hendiadys in v. 4, they suggest a structure based around pairs of lines.[68]

Trublet and Aletti take this psalm as an illustration of the way in which a linear, progressive development of a theme may overlay a concentric rhetorical structure.[69] They highlight the alternation of grammatically negative and positive clauses through vv. 3–8 and offer the following thematic chiastic structure:[70]

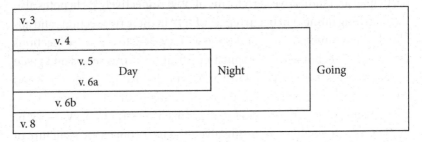

Summary

The first two lines of this psalm are generally recognised as a distinct section, being rhythmically (3+3) and grammatically (1c.s.) distinguished from the remainder.[71]

The other six lines present a range of possible structures due to the high degree of repetitions and thematic connections between lines. All these lines are either a 3+2 bicolon or a 2-2-2 para-tricolon, but v. 5 and v. 8 are ambiguous in this respect.

The strophic division is best interpreted as four strophes of two lines each. Rhetorically, there is a distinction between statements about "Yahweh the keeper" and statements that "Yahweh will keep," but other thematic connections are also apparent.

68. Ibid., 16, and 20–21; cf. Maré, "Some Remarks," 171–72.

69. Trublet and Aletti, *Approche Poétique*, 110–11.

70. Ibid., 96–97.

71. Although Anderson, *Psalms: Volume 2*, 851, regards vv. 2–8 as the answer to v. 1

Strophic structure	Thematic structure	Rhetorical structure
1a 1b 2a 2b	1–2	1 2
3a 3b	3–8	3
4a–4b–4c		4
5a–5b–5c		5
6a 6b		6
7a 7b		7
8a–8b–8c		8

Psalm 122

Colometric Analysis

1 שִׁיר הַמַּעֲלוֹת לְדָוִד

שָׂמַחְתִּי בְּאֹמְרִים לִי   בֵּית יְהוָה נֵלֵךְ:

2 עֹמְדוֹת הָיוּ רַגְלֵינוּ   בִּשְׁעָרַיִךְ יְרוּשָׁלָ͏ִם:

3 יְרוּשָׁלַ͏ִם הַבְּנוּיָה כְּעִיר   שֶׁחֻבְּרָה־לָּהּ יַחְדָּו:

4 שֶׁשָּׁם עָלוּ שְׁבָטִים   שִׁבְטֵי־יָהּ עֵדוּת לְיִשְׂרָאֵל   לְהֹדוֹת לְשֵׁם יְהוָה:

5 כִּי שָׁמָּה יָשְׁבוּ כִסְאוֹת לְמִשְׁפָּט   כִּסְאוֹת לְבֵית דָּוִיד:

6 שַׁאֲלוּ שְׁלוֹם יְרוּשָׁלָ͏ִם   יִשְׁלָיוּ אֹהֲבָיִךְ:

7 יְהִי־שָׁלוֹם בְּחֵילֵךְ   שַׁלְוָה בְּאַרְמְנוֹתָיִךְ:

8 לְמַעַן אַחַי וְרֵעָי   אֲדַבְּרָה־נָּא שָׁלוֹם בָּךְ:

9 לְמַעַן בֵּית־יְהוָה אֱלֹהֵינוּ   אֲבַקְשָׁה טוֹב לָךְ:

This psalm of celebration of, and intercession for, the city of Jerusalem, opens with a scene-setting pair of bicola (3+2 / 3+2).[72] These lines describe arrival at Jerusalem at the end of a journey. The following lines, vv. 3–5, rejoice over Jerusalem as the appointed place for worship and the seat of the monarch.[73] The colometry within this section is not immediately apparent, and is considered below. Verses 6–9 focus on prayer

---

72. Sievers considered it important to retain the full stress on a preposition with pronominal suffix; Sievers, *Metrische Studien*, 204. The consequent juxtaposition of stressed syllables at the end of v. 1a would be accommodated by "stretching" this monosyllabic word to create a slurred disyllable; Sievers, *Metrische Studien*, 226.

73. Allen, *Psalms 101–50*, 211.

for the peace of Jerusalem, each verse being a bicolon. Verses 6–7 have rhythm 3+2.[74] Verse 8 could be read as 3+3, treating the juxtaposition of stressed syllables at the end of the line in the same manner as v. 1a. The end of v. 9 presents greater difficulty, with three successive stressed syllables. This problem may be overcome by the omission of a stress on טוֹב. Whilst it is implicit in Sievers' thesis that every substantive in the absolute state should carry a stress, he does very occasionally deviate from this principle in the case of a monosyllabic substantive that is closely connected to the following word.[75] Therefore, a reading of v. 9 as 3+2 is conceivable. The same approach could be taken with v. 8, but this would involve leaving a disyllabic substantive unstressed, which is probably a step too far. So it is clear that vv. 1–2 and vv. 6–9 are all bicola. They can *conceivably*, but not *clearly*, all be read as 3+2 and doing so may suggest a greater degree of uniformity than is the case.

The approximate rhythmical regularity of vv. 1–2 and vv. 6–9 have strongly influenced many analyses of the intermediate lines. A preference for finding a regular 3+2 rhythm throughout the psalm has clearly influenced some.[76] The foregoing analysis demonstrates that this may not be justified. Verse 3 introduces Jerusalem as the subject of the central section with a bicolon (3+2).[77] Verse 4 is a long line and difficult to divide into cola. Within it, there is a delicate interaction between the options for colometry and the resolution of a textual ambiguity. Following the criteria for colometry established above (see the section "Basis of Analysis: Colometry" on pp. 66–67), the eight or nine stresses in the verse (depending on how לְּשֵׁם יְהוָה is treated) and the twenty three syllables indicate that it is too long for a bicolon, unless they are exceptionally long cola. Equally a division into two bicola would produce noticeably short cola. A division into three cola therefore suggests itself as the means to produce cola that broadly match those of the remainder

---

74. Verse 7 could also legitimately be read as 3+3, due to the length of the final word; Sievers, *Metrische Studien*, 177.

75. See his treatment of Ps 25:11b and 25:15b, Sievers, *Metrische Studien*, 519.

76. E.g., Jacquet, *Les Psaumes*, 426–29; Kraus, *Psalms 60–150*, 432; and to some extent Allen, *Psalms 101–50*, 210.

77. Masoretic accentuation presents this line as 2+3; but it is certainly a bicolon in either case. Kugel, *Idea*, 66–68, combines vv. 2–3 and creates a tricolon without offering any justification, and then comments that this composite line could be read as two lines. The proposals of Donner, "Psalm 122," 84–86, and Marrs, "Psalm 122," 109 concerning the meaning of the line do not influence the colometric considerations.

of the psalm.[78] This is supported by the Masoretic accentuation: there are three disjunctive accents in the line, but with two occurring on adjacent words, only two can indicate a caesura. Such a reading as a tricolon is attested by both MA and ML, which follow, no doubt, the accentuation.

The immediate repetition within the line of the lexeme שֵׁבֶט is an unusual feature of Hebrew poetry, but fits the pattern of "expanded repetition" identified by Yona. In this literary device a lexeme is introduced in a deliberately vague fashion, and is then repeated as part of a parallel construct chain in order to provide greater clarity or definition.[79] The identification of such a device in this line would strongly suggest that the two instances of the lexeme should be split between different cola (all of Yona's examples are formed thus) and that these two cola should in some way match each other so that the initial lexeme and the construct chain within which it is repeated are parallel.

The presentation of the verse as a tricolon does produce a semantically difficult middle colon placing two noun phrases in apposition (שִׁבְטֵי־יָהּ and עֵדוּת לְיִשְׂרָאֵל) when there is no syntactic connection between them.[80] The first phrase is clearly a synonym for the preceding word; the second phrase can be read as a nominal clause commenting on the initial colon.[81] Taken together they can possibly be understood as a parenthetical expansion of the initial colon: the tribes of Yah (go up) (as) an ordinance for Israel. This would be commensurate with the pattern for "expanded repetition." If the alternative text of 11QPs[a] is adopted[82], the sense would be easier as the colon would expand only the preceding noun by means of two paraphrases: tribes—tribes of Yah, the congregation of Israel.[83] Booij argues for the priority of the Qumran reading, and

---

78. Excepting vv. 4–5, all cola have two or three stresses and five to ten syllables, typically eight.

79. Yona, "Expanded Repetition," 586–89. Berlin, *Dynamics*, 69–71, also demonstrates that repetition of a lexeme is an acceptable form of lexical parallelism.

80. Kugel, *Idea*, 67, in support of a tricolon overcomes this difficulty by a more radical amendment of the text to read שבטי העדות לישראל "the tribes of Israel's assemblies." No textual evidence is cited for such an amendment. The use of the plural form "assemblies" is unattested. Weiser, *The Psalms*, 749, presents the verse as a tricolon (4+2+2), but by placing "tribes" and "tribes of Yah" in apposition in the first colon. This seems even less likely, producing an unusually long colon by means of almost verbatim repetition.

81. Delitzsch, *Commentary*, 271; Hossfeld and Zenger, *Psalmen*, 450.

82. Reading עדת ישראל in place of עֵדוּת לְיִשְׂרָאֵל.

83. However, the text of 122:3–4 in 11QPs[a] is incomplete and canot be fully com-

considers that the semantic structure of the verse then requires a caesura after שִׁבְטֵי־יָהּ to become two lines. However, he is silent on how those lines should be divided into cola (if at all) and does not adequately address rhythmical considerations.[84]

A common alternative approach to v. 4 is to read the verse as a pair of bicola, thus:

שֶׁשָּׁם עָלוּ שְׁבָטִים   שִׁבְטֵי־יָהּ
עֵדוּת לְיִשְׂרָאֵל לְהֹדוֹת   לְשֵׁם יְהוָה׃

This colometry can be arrived at from two perspectives. Principally it is motivated by rhythmical considerations, seeking to perpetuate the perceived regularity of 3+2 rhythm throughout the psalm. However, not only does the remainder of the text fail to clearly exhibit 3+2 rhythm, neither does this reading of v. 4. The allocation to two stresses to the construct phrase שִׁבְטֵי־יָהּ unnecessarily results in adjacent stressed syllables, creating a very jarring effect and contradicting a key principle of Sievers' approach to rhythmical analysis. The rhythm of these bicola is rightly 3+1 / 3+2,[85] and the creation of a single-stress colon is highly questionable.[86] Secondarily, this colometry is motivated by semantic considerations. For example Crow, adopting the text of 11QPsᵃ comments on the "excellent parallelism" by which he means semantic parallelism.[87] However, the creation of a single word-unit colon makes it more difficult to explain the reason for an immediate repetition of a lexeme when not set within a parallel colon. Moreover, it is apparent that the colometry presupposes the semantic relationships, which in turn presupposes the resolution of textual variants. As discussed above, it is considered more appropriate to consider the colometry and textual variants with greater independence. The presentation of a pair of bicola is not considered justifiable and on the basis of established criteria the verse is judged to be a tricolon.

---

pared with MT. From what is available, Skehan, "Gleanings," 449–52, has interpolated a text that is secondary, reflecting Essene community concerns.

84. Booij, "Psalm CXXII," 262–63.

85. Following the BHS suggestion to relocate the 'atnach. Otherwise the rhythm is 3+1 / 2+3.

86. Having only three syllables it also fails Fokkelman's criterion for a valid colon.

87. Crow, Songs of Ascents, 45.

Verse 5 can be construed as a bicolon (4+3), a bicolon (3+3) with בִּי שָׁמָּה read as an anacrusis, a para-tricolon (2–2–2) or a tricolon (2+2+3).[88] The variation in the total stress count is due to ambiguity in the rhythm at the end of the verse, where the construct phrase לְבֵית דָּוִד could be allocated either one stress or two. The bicolon option follows the Masoretic accentuation. It would consist of a syntactically compete clause in the initial colon followed by a parallel noun phrase in the second. The initial colon would have eleven syllables, such that this is a legitimate but questionable reading, according to the established criteria. A bicolon with anacrusis would possibly be Sievers' treatment of the line. However, there does not seem adequate reason to read such a strong two-word anacrusis in the middle of the psalm, particularly as the line develops the preceding line and is linked to it by the repetition of a cognate adverb (שָׁם v. 4). The reading of a para-tricolon is an unusual example of Sievers' scheme for this type of line, requiring as it does the allocation of a single stress to a construct phrase. However, it is comparable with a four-syllable chain that he cites.[89] The line comprises three phrases. The first is a potentially complete, albeit semantically ambiguous, verbal clause. The other two are noun phrases with a degree of synonymy, both of which relate equally to the opening verbal phrase. Together the phrases form a single complete clause, and the two caesurae can be regarded as minor, without any significant syntactic pause coinciding.

Reading v. 5 as a para-tricolon thus reflects the unity of the line as a single clause whilst also highlighting the parallelism of the two noun phrases. It offers good regularity of syllable count (6/5/6) as well as stresses (2–2–2).[90] As such it is considered marginally preferable to the reading as a 4+3 bicolon. However, it does create an apparent conflict with the accentuation, placing a minor caesura after the verb that carries a conjunctive accent. Some more detailed consideration of the implications of the accentuation is therefore required. Firstly, it is noted that

88. Watson, *Classical*, 181, reads a (para)-tricolon; so also Allen, *Psalms 101–50*, 210, and Dahood, *Psalms*, 203 (based on syllable count). Fokkelman, *Major Poems II*, 295, reads a bicolon.

89. In Ps 2:7 אֶל חֹק יְהוָה is treated as a single stress word-unit; Sievers, *Metrische Studien*, 501.

90. The relatively short cola (in terms of syllable count) militate against reading a full tricolon rather than a para-tricolon. However, a 2+2+3 full tricolon is a legitimate reading according to the established criteria.

the accents indicate the division of the text into semantic units. As such they are to some degree interpretative of the meaning of the text, and do not necessarily coincide with the syntactic division of the text.[91] Indeed, it is plausible that the rhythmical, syntactic, and semantic divisions of the text could all be different, and the interplay between them put to use for aesthetic and rhetorical effect. Secondly, taking the instance of an indicative verb followed by a word or phrase that it governs, there is inconsistency in the accentuation. While such a verb is usually assigned a conjunctive accent, within the Psalms of Ascents there are examples of a verb with a disjunctive accent directly followed by its subject (121:4; 125:3;[92] 129:8a), its direct object (121:7b; 128:5b; 129:3b; 131:2b), its indirect object (132:2a) or its adverbial modifier (126:1; 129:6; 131:1c; 132:3a; 133:2). Therefore, the accentuation clearly does not regard a verb as being universally semantically integrated with a following word/ phrase that it governs. Thirdly, the accentuation represents one particular tradition of reading and may well be influenced by an assumed colometric division of the text. It is plausible that an alternative rhythmical analysis is valid and that this would have a bearing on the intonation of the text.[93] In light of these observations, it is considered appropriate, at least in terms of allowing an exploration of the phenomenon of the para-tricolon, to nuance the original criteria for colometry (in the section "Basis of Analysis: Colometry" on pp. 66–67) so as to allow a minor caesura to follow an indicative verb that carries a conjunctive accent. Verse 5 of this psalm is therefore identified as a possible para-tricolon.

Structural Analyses

THEMATIC ANALYSIS

Gerstenberger reads the psalm as an account of pilgrimage followed by a two-part hymn to Jerusalem, each part opening with mention of the city by name, thus:

---

91. Scott, *Simplified Guide*, 25; Yeivin, *Introduction*, 158.

92. The contrast in accentuation of the verbs in 122:5a and 125:3a for very similar syntactic structures exemplifies the point.

93. As discussed in the section "Masoretic Accentuation in a Canonical Approach" on pp. 16–17.

vv. 1–2   Account of pilgrimage

vv. 3–5   Hymn to Jerusalem I

vv. 6–9   Hymn to Jerusalem II

The two parts of the hymn are distinguished by the change of discourse: objective affirmations in vv. 3–5 and direct address in vv. 6–9.[94] Kraus adopted the same structure, but read vv. 6–9 as prayers and blessings rather than praise.[95]

STROPHIC ANALYSIS

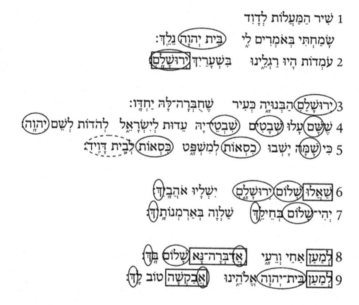

Structure: Van der Lugt reads 2|2.2|2.2, but this is dependent upon the colometry of v. 4 as a pair of bicola. Applying the same principles to the preferred colometry, a structure of 2.3|2.2 can be discerned. There are clearly three sections to the psalm: a scene-setting opening that places the psalmist in Jerusalem (vv. 1–2); a eulogy to Jerusalem (vv. 3–5); and a call to prayer for Jerusalem (incorporating both the call, vv. 6–7, and its reasons, vv. 8–9).

94. Gerstenberger, *Psalms*, 326–29.

95. Kraus, *Psalms 60–150*, 432. So also Weiser, *The Psalms*, 750–51 and Allen, *Psalms 101–50*, 212–13.

Strophe 1 sets the context for the psalm and is worded in the first person. It introduces the thematic reference to Jerusalem as a vocative. This transition marker indicates the end of this single strophe canto (in Van der Lugt's structure), and by means of concatenation provides continuity with the following strophes.

Strophe 2 comprises a eulogy to Jerusalem. The opening nominative form is not strictly a transition marker, but carries some of the exclamatory force of the vocative that it repeats. The strophe is bound together by the repeated שָׁם referring to Jerusalem. The reference to the house of David is not an exact repetition but carries an echo of the opening reference to house of Yahweh.[96]

Strophes 3 and 4 are clearly marked by the opening imperative of v. 6 and by the explanatory particle repeated in vv. 8 and 9 that implies closure. The four lines are knit together by the repeated 2f.s. suffix at the end of each line. Strophe 4 is also characterized by the 1c.s. cohortative in each line. According to Van der Lugt's criteria, cohortatives normally function as a marker of opening and these could be regarded as contra-indications; but they can also be seen to function in relation to the lines' opening explanatory particles.

Most other analyses produce the same result.[97] A notable exception is that of Kissane, who divides the psalm into two sections: vv. 1–4 and vv. 5–9. This results from linking the reference to David (v. 5) with the concern for kinsmen (v. 8). Whilst this link is imaginative, it is somewhat weaker than the more apparent link between v. 4 and v. 5, each of which expands the meditation on Jerusalem. It also neglects the change of topic and change of mood marked by the imperative at the opening of v. 6.

RHETORICO-STRUCTURAL ANALYSIS

The psalm is framed by references to בֵּית יְהוָה and the divine name also occurs near the middle of the psalm.[98] Based on the principal thematic repetition of יְרוּשָׁלַם Girard splits the psalm into three sections: vv. 1–2/

---

96. Hunter, *Psalms*, 198, suggests that reference to the "house of David" complements the references to the temple and the city in order to epitomise respectively the royal, priestly and civic aspects of Jerusalem.

97. Allen, *Psalms 101–50*, 213; Fokkelman, *Psalms in Form*, 133; Goldingay, *Psalms*, 461–62; Hunter, *Psalms*, 197; Jacquet, *Les Psaumes*, 426; Terrien, *Strophic Structure*, 814.

98. Girard, *Psaumes 3: 101–150*, 305–6.

vv. 3–5/vv. 6–9. He notes that the middle section coheres by means of matching syntactical constructions in v. 4ab and v. 5. The final section is tied together by the sequence of imperative/jussive/cohortative verb forms, and can be seen to divide into two sub-sections. The repetitions of שלה / שָׁלוֹם identify vv. 6–7 as parallel lines, and the repetition of לְמַעַן together with the synonymy and rhyme of טוֹב לָךְ / שָׁלוֹם בָּךְ identify vv. 8–9 as parallel lines.[99] The result is therefore identical to the strophic analyses.

Auffret and Trublet and Aletti offer very similar analyses.[100] Alden produces a slightly different structure by linking the explicit references to Jerusalem in vv. 2–3.[101]

Summary

The various analyses of the structure of this psalm have a high degree of uniformity. Two opening bicola set the narrative scene. There follow two sections respectively eulogizing Jerusalem and eliciting prayer for its well-being.

In the central section the colometry is irregular. The three lines comprise a bicolon, a tricolon, and a particularly ambiguous line. All other lines are clearly bicola.

Strophic structure			Thematic structure	Rhetorical structure
1a	1b		1–2	1
2a	2b			2
3a	3b			3
4a	4b	4c	3–5	4
5a–5b–5c				5
6a	6b			6
7a	7b		6–9	7
8a	8b			8
9a	9b			9

99. Ibid., 303–4; so also Auffret, *Etude Structurelle*, 24.
100. Auffret, *Etude Structurelle*, 24–28; Trublet and Aletti, *Approche Poétique*, 97.
101. Alden, "Chiastic Psalms (III)," 206–7.

Psalm 123

Colometric Analysis[102]

1 שִׁיר הַמַּעֲלוֹת

אֵלֶיךָ נָשָׂאתִי אֶת־עֵינַי   הַיֹּשְׁבִי בַּשָּׁמָיִם׃

2 הִנֵּה כְעֵינֵי עֲבָדִים   אֶל־יַד אֲדוֹנֵיהֶם

כְּעֵינֵי שִׁפְחָה   אֶל־יַד גְּבִרְתָּהּ

כֵּן עֵינֵינוּ אֶל־יְהוָה אֱלֹהֵינוּ   עַד שֶׁיְּחָנֵּנוּ׃

3 חָנֵּנוּ יְהוָה חָנֵּנוּ   כִּי־רַב שָׂבַעְנוּ בוּז׃

4 רַבַּת שָׂבְעָה־לָּהּ נַפְשֵׁנוּ   הַלַּעַג הַשַּׁאֲנַנִּים   הַבּוּז לִגְאֵיוֹנִים׃

This short psalm addresses Yahweh by means of the epithet הַיֹּשְׁבִי בַּשָּׁמָיִם,
describes by a pair of similes the process of looking to Yahweh for help
and then directly intercedes for help in face of opposition.

The opening verses, vv. 1–2, consist of a chiastic set of four bicola,
having an ABB'A' pattern.[103] The rhythm is quite regular. Allowing for
anacrusis at the beginning of the second line (הִנֵּה being extra-rhythmical), the rhythm pattern is 3+2 / 2+2 / 2+2 / 3+2.[104] This colometry
ensures that each caesura coincides with a disjunctive accent. Some have
preferred to combine v. 2a–d into a single bicolon with rhythm 4+4,
but this produces a pair of cola that are close to the limit of acceptable
length (in terms of syllables) and produce a very irregular reading in
the context of surrounding shorter cola.[105] Therefore in this instance the
division into shorter cola is preferred, whilst also noting that the alternative reading of a 4+4 bicolon does not significantly affect the overall
structure of the psalm, nor create a possibility of any tricola.

Reading vv. 1–2 in this way, the chiastic pattern of the four lines
is also apparent semantically and syntactically. The central two lines

102. Vocalization of v. 4 has been amended from the MT *qere* to match the *kethib*,
as suggested by BHS apparatus.

103. Allen, *Psalms 101–50*, 216.

104. The monosyllabic particle כֵּן opening the fourth line is unstressed (according
to Sievers) as it stands before a single unstressed syllable. In contrast עַד attracts a full
stress since it is followed by three unstressed syllables; although Sievers might well have
avoided a colon beginning with a stressed syllable by shifting the stress from עַד onto שֶׁ.
Sievers, *Metrische Studien*, 188–93.

105. E.g., Crow, *Songs of Ascents*, 48.

parallel each other, having identical syntactic structures and gender-matched parallel semantic content (servants / masters // maidservant / mistress). The relationship between the cola within each line is one of narrative development of the particular image being described. The two together combine to form the comparison with the psalmist's relationship to Yahweh. The outer two lines of the chiasm also match each other, although not so exactly. Each describes, in its first colon, an action of looking towards Yahweh expressed in the first person, followed in its second colon by a verbal ascription to Yahweh. The development between the cola in each line, and between the two lines, can be seen as one of increasing specificity.[106] The "you" of v. 1a is specifically "the one dwelling in heaven" (v. 1b); who is specifically "Yahweh our God" (v. 2e) who will specifically "have mercy on us" (v. 2f). The development from an intransitive past/present time reference to a transitive future time reference gives the psalm a dynamically forward-looking impulse.

It is possible to read v. 2e–f as a tricolon, as Goldingay does. He does not provide any reasoned substantiation for his colometry, but has possibly been attracted by the idea of the psalm having two sections, each one concluded by a tricolon. He does note that, in contrast to the weightier v. 4 (discussed below), the rhythm of this line is "merely" 2+2+2.[107] However, there is not a clear basis for reading a six-stress line. The allocation of a full stress to the opening particle, without any preceding unstressed syllables, would produce awkward disjunction in the rhythm and would not accord with Sievers' approach. The line more readily scans as a 3+2 bicolon, matching v. 1.

Watson reads the whole of v. 2 as a tricolon, apparently in order to highlight the alliterative opening (כ) of its three lines.[108] He comments that this creates "excessively long lines; no natural division which also respects parallelism appears to break them into smaller units."[109] Watson seems to have created confusion from unspecified priorities between, for example, colon length and prominence of poetic devices such as alliteration and repetition. Watson's tricolon is not substantiated and fails to meet the established criteria for colon length.

---

106. Cf. Clines, "Greater Precision."

107. Goldingay, *Psalms*, 469–70.

108. Watson, *Classical*, 366–67.

109. Ibid., 367.

Returning to the present analysis, the remaining verses, vv. 3–4, comprise one line each. Verse 3 is a bicolon with 3+3 rhythm.[110] Verse 4 has a lexical ambiguity in the final word. The choice of the *kethib* or *qere* reading does not affect the rhythmical analysis of the line, although the *qere*, which reads two words in place of one, would allow the introduction of an additional stress. In the present analysis, the commonly endorsed proposal of BHS, to maintain the *kethib*, is adopted.[111] Notwithstanding this ambiguity, three distinct phrases can clearly be identified with parallelism between the second and third.[112] The initial phrase develops the closing thought of the previous line: the psalmist and companions' satiation with scorn. The second and third phrases offer synonymous explications of that scorn.[113] The rhythm of the line is 3+2+2.

The combination of the first and second phrases would produce a five-stress colon of excessive length (sixteen syllables). The combination of the second and third phrases, to create a 3+4 bicolon,[114] would comply with the basic criteria established above for the treatment of four-word cola that exhibit internal parallelism. However, in this instance the resulting colon is noticeably long and dense, having fifteen syllables (which exceeds Fokkelman's limit) in a poem where no other colon exceeds eleven syllables or three word-units. Note also the influence of the *qere*: should the final word be split into two there is the possibility of an additional stress and the hypothetical colon becomes even weightier.[115]

---

110. BHS apparatus suggests deletion of the (tautological?) רַב in order to maintain a 3+2 rhythm. Such a proposal embodies significant assumptions about the existence and nature of metre in Hebrew poetry. However, in this instance it does not affect the identification of the line as a bicolon. Dahood, *Psalms*, 208, reads a tricolon based on reading רַב as a divine title. His treatment of כִּי is ambiguous.

111. Crow, *Songs of Ascents*, 49; Keet, *Study*, 40. Similarly, the introduction of a conjunction, attested in some mss, does not affect the rhythmical analysis.

112. Jacquet, *Les Psaumes*, 439, citing Gunkel, deletes the third phrase as a gloss. There is no textual evidence for this emendation.

113. Weiser, *The Psalms*, 751, omits the second colon entirely on the grounds that it is a later addition, citing Kittel. However, BHS offers no comment. Allen, *Psalms 101–50*, 216, supports the retention of the full text as a tricolon. Our concern is with the final form of the text, excepting only where manuscript evidence casts significant doubt on its accurate transmission.

114. This is possible within Sievers' system but regarded as very unusual.

115. Having assessed the relative merits of the *kethib* and *qere*, Briggs and Briggs, *Exegetical Commentary*, 452, comment, "In any case two accents are needed for the measure."

Therefore the context of this line determines that a combination of any of the three phrases is not appropriate, and the line is rightly read as a tricolon.[116]

Structural Analyses

THEMATIC ANALYSIS

Gerstenberger structures the text by verses, reading them as an introduction and summons (v. 1), an affirmation of confidence (v. 2), a petition (v. 3), and a complaint (v. 4).[117] Kraus links v. 3 and v. 4 as a communal complaint.[118]

STROPHIC ANALYSIS

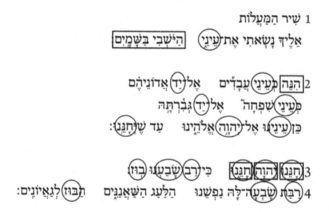

Structure: 1.3.2; Van der Lugt reads the middle strophe as having only two lines but it is actually three. However, this does not affect the division into strophes.

Strophe 1 consists of a single line and states the theme of the psalm: looking to Yahweh for mercy. The thematic word עֵינַי (here with a 1c.s. suffix) is introduced, and Yahweh is addressed at the end of the line by means of an epithet.

---

116. As do Allen, *Psalms 101–50*, 216; Delitzsch, *Commentary*, 73; Fokkelman, *Psalms in Form*, 133; Goldingay, *Psalms*, 469; Hossfeld and Zenger, *Psalmen*, 466 (despite the line having only one clause—see comment on their treatment of 121:5 in the section "Psalm 121: Colometric Analysis" on pp. 77–82); Kissane, *Book of Psalms*, 572.

117. Gerstenberger, *Psalms*, 330.

118. Kraus, *Psalms 60–150*, 438; so also Weiser, *The Psalms*, 753.

Strophe 2 is clearly marked by the opening particle and bound to-gether by the three-fold comparison of servants' eyes being raised to their masters. The strophe is closed by a reference to an indeterminate time of waiting, and the introduction of the next thematic word חנן pro-vides a link with the following strophe.

Strophe 3 is very strongly marked at its opening by two imperatives and a vocative, all of which are repeated key words. The remainder of the strophe explains the reason for this emphatic plea, בוז . . . שׂבע being the repeated key phrase. There is no lexical marking of closure, but v. 4 may be read as a tricolon to this effect.

Most other strophic analyses are similar. Fokkelman and Kissane offer the same structure as Van der Lugt.[119] Allen, citing Magne, reads vv. 1–2 as a single four-line strophe, but the basis of this is the disposi-tion of formal elements and so rather represents a rhetorico-structural approach.[120] Goldingay follows Allen in his presentation, but analyzes and comments on v. 1 separately from v. 2, indicating some tension in the demarcation of strophes.[121]

RHETORICO-STRUCTURAL ANALYSIS

Girard highlights the three key repeated words/phrases that divide the psalm into three sections: עֵינֵי (vv. 1–2e), חנן (vv. 2f–3a), and רַב שֹׂבַע (vv. 3b–4).[122] These three words characterize the three sections as affir-mation of confidence, prayer and lament. However, v. 2f clearly relates to the extended picture of observant trust in vv. 1–2, and so he also proposes a structure with v. 3a standing alone as a pivot between the preceding affirmation of confidence and the following complaint:

vv. 1–2	Confidence
v. 3a	Prayer
vv. 3b–4	Lament

In this case, the repetition of חנן functions as a concatenation to link the first section with the pivot.

---

119. Fokkelman, *Psalms in Form*, 133; Kissane, *Book of Psalms*, 572.

120. Allen, *Psalms 101–50*, 216.

121. Goldingay, *Psalms*, 469–70.

122. Girard, *Psaumes 3: 101–150*, 313.

Girard's analysis of the structure of vv. 1–2 reveals a chiastic arrangement:

v. 1	"My" eyes lifted to heaven	singular
v. 2ab	Servants' eyes lifted to master	masculine plural
v. 2cd	Handmaid's eyes lifted to mistress	feminine singular
v. 2e	"Our" eyes lifted to Yahweh	plural

Similarly he identifies vv. 3b–4 as a unit based on the parallel phrases.[123]

Given that Girard accepts that v. 2f belongs in the unit vv. 1–2, despite not forming part of the chiasm outlined above, it seems odd that he is not also willing to consider that v. 3a can be part of the unit vv. 3–4. To do so would yield a simpler division of the text into two sections, vv. 1–2 and vv. 3–4, with חנן functioning as a link between the two. However, Girard's proposal may be an instance of a rhetorical structure that does not overlay exactly onto a colometric analysis of the text. Indeed, Auffret presents a similar case but goes further to suggest that v. 2f be separated from vv. 1–2e. This results in a four-section rhetorical structure that underlies the principal division of the psalm into two parts, thus:[124]

vv. 1–2e	expression of confidence
v. 2f	waiting for mercy
v. 3a	prayer for mercy
vv. 3b–4	complaint (reason for prayer).

This analysis is more self-consistent than that of Girard and allows an appreciation of the interaction between rhetorical structure and strophic structure.

Summary

The psalm divides thematically into two sections. The strophic division matches this overall structure, but additionally subdivides the opening section. The initial address stands slightly separate, with a strongly marked opening to the descriptive image of trust in v. 2. Rhythmically the psalm is consistent throughout with cola of two or three stresses.

123. Ibid., 310–12. Trublet and Aletti, *Approche Poétique*, 97, offer a very similar analysis.

124. Auffret, *Etude Structurelle*, 31–32.

Rhetorically the two thematic sections are also followed. The first section exhibits a chiasm of formal elements. The two sections are connected by means of a pivot comprising the closing colon of the first section and the opening colon of the second.

Strophic structure			Thematic structure	Rhetorical structure	
1a	1b			1	
2a	2b		1–2	2ab	
2c	2d			2cd	
2e	2f			2e	2f
3a	3b		3–4		3a
4a	4b	4c		3b–4	

Psalm 124

Colometric Analysis

1 שִׁיר הַמַּעֲלוֹת לְדָוִד

לוּלֵי יְהוָה שֶׁהָיָה לָנוּ   יֹאמַר־נָא יִשְׂרָאֵל:

2 לוּלֵי יְהוָה שֶׁהָיָה לָנוּ   בְּקוּם עָלֵינוּ אָדָם:

3 אֲזַי חַיִּים בְּלָעוּנוּ   בַּחֲרוֹת אַפָּם בָּנוּ:

4 אֲזַי הַמַּיִם שְׁטָפוּנוּ   נַחְלָה עָבַר עַל־נַפְשֵׁנוּ:

5 אֲזַי עָבַר עַל־נַפְשֵׁנוּ   הַמַּיִם הַזֵּידוֹנִים:

6 בָּרוּךְ יְהוָה   שֶׁלֹּא נְתָנָנוּ   טֶרֶף לְשִׁנֵּיהֶם:

7 נַפְשֵׁנוּ כְּצִפּוֹר נִמְלְטָה   מִפַּח יוֹקְשִׁים

הַפַּח נִשְׁבָּר   וַאֲנַחְנוּ נִמְלָטְנוּ:

8 עֶזְרֵנוּ בְּשֵׁם יְהוָה   עֹשֵׂה שָׁמַיִם וָאָרֶץ:

The opening pair of lines introduces the theme of this psalm: Yahweh's presence and deliverance in times of peril. These two lines form a classic example of "staircase parallelism," with an identical opening colon in each line.[125] The rhythmical analysis, and therefore colometry, of these lines is somewhat ambiguous. The normal allocation of one stress to each word yields six stresses in v. 1 and seven in v. 2. However it is also possible to leave the opening disyllabic particles unstressed. The various

---

125. Watson, *Classical*, 150.

stress counts therefore give rise to several possible colometries. Given the close connection between the two lines, it is considered appropriate that they should be read with similar forms. Since v. 1 appears to form a liturgical introduction, with v. 2 being the more coherent part of the psalm, it is the analysis of v. 2 that will be considered dominant. Therefore v. 2 will be considered in detail with the hypothesis that the corresponding part of v. 1 should match its form.[126]

With either six or seven stresses, it is possible to read v. 2 as either a bicolon (3+3 or 4+3) or a tricolon (2+2+3).[127] The option of a para-tricolon (2–2–2) does not come into consideration since if the line is read with only six stresses it does not syntactically divide into three phrases of two stresses each. At nine syllables long, the first "half" of the line could reasonably be represented by a single colon or by two short cola. The syntactic construction of the line with a relative clause rather than a simple continuing verbal clause, thereby creating an additional syntactic pause at this point, is evidence for separate cola. This syntactic pause potentially justifies splitting the four words between two cola in this instance. The decision comes down to the strength of the pause prior to the relative pronoun. The reason for the disjunctive accent here is probably to distinguish the following relative clause from the (incomplete) main clause. But the question remains whether the pause is significant enough to be regarded as a colon division rather than a mid-colon pause. There does not appear to be any strong reason to decide one way or the other, and so for now this verse, and therefore the preceding part of v. 1 also, is identified as a possible tricolon.

The following three lines are bicola (vv. 3–5). They are tightly bound together by the repetition of the same opening particle and together describe what perils had been faced in a series of imaginative descriptions. The rhythm of these lines is 3+3 / 3+3 / 3+2, the shorter final colon possibly marking closure of the section by creating a slightly longer pause.[128] Curiously Dahood reads v. 4 as a tricolon citing syllable

126. Curiously Kraus, *Psalms 60–150*, 440, takes the opposite view, commenting first on v. 1 (and relating it to v. 6) and then adopting a tripartite reading of v. 2 to match.

127. Allen, *Psalms 101–50*, 218, and Kraus, *Psalms 60–150*, 440, identify vv. 1–2 as tricola. Watson, *Classical*, 151–53, appears to state that they should be read as a single bicolon.

128. Alternatively, a secondary stress may be read in the final word, as indicated by a *metheg*, thus maintaining the 3+3 rhythm.

count as the reason. However, with eight syllables each the two cola are perfectly acceptable, and indeed fall within the most common range. [129]

Verse 6 marks a disjunction in the flow of the psalm, exclaiming a blessing on Yahweh who has saved. The Masoretic accentuation of v. 6 as a bicolon produces an unusual rhythm (2+4).[130] But as a six-word line that has a syntactic division into three phrases of two words, it can be seen to follow the pattern of a para-tricolon (2–2–2). The line is a single sentence comprising a main clause and a subordinate relative clause. The first caesura coincides with a syntactic pause but only a slight one; interestingly the syntactic and lexical construction here (שֶׁ יְהוָה) is identical to that in vv. 1–2 where it was not possible to determine whether a full caesura between cola was warranted or not. The second caesura occurs within the relative clause but at a point where it is theoretically syntactically complete, albeit semantically ambiguous. It also follows an indicative verb that carries a conjunctive accent. In both these respects it matches the situation found in 122:5a, in relation to which the apparent conflict with the accentuation has been provisionally accepted (see the section "Psalm 122: Colometric Analysis" on pp. 87–92). A minor caesura is adjudged to be appropriate at these two points in the line, and it is regarded as a para-tricolon. This perspective is reinforced by the analysis of others: Watson cites v. 6 as an example of a "staccato" tricolon, having a 2+2+2 rhythm, and Weiser and Dahood are in agreement.[131] Dahood typically cites the syllable count as evidence (4/6/6) but in this case also notes that the tricolon has "two beats in each colon." The greater uniformity of the accentual measure compared with the syllabic measure is striking.

In v. 7 the salvation of Yahweh is described figuratively in a pair of bicola (3+2 / 2+2).[132] These lines together have a clear chiastic structure, with lexical repetition/matching in v. 7a and v. 7d and lexical repetition in v. 7b and v. 7c. To read the verse as a single 5+4 bicolon does not appear reasonable in the light of the consistency of two- and three-stress

---

129. Dahood, *Psalms*, 211–12. Watson, *Classical*, 179 and 183, also cites v. 4 as a tricolon, but without explanation.

130. Kugel, *Idea*, 3, identifies the line as a bicolon following the Masoretic accentuation and comments on the "lopsided" result.

131. Watson, *Classical*, 178fn; Weiser, *The Psalms*, 754; Dahood, *Psalms*, 213.

132. The layout of the text in ML and MA suggests this, as reflected in BHS. Prinsloo, "Historical Reality," 183, 188, reads a tricolon but without explicit justification.

cola throughout the remainder of the psalm, and the five-stress colon would exceed Fokkelman's syllable limit. There is no evidence of the line being a tricolon. The reading of the verse as a double bicolon is evidenced by the fact that the pronoun in v. 7d is redundant, semantically, syntactically, and pragmatically. It therefore appears to have been used as rhythmical ballast and as a complement for נַפְשֵׁנוּ in v. 7a in the chiastic structure of the verse. Were v. 7cd intended as a single colon, this redundant pronoun would lengthen it quite unnecessarily and so militates against such a reading.

The psalm closes with a 3+3 bicolon aphorism in v. 8.

Structural Analyses

THEMATIC ANALYSIS

Gerstenberger asserts this psalm's congregational use, regarding the first line as an introduction intoned by a worship leader with the remainder of the psalm recited communally.[133] The division of the psalm is into three sections: vv. 2–5 supposed conditions and consequences; vv. 6–7 hymn of thanksgiving; v. 8 well-wish.[134]

---

133. Gerstenberger, *Psalms*, 334–35.
134. Ibid., 333; Kraus, *Psalms 60–150*, 441–42; Weiser, *The Psalms*, 755–56.

Strophic Analysis

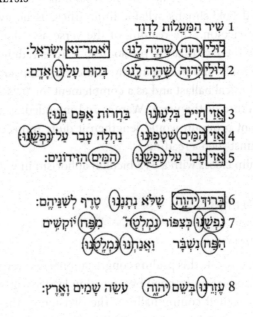

1 שִׁיר הַמַּעֲלוֹת לְדָוִד
לוּלֵי יְהוָה שֶׁהָיָה לָנוּ יֹאמַר־נָא יִשְׂרָאֵל:
2 לוּלֵי יְהוָה שֶׁהָיָה לָנוּ בְּקוּם עָלֵינוּ אָדָם:

3 אֲזַי חַיִּים בְּלָעוּנוּ בַּחֲרוֹת אַפָּם בָּנוּ:
4 אֲזַי הַמַּיִם שְׁטָפוּנוּ נַחְלָה עָבַר עַל־נַפְשֵׁנוּ:
5 אֲזַי עָבַר עַל־נַפְשֵׁנוּ הַמַּיִם הַזֵּידוֹנִים:

6 בָּרוּךְ יְהוָה שֶׁלֹּא נְתָנָנוּ טֶרֶף לְשִׁנֵּיהֶם:
7 נַפְשֵׁנוּ כְּצִפּוֹר נִמְלְטָה מִפַּח יוֹקְשִׁים
הַפַּח נִשְׁבָּר וַאֲנַחְנוּ נִמְלָטְנוּ:

8 עֶזְרֵנוּ בְּשֵׁם יְהוָה עֹשֵׂה שָׁמַיִם וָאָרֶץ:

Structure: 2.3|3.1

Strophe 1 is marked by the opening particle and also by the jussive verb form. The second line is clearly closely bound to the first, with the verbatim repetition of the opening colon, and also adds a further 1c.p. suffix that is often repeated through the psalm. Thus the theme is defined as the implications of Yahweh being for "*us.*"

Strophe 2 is similarly marked by the "emphatic" particle that is repeated at the head of each line in the strophe. The ongoing use of the 1c.p. suffix is further emphasised by the repeated use of נַפְשֵׁנוּ in vv. 4–5. It details the potential consequences of Yahweh *not* having been for "us."

Strophe 3 has a clearly marked opening with its exclamatory blessing. It describes the actual consequences of Yahweh *having* been for "us" through the metaphor of Yahweh setting free captured prey. The further repetition of נַפְשֵׁנוּ and 1c.p. suffixes provides continuity with the preceding strophe.

Strophe 4 is a single line aphorism that summarises the content of the psalm. The psalm thus has a linear structure leading to this concluding thought.

Several other analyses produce the same result.[135] Some have combined vv. 2–5 as a single strophe, reading v. 1 as a separate liturgical introduction.[136]

RHETORICO-STRUCTURAL ANALYSIS

Girard proposes that the rhetorical structure of the psalm is a diptych with two sections to each side, the overall pattern being AB//AB. The first side, vv. 1–5, is about life imagined without Yahweh, and is divided into two sections, vv. 1–3 and vv. 4–5. The second side, vv. 6–8 is about life with Yahweh, and is divided into sections, v. 6 and vv. 7–8.[137]

The divine name forms an inclusion both to the entire psalm and to the second side. The first side is unified by the anaphora of vv. 3–5. Girard finds the following parallels between the respective sections of the two sides: between vv. 1–3 and v. 6, the repetition of יְהוָה שֶׁ and the theme of being consumed; between vv. 4–5 and vv. 7–8, the repetition of נַפְשֵׁנוּ and an antithesis between life imperilled and life saved.[138] There are chiasms in vv. 4–5, הַמַּיִם - נַפְשֵׁנוּ - נַפְשֵׁנוּ - הַמַּיִם, and in v. 7, נִמְלָטָה - פַּח - פַּח - נִמְלָטְנוּ.[139]

The division between the two sides of the diptych is clear, but the division of the sides into sections, less so. In the first side, v. 3 might as well be grouped with vv. 4–5, and all the formal elements of the structure would remain the same, although the thematic correspondence of being consumed would be lost. However, a greater degree of cohesion of the thematic elements of the psalm could be highlighted by proposing a chiastic structure based around the fundamental antithesis of life without Yahweh versus life with Yahweh. Thus, vv. 1–2 / vv. 3–5 // vv. 6–7 / v. 8 would incorporate two outer sections that proclaim Yahweh's help, first

---

135. Fokkelman, *Psalms in Form*, 134; Hunter, *Psalms*, 202. Terrien, *Strophic Structure*, 820, reads v. 7 as a single bicolon and includes v. 8 with vv. 6–7 in the third strophe.

136. Allen, *Psalms 101–50*, 220; Crow, *Songs of Ascents*, 51–52; Kissane, *Book of Psalms*, 574. Allen and Kissane also add v. 8 to vv. 6–7, attracted by the notion of two equal strophes of four lines each. Briggs and Briggs, *Exegetical Commentary*, 452, achieve this same form by deleting v. 5 as a "gloss of repetition"; so also Jacquet, *Les Psaumes*, 443, who deletes v. 4b and v. 5a.

137. Girard, *Psaumes 3: 101–150*, 316–17.

138. Ibid., 317–19. Prinsloo, "Historical Reality," 187–88, makes similar observations.

139. Girard, *Psaumes 3: 101–150*, 318.

negatively then positively, and two inner sections that describe life imperilled without Yahweh and secure life with Yahweh. Such a structure would be denoted A– B– // B'A. Allowing for the introductory summons, the lengths of the corresponding sections would match, and almost all the formal structural aspects, the word repetitions, would remain.

Auffret proposes a similar structure, arguing for the cohesion of vv. 3–5 and vv. 6–7.[140] However, he also splits v. 2 between sections, and separates v. 6a as a central pivot, losing the correspondence between the openings of the two sides. VanGemeren, who proposes a concentric structure on a thematic basis, also identifies v. 6a as a central pivot and identifies framing references to Yahweh's presence and protection.[141]

Trublet and Aletti note many of the same features, but also propose an overall thematic chiastic structure in the psalm:[142]

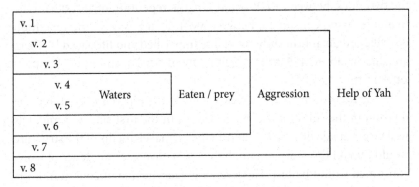

Whilst this points up some thematic connections, the correspondence between v. 2 and v. 7 is a little forced, and the whole structure is based on verses rather than lines, neglecting that v. 7 comprises two lines whilst all other verses comprise one.

Summary

The opening two lines in this psalm are ambiguous both in their colometry and in their relationship to the structure of the remainder of the psalm. The remaining lines are all bicola, apart from the para-tricolon of v. 6, which marks the central acclamation and turning point from

---

140. Auffret, *Etude Structurelle*, 36–40.

141. VanGemeren, "Psalms," 784.

142. Trublet and Aletti, *Approche Poétique*, 97–98.

strophic, thematic, and rhetorical perspectives. Its opening phrase, v. 6a, could possibly be regarded as a central pivot for the whole psalm.

There are a high number of thematic links between different parts of the psalm, with clear chiastic patterns within pairs of lines, such that no single rhetorical structure dominates.

Strophic structure			Thematic structure	Rhetorical structure
1a	1b	1c	1	1
2a	2b	2c		2
3a	3b		2–5	3
4a	4b			4
5a	5b			5
6a–6b–6c				6
7a	7b		6–7	7ab
7c	7d			7cd
8a	8b		8	8

Psalm 125

Colometric Analysis

1 שִׁיר הַמַּעֲלוֹת

הַבֹּטְחִים בַּיהוָה   כְּהַר־צִיּוֹן לֹא־יִמּוֹט   לְעוֹלָם יֵשֵׁב:

2 יְרוּשָׁלַ͏ִם הָרִים סָבִיב לָהּ   וַיהוָה סָבִיב לְעַמּוֹ   מֵעַתָּה וְעַד־עוֹלָם:

3 כִּי לֹא יָנוּחַ שֵׁבֶט הָרֶשַׁע   עַל גּוֹרַל הַצַּדִּיקִים

לְמַעַן לֹא־יִשְׁלְחוּ הַצַּדִּיקִים   בְּעַוְלָתָה יְדֵיהֶם:

4 הֵיטִיבָה יְהוָה לַטּוֹבִים   וְלִישָׁרִים בְּלִבּוֹתָם:

5 וְהַמַּטִּים עֲקַלְקַלּוֹתָם   יוֹלִיכֵם יְהוָה   אֶת־פֹּעֲלֵי הָאָוֶן

שָׁלוֹם עַל־יִשְׂרָאֵל:

This psalm opens with an assertion about the security of those who trust in Yahweh. The syntax of the line is ambiguous, appearing to comprise a nominal clause and two verbal clauses but with no indication of the relationships between them.[143] The initial nominal clause has הַבֹּטְחִים

143. Crow, *Songs of Ascents*, 55, discusses the LXX reading of יֵשֵׁב at the end of v. 1 as belonging at the beginning of v. 2. Both he and Allen, *Psalms 101–50*, 224, conclude that it rightly belongs in v. 1, due to the clear parallelism of v. 2. For a radical reconstruction of vv. 1–2, see e.g., Jacquet, *Les Psaumes*, 450–52.

בַּיהוָה as the subject and הַר־צִיּוֹן as part of the complement. The following verbal clauses are best judged to have הַר־צִיּוֹן as the subject and so are implicitly relative to that phrase in the initial clause. A common approach, therefore, is to separate the apparent nominal clause from the verbal clauses and to read a balanced bicolon (3+3).[144] However, the Masoretic accentuation presents the line quite differently, as an unusual 2+4 bicolon, with an additional disjunctive accent in the second colon. The presentation of three phrases with two stresses each raises the possibility of the line being a para-tricolon with 2–2–2 rhythm.[145] This would correctly observe each of the disjunctive accents and would avoid the anomaly of a caesura coinciding with a conjunctive accent that is a feature of the 3+3 bicolon reading. It would not be so well matched to the supposed syntax of the line, but rather would bring out its syntactic ambiguity. In this presentation the central colon in the line would act as a pivot, completing the initial nominal clause and opening the following verbal clauses. Such close interaction between the cola would justify the presence of only minor caesurae between them. Therefore v. 1 is identified as a possible para-tricolon, with further detailed examination of the syntactic and semantic structure of the line required.

Both possibilities for v. 1 are reflected in the presentation of the text in BHS. A gap is indicated after the *'atnach* (in light of the accent and the presentation in M^A), but also after צִיּוֹן, presumably reflecting the editors' support for a 3+3 reading of the line. Possibly because of this, and in the light of the following line, Allen has read v. 1 as a tricolon with rhythm 2+2+3 by allocating two full stresses to כְּהַר־צִיּוֹן.[146] However, this seems unlikely since a line of three clauses is being split into three cola without coincidence of clauses and cola. A review of syllable counts also assists in the evaluation of this, and the other options. The tricolon reading has 7/4/8 syllables, indicating a particularly short middle colon. The bicolon reading has 11/8 syllables, revealing a long initial colon. The para-tricolon has 7/7/5 syllables, achieving the best balance of the three options.

---

144. So Fokkelman, *Major Poems III*, 278, for this syntactic reason; and Kraus, *Psalms 60–150*, 443, who in translation renders the two verbal clauses explicitly relative. Analysis of rhythm here assumes that כְּהַר־צִיּוֹן is maintained as a bound phrase with single stress.

145. Goldingay, *Psalms*, 485, and Hossfeld and Zenger, *Psalmen*, 487, note this as a possibility; the translation of Alter, *Book of Psalms*, 445–46, implies this colometry.

146. Allen, *Psalms 101–50*, 223.

Verse 2 extends the imagery of v. 1 and makes an assertion about Yahweh; it has three distinct phrases. All other cola in this psalm have either two or three word-units, and this line of eight stresses cannot be read as a bicolon without producing an unusually long colon. The BHS apparatus, along with Kraus and Gunkel, suggest deleting the final phrase as being a gloss.[147] This suggestion is offered on the grounds of metre.[148] Crow disagrees with this approach whilst maintaining that the "extra" colon is evidence of redactional activity.[149] Similarly, Allen argues for its retention, noting that it balances the tricolon of v. 1 (as he reads it) and provides parallelism of עוֹלָם in the final colon of each verse.[150]

The evidence for a tricolon is strong in this instance. The Masoretic accentuation divides the line at the end of the second phrase (עַמּוֹ), thus generating an initial colon that is too long according to almost any measure. It exceeds O'Connor's constraints on word-units, constituents, and predicates that govern a nominal phrase; it exceeds Fokkelman's limit on word-units; and at seventeen syllables it considerably exceeds his normal limit of twelve.[151] In a metrical analysis, Sievers would probably present the first two phrases as a 3+3 bicolon (omitting any stress within the initial סָבִיב in order to avoid consecutive stressed syllables) followed by a three-stress monocolon.[152] Gray would go along with a desire to separate the first two phrases in order to highlight their parallelism; his treatment of the third phrase can only be speculated.[153] The absence of any pausal forms makes it impossible to apply Revell's theory to this line.

By almost all accounts, therefore, it seems appropriate to read this line as a tricolon. The first two phrases exhibit parallelism at semantic, lexical, and syntactic levels, and the third phrase is closely connected with them, as it qualifies the metaphor thereby created. The resulting three cola are reasonably balanced, numerically speaking, exhibiting a

---

147. Kraus, *Psalms 60–150*, 443.

148. Such a proposal embodies significant assumptions about the existence and nature of metre in Hebrew poetry. Tov, *Textual Criticism*, 368, regards textual emendation on such grounds as untenable. See also the discussion of 126:2–3 in the section "Psalm 126: Colometric Analysis" on pp. 117–22."

149. Crow, *Songs of Ascents*, 55.

150. Allen, *Psalms 101–50*, 224.

151. Fokkelman, *Major Poems II*, 25.

152. Cf. Sievers' treatment of Ps 2:2 and 4:1; Sievers, *Metrische Studien*, 500–503.

153. See Gray's discussion of four-word cola; Gray, *Forms*, 161–63.

gradual decrease in word-count (4/3/2) and syllable count (9/8/7). The omission of the final colon on metrical grounds cannot be substantiated.

Verse 3 gives reasons for Yahweh's protection in a pair of lines. The second is a bicolon with 3+2 rhythm, but the nature of the first is ambiguous. The opening two particles may be assigned a stress or may be bound with the following verb as a single word-unit. The alternatives give rise to readings of a 2–2–2 para-tricolon and a 3+2 bicolon respectively. These two options are equally plausible. They both provide a reading commensurate with the accentuation and both satisfy O'Connor's and Fokkelman's constraints. The initial colon of the para-tricolon option has the lowest acceptable number of syllables, but other such cola in para-tricola have already been verified (120:7a; 121:4b; 124:6a). The very nature of cola in para-tricola being limited to two word-units inevitably results in typically shorter cola than is the case generally. Given that the line comprises a single clause without any parallelism between its phrases, there is not internal evidence of parallelism that might affect the rhythmical analysis. Kraus and Allen read a 2+2+2 tricolon, while Fokkelman, Jacquet, Goldingay, and Crow read a bicolon.[154] From a subjective point of view, a case can be made for either option. A para-tricolon could be seen to match those of v. 1 (potentially) and v. 5 (see below), while a bicolon can be regarded as matching the following two lines (remainder of v. 3 and v. 4). A judgement has been made between the two alternatives based on the syntactic structure of the line (conjunction – negative verb – subject noun phrase – adverbial phrase) being almost identical to the following line, which is a bicolon. Therefore the line is read as a 3+2 bicolon.

Verse 4 is a prayer addressed to Yahweh and is also a bicolon, again with 3+2 rhythm.

Verse 5 makes an assertion about Yahweh's dealings with the wicked, and concludes the psalm with an aphoristic monocolon. This final phrase has no direct syntactic or semantic connection with the main clause of the line and so is rightly presented separately. The monocolon probably has a closing function.[155]

---

154. Kraus, *Psalms 60–150*, 444; Allen, *Psalms 101–50*, 223; Fokkelman, *Psalms in Form*, 134; Jacquet, *Les Psaumes*, 450; Goldingay, *Psalms*, 483; Crow, *Songs of Ascents*, 54.

155. Watson, *Classical*, 168–72. Allen, *Psalms 101–50*, 224, erroneously cites this reference as Watson, *Classical*, 70–72.

Turning to the main part of v. 5 the accentuation indicates three phrases, each of two word-units. The third phrase can be regarded as redundant: Crow reads it as a scribal gloss "clarifying the referent of the accusative 'them'" and favors its deletion, but notes that "all other commentators" retain it, reading אֵת as the preposition "with."[156] Subsequently, Goldingay has concurred with Crow's reading of אֵת as the definite object marker, but without wishing to excise the phrase.[157] It is retained here, due to the lack of any textual evidence to the contrary. The division of the line into three two-stress phrases indicates its character as a para-tricolon. This reading is supported by the line's being a single clause, such that only minor caesurae are appropriate. The central verbal phrase relates equally to the preceding colon, identifying its object, and the following colon, adverbially modifying it. Kraus and Allen read the line as tripartite but cite a rhythm of 3+2+2.[158] They presumably wish to allocate a secondary stress to עֲקַלְקַלּוֹתָם but this is not necessary. With four unstressed syllables before the stress, a secondary stress is possible but not required, according to Sievers' system.[159] And despite the length of this word, the initial colon, having nine syllables, is not unusually long. Therefore v. 5 as a whole is a para-tricolon plus monocolon.

Structural Analyses

THEMATIC ANALYSIS

Gerstenberger discerns five elements in the psalm, corresponding to the five verses: felicitation, assurance, threat to evildoers, petition and imprecation. He also notes that vv. 1–2 stand together as a meditation on blessedness and vv. 4–5 as prayer.[160]

---

156. Crow, *Songs of Ascents*, 55–56.

157. Goldingay, *Psalms*, 483 n. 2.

158. Kraus, *Psalms 60–150*, 43–44; Allen, *Psalms 101–50*, 223.

159. Sievers, *Metrische Studien*, 177.

160. Gerstenberger, *Psalms*, 336–38. Kraus, *Psalms 60–150*, 445, and Weiser, *The Psalms*, 757–58, adopt similar structures.

STROPHIC ANALYSIS

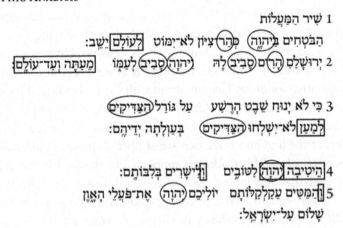

Structure: 2.2.3 assuming the final colon stands apart as a monocolon. Van der Lugt reads v. 5 as a single line, but there is not sufficient syntactic or semantic connection between the final colon and the rest of the line to warrant this approach, as discussed above.

Strophe 1 describes the certainty of Yahweh's steadfastness, using the imagery of mountains. The reference to eternity in v. 1 does not mark closure, occurring in the first line of a higher rhetorical unit. The closure of the strophe is marked strongly by the reference to eternity at the end of v. 2. Whilst many commentators regard this phrase as a late addition to the text, it is interesting to note that it performs this marking function, given that the opening of the following strophe is not marked.

Strophe 2 expounds Yahweh's dealings with righteous and wicked people, thus providing the substantiation for the assertions of v. 1. The closure of the strophe is marked by the explanatory particle.

Strophe 3 comprises a prayer for Yahweh to act in the interests of the "righteous," and a statement that Yahweh will act against the interests of the wicked. The opening of the strophe is clearly marked by an imperative and vocative. The conjunction of v. 5, which can be a marker of opening, here would mark the concluding line of a higher unit, were it not for the final colon. Perhaps this colon is included due to the lack of any other strong indication of closure (cf. 124:8).

Most other strophic analyses are similar. Allen, Fokkelman, Goldingay, and Kissane offer the same structure as Van der Lugt.[161]

---

161. Allen, *Psalms 101–50*, 224; Fokkelman, *Psalms in Form*, 134; Goldingay, *Psalms*, 483; Kissane, *Book of Psalms*, 576.

Terrien connects v. 3 with vv. 1–2, reading it as a tricolon.[162] Conversely, Hunter connects v. 3 with vv. 4–5 based on the thematic appraisal of "dramas of instability."[163]

RHETORICO-STRUCTURAL ANALYSIS

The relative dearth of repetitions within this psalm makes analysis very difficult. Girard struggles to derive a clear overall structure, positing three possibilities and depending upon an unusual reading of the text (מַטִּים v. 5 as the plural of מַטֶּה) in order to suggest any internal cohesion.

The unity of vv. 1–2 is apparent in the repetitions of יְהוָה and הַר, the synonymous terms צִיּוֹן and יְרוּשָׁלַם and in the corresponding rhetorical function of each line making a comparison.[164] Girard reads these lines as an independent part of the psalm, as he does with the closing benediction, and structures the remaining lines concentrically (v. 3/v. 4/v. 5) according to an A/B/A' pattern. However, his link between v. 3 and v. 5 is tenuous, resting on the reading mentioned above and further interpretive propositions.[165] An overall structure for the psalm is best found in an antithetic inclusion that contrasts הַבֹּטְחִים בַּיהוָה (v. 1) with הַמַּטִּים עֲקַלְקַלּוֹתָם (v. 5).[166] Allen suggests an alternative inclusion based on a wordplay between מוֹט (v. 1) and מַטִּים (v. 5), but it is not reasonable to suppose that an alliterative link could be sustained over such a textual distance. A better observation is that the divine name is repeated twice, in similar positions, in vv. 1–2 and vv. 4–5. Allen also notes that the central pair of lines, in v. 3, have a thematic/lexical chiasm "which befits its central position": רֶשַׁע - צַדִּיקִים - צַדִּיקִים - עַוְלָתָה.[167] Thematically-based concentric structures, with v. 3 as the focus, are also offered by VanGemeren and Alden.[168]

Trublet and Aletti adopt a distinct approach, finding thematic parallels between v. 1 and v. 3—confidence, faithfulness—and between v. 2 and vv. 4–5—assertions about Yahweh.[169] These interpreted con-

162. Terrien, *Strophic Structure*, 822.

163. Hunter, *Psalms*, 203.

164. Girard, *Psaumes 3: 101–150*, 323; Auffret, *Etude Structurelle*, 43.

165. Girard, *Psaumes 3: 101–150*, 325.

166. Ibid., 327.

167. Allen, *Psalms 101–50*, 224; cf. Auffret, *Etude Structurelle*, 44.

168. Alden, "Chiastic Psalms (III)," 207; VanGemeren, "Psalms," 787.

169. Trublet and Aletti, *Approche Poétique*, 98.

nections are by no means clearly apparent, and seem somewhat weaker than those identified by Girard and Allen. Auffret produces a similar, but more complicated, analysis based on the identification of word-pairs and thus depending upon an assumption of the accepted identification of such pairs more than any features of the text of the psalm alone.[170]

Summary

The psalm is marked out in three clear sections and is concluded by a separate monocolon. The main body of the psalm is bounded by para-tricola and an antithetic inclusio. Within each of the three pairs of lines there are linking lexical or thematic features, and an overall chiastic structure of the psalm is suggested by the central chiasm in v. 3 and the overall inclusio. Verse 2 stands out from the others as a tricolon, the function of which is not immediately apparent.

Strophic structure	Thematic structure	Rhetorical structure		
1a–1b–1c 2a 2b 2c	1–2	1 2		
3a 3b			3a	3b
3c 3d	3–5c		3d	3c
4a 4b		4		
5a–5b–5c		5a–c		
5d	5d			5d

---

170. Auffret, *Etude Structurelle*, 44–46.

Psalm 126

Colometric Analysis

שִׁיר הַמַּעֲלוֹת 1

בְּשׁוּב יְהוָה אֶת־שִׁיבַת צִיּוֹן הָיִינוּ כְּחֹלְמִים׃

אָז יִמָּלֵא שְׂחוֹק פִּינוּ וּלְשׁוֹנֵנוּ רִנָּה 2

אָז יֹאמְרוּ בַגּוֹיִם הִגְדִּיל יְהוָה לַעֲשׂוֹת עִם־אֵלֶּה׃

הִגְדִּיל יְהוָה לַעֲשׂוֹת עִמָּנוּ הָיִינוּ שְׂמֵחִים׃ 3

שׁוּבָה יְהוָה אֶת־[כ= שְׁבוּתֵנוּ] [ק= שְׁבִיתֵנוּ] כַּאֲפִיקִים בַּנֶּגֶב׃ 4

הַזֹּרְעִים בְּדִמְעָה בְּרִנָּה יִקְצֹרוּ׃ 5

הָלוֹךְ יֵלֵךְ וּבָכֹה נֹשֵׂא מֶשֶׁךְ־הַזָּרַע 6

בֹּא־יָבוֹא בְרִנָּה נֹשֵׂא אֲלֻמֹּתָיו׃

This psalm looks back to some previous (unspecific) restoration of Zion, and intercedes with Yahweh to act in the same way again.[171] The translation of v. 1 is particularly difficult due to the lexical ambiguity of the terms שִׁיבַת and כְּחֹלְמִים, with at least two variants of each attested in ancient versions.[172] However, adoption of any of the variants does not affect the rhythm of the line.[173] The line has six stresses and may be read as a 4+2 bicolon[174] or as a para-tricolon (2–2–2).[175] Both options satisfy O'Connor's and Fokkelman's numerical constraints and place caesurae coincident with disjunctive accents. Syntactically the line comprises a temporal subordinate clause followed by a main clause. Therefore, it naturally lends itself to division as a bicolon, matching this syntactic structure. Reading the line as a para-tricolon creates a seemingly unnecessary mid-clause division after the divine name. However, it does reflect the fact that the line comprises three distinct phrases and is not

171. The tenses of the psalm are notoriously difficult to interpret. The most common approach of a past reference for vv. 1–3 is adopted here, based primarily on the perfectives of v. 3. See discussions in Allen, *Psalms 101–50*, 228–30; Beyerlin, *Dreamers*, 15–23; Hossfeld and Zenger, *Psalmen*, 503–05; Prinsloo, "Analyzing," 226–27.

172. See BHS apparatus; Crow, *Songs of Ascents*, 59–60, discusses the variants.

173. Dahood, *Psalms*, 217–20, proposes that כְּחֹלְמִים should be split into two words forming a construct chain that could reasonably be read as a single stress word-unit.

174. Thus Weiser, *The Psalms*, 759; Terrien, *Strophic Structure*, 824; Crow, *Songs of Ascents*, 58–59.

175. Thus Allen, *Psalms 101–50*, 227; Kraus, *Psalms 60–150*, 447.

altogether inappropriate. In view of this, and of the possible matching with the following lines (see below), the line is classified at this stage as a possible para-tricolon.

Verse 2 is clearly too long to be a single line. It readily divides into two lines as evidenced by the repeated particle אז at the beginning of each. The first line may be read as a typical form of bicolon with rhythm 3+2 if the opening particle remains unstressed.[176] It would comprise a complete clause in the initial colon, followed by a parallel clause with elided verb in the following colon. The order of the parallel elements, subject and object of the verb, are inverted in the following colon to create a chiasm. However, it is also possible to allocate a full stress to the opening particle and to read the line as a para-tricolon (2–2–2). Whilst it would be unusual to begin a line with a stressed syllable, this is exactly the analysis offered by Sievers of Ps 2:5, which has a similar syntactic structure and begins with the same particle אז followed by an indicative verb.[177] Whereas Ps 2:5 comprises two distinct verbal clauses with different verbs and different modifiers, the line in question here can be read as a single verbal clause with conjoined objects. Therefore, this line has a greater syntactic coherence than Ps 2:5 and warrants being read as three phrases with only minor caesurae between them. The initial phrase is potentially syntactically complete, albeit semantically ambiguous. The following two phrases relate to it with equal prominence. Therefore, the line may legitimately be read as a para-tricolon. The only contraindication of this reading is the coincidence of the first minor caesura with a conjunctive accent, a feature that applies to Ps 2:5 also. Such a situation has already been addressed and validated in the analysis of Ps 122:5, which has a very similar syntactic structure to this line (see the section "Psalm 122: Colometric Analysis" on pp. 87–92). It is curious that an initial stressed syllable has not been avoided by the use of a variant lexeme אזי but the explanation possibly lies in the following line.[178]

The second line in v. 2 is more difficult to analyze. Curiously the opening particle carries a disjunctive accent, despite its syntactic and semantic relationship to the following verb being the same as that of

176. Thus Allen, *Psalms 101–50*, 227.

177. Sievers, *Metrische Studien*, 501. In doing so, he follows his normal practice of allocating a full stress to particles when followed by two unstressed syllables; Sievers, *Metrische Studien*, 188–93.

178. Cf. 124:3–5.

the particle at the beginning of the preceding line, where the particle carries the expected conjunctive accent. This variation possibly provides evidence of the flexibility inherent in such monosyllables to either provide a stressed beat or not.[179] Such flexibility is integral to Sievers' system. While a stress has been allocated to the particle in the preceding line, a rhythmical consistency is achieved by leaving it unstressed in this line. By this means the line has six stresses, matching the others in the first half of the psalm. It is possibly the need to leave the particle unstressed in this line that has dictated the use of the shorter particle אַז rather than אֲזַי.

The accentuation of the second line of v. 2 implies reading a 2+4 bicolon, a colometry that matches the syntactic and semantic division of the line between the introduction of direct speech and the speech itself. This produces an unbalanced bicolon, with the unusual characteristic of the second colon being longer than the first. Most scholars agree that long second cola are unusual. Whether they represent aberrations or deliberate ploys to draw attention to the line can only be a matter of speculation. However, this long second colon still forms a valid colon by any standard. Perhaps the Masoretic disjunctive accent on the opening particle in this line is an attempt to achieve a better rhythmical balance if the line is read as a bicolon.

The possibility of the line being a para-tricolon warrants exploration. The line apparently can be regarded as comprising three phrases of two word-units each. What is less apparent is the syntactic relationship between the second and third phrases. Fokkelman argues that the phrases together constitute an idiomatic expression the integrity of which should not be corrupted by dividing it.[180] However, the infinitive construct עֲשֹׂות may simply be a complement to the main verb (cf. Gen 19:19). In contrast, Dahood does split the phrase arguing that it is formed of two separate verbal phrases: הִגְדִּיל being a "hiphil elevative" meaning "showed his greatness" and לַעֲשֹׂות being an infinitive construct of circumstance meaning "by working."[181] Without any strong evidence

---

179. It may also be another example of accentuation being varied depending on the context, as discussed in relation to indicative verbs in the section "Psalm 122: Colometric Analysis" on pp. 87–92.

180. Fokkelman, *Major Poems III*, 280–81. He also argues for the phrase to be treated in the same way in v. 3.

181. Dahood, *Psalms*, 220. This construction can also be known as epexegetical; see Waltke and O'Connor, *Syntax*, 608.

that הִגְדִּיל לַעֲשׂוֹת is indeed an inseparable idiomatic phrase, there is cause to follow Dahood's view on the syntax, and to allow the line to be split into three phrases. However, it is arguable in this instance that there is naturally a stronger pause between the report of speech and the speech itself than there is in the middle of the speech. This would militate against reading a para-tricolon. The point is a difficult one to judge, and the possibilities for the line being a 2+4 bicolon and being a 2–2–2 para-tricolon seem fairly evenly balanced. A syllable count yields little additional insight. In the case of reading a para-tricolon the medial colon has only four syllables, but this is acceptable.[182]

Verse 3 contains the same syntactic construction as the preceding line, and so the same issues pertain to its rhythmical analysis. The two alternatives for reading the line are as a 4+2 bicolon or a 2–2–2 para-tricolon. The similarity between the two lines suggests that they should be treated in the same way, and many scholars do this. Weiser, Fokkelman, and Crow read both lines as bicola, following the Masoretic accentuation; Kraus, Dahood, and Allen read both lines as tricola.[183] The irregular rhythm created by reading these lines as bicola does create doubt as to the validity of doing so. [184] But although reading a pair of para-tricola produces rhythmical consistency, such colometry has not yet been fully substantiated. Therefore it is concluded that these lines are possible para-tricola, and will be subject to more detailed scrutiny.

In passing, it is noteworthy that the ambiguity in the colometry of these lines has implications for certain views of poetic structure. Firstly it is apparent that no single system of counting syllables, words, stresses, or syntactic components can unequivocally define the colometry of these lines. This reinforces the view that no existing single approach to colometry can be regarded as consistently valid, and that therefore significant textual emendation on the grounds of metre, for instance, cannot be substantiated.

182. See comment on 125:3ab in the section "Psalm 125: Colometric Analysis" on pp. 109–13.

183. Weiser, *The Psalms*, 759; Fokkelman, *Psalms in Form*, 135; Crow, *Songs of Ascents*, 58–59; Kraus, *Psalms 60–150*, 447–48; Dahood, *Psalms*, 217; Allen, *Psalms 101–50*, 227.

184. Jacquet, *Les Psaumes*, 459, and Terrien, *Strophic Structure*, 824–26, argue for a consistent 4+2 rhythm for the first four lines (vv. 1–3). This approach embodies a mistreatment of the opening particle of v. 2, goes against the accentuation in the second line of v. 2, and treats the repeated phrase in two different ways.

Secondly, the common, though often unstated, assumptions adopted by analysts of Hebrew poetry—that the Masoretic accentuation provides the key indication of colometry and that we should expect to find some form of regularity of structure—are mutually incompatible in the case of these lines. If they are read as bicola, following the accentuation, they are unbalanced and inconsistent bicola. The pattern for the first four lines of the psalm is 4+2 / 3+2 / 2+4 / 4+2. There is matching neither between cola in a line nor between the form of adjacent lines, despite the fact that these lines clearly form a unit, knit together by the repetition of the opening particle in two lines and by the repetition of the phrase describing Yahweh's dealings. Therefore a more sophisticated approach may be required, but without having recourse to speculative emendation of the text.

Thirdly, however, there is a means of reading regularity in the structure of the text, without directly contradicting the accentuation, by reading each line as a para-tricolon. Verse 1, which introduces these lines, potentially has this form, as does the first line of v. 2 when the initial occurrence of the temporal particle at the beginning of the line is allocated a full stress.[185] Such a nuanced rhythmical analysis represents a very modest "emendation" of the Masoretic text and accentuation compared to the more radical alterations that are often proposed *metri causa*. The presentation of four para-tricola forms a unified and consistent structure for the first half of this psalm. It differs from any previous approach, probably due to the commonly held dichotomy between bicolon and tricolon, and due to the near impossibility of a translation of these lines that reproduces both content and structure.

Returning to the present analysis of the psalm, vv. 4–5 are a pair of bicola with rhythm 3+2 / 2+2.[186] The concluding verse of the psalm, v. 6, develops the image of sowing and reaping from v. 5. The verse is too long to constitute a single bicolon (nine or ten stresses, twenty six syllables), and its syntactic composition of two very similar structures indicates that it comprises two lines rather than a tricolon.[187] The rhythm of the

185. It may be noted that in terms of pragmatic structuring, this actually makes more sense than the opposite accentuation evidenced in the MT; the first instance of the particle is a focus-marker and can reasonably be stressed, whereas the second instance provides no new information.

186. The textual variants in v. 4, as v. 1, not affecting the rhythm.

187. Willis, "Alternating Parallelism," 59, cites the lines as an alternating aba'b' pattern that emphasises the consequences of human activity.

two lines is 3+2 / 2+2. The ambiguity attested in 11QPs[a] and LXX over whether the participles in the line should be singular or plural has no bearing on this analysis.

Structural Analyses

THEMATIC ANALYSIS

Gerstenberger favors a reading with a past reference and discerns clear differences between vv. 1–4, being first person expressions of immediate experiences, and vv. 5–6, being an impersonal descriptive song dealing with general human truths.[188] Kraus makes a threefold division, vv. 1–3 historical retrospect, v. 4 petition, vv. 5–6 comforting promises, noting a correspondence with the structure of Psalm 85.[189] Hossfeld and Zenger read vv. 5–6 as an expansion of the petition of v. 4.[190]

STROPHIC ANALYSIS

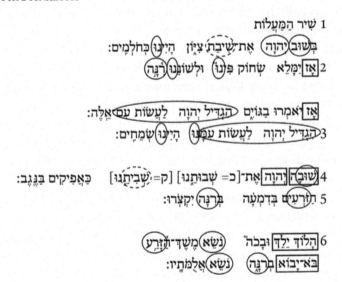

Structure: 2.2|2.2

Strophe 1 recounts a non-specific past occasion of Yahweh's restoring Zion's fortunes and the joy that it brought. Thematic words are intro-

---

188. Gerstenberger, *Psalms*, 339–40.

189. Kraus, *Psalms 60–150*, 448–49; so also Weiser, *The Psalms*, 760–63.

190. Hossfeld and Zenger, *Psalmen*, 505; cf. Prinsloo, "Analysing," 235–37.

duced in this strophe, but there is no marking of opening or closure. The particle אָז at the head of v. 2 must be regarded as a contra-indication of its normal marking function; instead it acts in concatenation with the repetition in the following line in order to provide continuity. It might also have a rhythmical purpose.

Strophe 2 continues the account of the effects of Yahweh's past dealings, broadening the horizon to the effect on other nations. The theme of rejoicing is continued. The opening of the strophe is marked but not the closing.

Strophe 3 is clearly marked out by its opening imperative and vocative, and is a prayer for renewed restoration. Re-use of the opening two lexemes of the psalm indicates that it is the same sort of restoration that has been celebrated before that is being sought again. This is further emphasised by the repetition of the thematic word רִנָּה. The finite verb in v. 5 should be read with jussive meaning, thus continuing the supplication of v. 4.

Strophe 4 describes the hoped-for effects of restoration in a more vividly detailed picture. The opening of the strophe is marked by a paranomastic infinitive construction. The final line creates a sense of closure by means of a closely matched contrast, using the same opening syntactical form and repeating the participle נֹשֵׂא whilst returning from בָּכֹה to the thematic רִנָּה (cf. 120:7 for contrast as closure).

A high number of other strophic analyses produce the same result, either as a result of observing matching between the two halves of the psalm (vv. 1–3 and vv. 4–6) or as a result of interpreting the verbs of the two halves to have past and future reference respectively.[191]

Rhetorico-Structural Analysis

Girard separates the psalm into two parts, vv. 1–4 and vv. 5–6, each part being a diptych. The first diptych is structured chiastically based around the repetitions: שׁוּב - הָיִינוּ - הִגְדִּיל - הִגְדִּיל - הָיִינוּ - שׁוּב and is thus denoted ABC/CBA. However the disposition of these words in the text is such that this rhetorical structure does not match the lineation of the text. Lines are divided between the sections: v. 1ab, vv. 1c–2c, v. 2def / v. 3ab,

---

191. Allen, *Psalms 101–50*, 229–30; Briggs and Briggs, *Exegetical Commentary*, 455; Crow, *Songs of Ascents*, 58–59; Fokkelman, *Psalms in Form*, 135; Goldingay, *Psalms*, 789; Hunter, *Psalms*, 206; Jacquet, *Les Psaumes*, 459; Kissane, *Book of Psalms*, 578; Terrien, *Strophic Structure*, 824–25.

v. 3c, v. 4. Observation of the chiasm is valid, but need not lead to a suggestion that the text be divided into these sections. Rather this may be taken as an example of a rhetorical structure which overlays the strophic structure without matching it exactly. Curiously, Girard makes no mention at all of the repetition of the particle אָז.[192]

The second diptych comprises the two cola of v. 5 paralleling linearly the two lines of v. 6 and is denoted AB//A'B'. Each of these verses has internal chiasm and they are similarly structured. The only formal indicator of cohesion of the whole psalm is the repetition of רִנָּה; Girard emphasises the thematic integration around the return from exile, but this is interpretive and not commensurate with his own methodology for structuring a text.[193]

Trublet and Aletti deduce a very similar structure to that of Girard, but highlight different repetitions as the basis of it. In vv. 5–6 they particularly mention the alternating thematic motifs of distress (v. 5a, v. 6ab) and joy (v. 5b, v. 6cd).[194]

Auffret divides the psalm differently, seeing the two parts as vv. 1–3 and vv. 4–6. He notes that v. 1 and v. 4 not only begin with the same word but also conclude with a comparison, and he concludes that these two lines correspond and introduce the two parts of the psalm. The remainder of each part is structured by internal chiasms that are evident in v. 2abc, v. 5 and v. 6, and partially in vv. 2def–3.[195] Allen cites additional evidence for this structure, noting that רִנָּה occurs in corresponding locations, towards the end of the second line in each part.[196]

A similar approach had been adopted by Lund and is cited by Meynet. He made the same points but added a correspondence between the celebration of Yahweh's great dealings with Israel in vv. 2def–3 and the celebration of successful harvest in v. 6. He thus discerned an overall structure for the psalm v1, v. 2abc, vv. 2def–3 / v. 4, v. 5, v. 6, denoted ABC/A'B'C', that exhibits correspondence between sections in formal, thematic and quantitative aspects.[197]

---

192. Girard, *Psaumes 3: 101–150*, 330–31.

193. Ibid., 332–33.

194. Trublet and Aletti, *Approche Poétique*, 98–99.

195. Auffret, *Etude Structurelle*, 50–52.

196. Allen, *Psalms 101–50*, 230.

197. Lund, *Chiasmus in New Testament*, 107–08, cited in Meynet, *Rhetorical Analysis*, 156–57. The analysis is not Meynet's own, *contra* Allen, *Psalms 101–50*, 231.

Summary

This psalm has two sections; the location of the division is a matter of contention. Verse 4 can be related both to the preceding and to the following verses. From a rhythmical / strophic point of view, the psalm is clearly structured into four strophes of two lines each. The cola are all of two or three stresses, accepting the reading of some lines as para-tricola. The form of the lines is not consistent, but a degree of uniformity is apparent in the second section, and a hypothetical means of recognizing uniformity in the first section has been mooted. At least two different rhetorical structures can be observed: one that locates v. 4 in the first section, and another that regards it as part of the second section in a rhetorical structure that more closely corresponds with the strophic structure of the psalm. Perhaps v. 4 should be regarded as a pivot that does double-duty, thereby generating coherence and overall unity.

Strophic structure	Thematic structure	Rhetorical structure		
1a–1b–1c		1ab		
2a–2b–2c			1c–2c	
2d–2e–2f	1–3			2def
3a–3b–3c				3ab
4a 4b	4		3c	
5a 5b		4	5a	
6a 6b	5–6			5b
6c 6d			6ab	6cd

Psalm 127

Colometric Analysis

1 שִׁיר הַמַּעֲלוֹת לִשְׁלֹמֹה

אִם־יְהוָה לֹא־יִבְנֶה בַיִת   שָׁוְא עָמְלוּ בוֹנָיו בּוֹ

אִם־יְהוָה לֹא־יִשְׁמָר־עִיר   שָׁוְא שָׁקַד שׁוֹמֵר:

2 שָׁוְא לָכֶם מַשְׁכִּימֵי קוּם מְאַחֲרֵי־שֶׁבֶת

אֹכְלֵי לֶחֶם הָעֲצָבִים   כֵּן יִתֵּן לִידִידוֹ שֵׁנָא:

3 הִנֵּה נַחֲלַת יְהוָה בָּנִים   שָׂכָר פְּרִי הַבָּטֶן:

4 כְּחִצִּים בְּיַד־גִּבּוֹר   כֵּן בְּנֵי הַנְּעוּרִים:

5 אַשְׁרֵי הַגֶּבֶר   אֲשֶׁר מִלֵּא אֶת־אַשְׁפָּתוֹ מֵהֶם

לֹא־יֵבֹשׁוּ כִּי־יְדַבְּרוּ   אֶת־אוֹיְבִים בַּשָּׁעַר:

This psalm emphasizes Yahweh as the source of a person's fortune. Uniquely among the Psalms of Ascents it is ascribed to Solomon, perhaps because of the allusion Yahweh's involvement in building a "house" which has connotations of the construction of the temple.[198] It also has a sapiential tone. Lexical curiosities present a number of interpretive issues, and there are several difficulties in the psalm's rhythmical analysis.

Verse 1 asserts the necessity of Yahweh's involvement in building and guarding and is too long to be a single line. Its syntactic structure comprises two distinct sentences, each one having a protasis and an apodosis, with lexically matching openings between the two sentences in both clauses. This is strongly suggestive of a pair of bicola. The rhythmical analysis presents a number of noteworthy features when Sievers' principles are applied. The natural accentuation of the words produces consecutive stressed syllables at the end of v. 1a, v. 1b and v. 1c. This is possibly the reason for the introduction of an additional *maqqeph* in v. 1c. The problem in v. 1c can be overcome by "stretching" the monosyllabic עִיר into a disyllable[199] and in v. 1b simply by reading בוֹנָיו בּוֹ as a single stress word-unit.[200] Neither approach works so well in v. 1a, where Sievers would probably want to relocate the stress in either יִבְנֶה or בַיִת or

198. Kraus, *Psalms 60–150*, 453.

199. Sievers, *Metrische Studien*, 226.

200. The seemingly tautological particle בּוֹ could be regarded as an accretion to the original text.

both. Equally plausible is the rhythmical joining of the words, matching the Masoretic treatment of v. 1c, in order to read a two-stress colon. It is also apparent that v. 1b and v. 1d have the relatively unusual characteristic of beginning with a stressed syllable. This is appropriate given the semantic significance of the word שָׁוְא, and there is no need to combine it rhythmically with the following verbs. Indeed the abruptness of the stressed opening to the cola emphasises the blunt message of the lines.[201] The final rhythm of the lines will depend on how these matters are dealt with; a balanced rhythm of 3+3 / 3+3 is plausible.

Verse 2 expands the theme, describing excessive periods of working as being vain. It contains lexical problems and has an indeterminate rhythm. The verse is too long to be a single line, having at least eleven word-units, the precise number depending upon how the rhythm is analyzed. At this length, it is conceivable that the verse might be a tricolon, but there is no clear indication of a division of the line into three cola, and at thirty syllables in total the cola would be particularly long. Syntactically the verse comprises two clauses, and a tricolon would need to split the initial clause across two cola. The subject of the initial clause is a paratactic sequence of three participial noun phrases.[202] Since the first two participial noun phrases cohere semantically as a form of hendiadys, these should not be separated and would form the first colon along with the clause's complement that stands at the head of the verse.[203] This results in the following speculative colon:

שָׁוְא לָכֶם מַשְׁכִּימֵי קוּם מְאַחֲרֵי־שֶׁבֶת

This is theoretically possible as a colon having four or five stresses, depending upon whether both participles or just one participle is combined rhythmically with its following infinitive construct. However, at thirteen syllables long it stands out as an unreasonably long colon.

---

201. Cf. Sievers' allocation of a stress to אֵין at the opening of cola in Ps 14:1,3; Sievers, *Metrische Studien*, 513.

202. Fleming, "Psalm 127," 439, and Hossfeld and Zenger, *Psalmen*, 513–14, read this syntactic structure for the verse. Goldingay, *Psalms*, 497, reads the same relationships but כֶּם as the subject of v. 2a and the participles as substantives identifying that subject. In either case the final clause (v. 2e) is separate and read as a contrast.

203. Briggs and Briggs, *Exegetical Commentary*, 459, describe the relationship between the participles as antithetic. However, the two concepts of "rising early" and "staying up late" are not opposites, but mutually reinforcing illustrations of a common concept: over-working.

In addition the lack of any form of caesura after the opening phrase שָׁוְא לָכֶם is not commensurate with its rhetorical significance and function. Therefore the possibility of the verse being a tricolon is not accepted, and the verse is read as two lines.

The line division within the verse comes after שֶׁבֶת for the same reasons discussed above in the exploration of the possibility of a tricolon. The common rendering of the verse is as two bicola, but the syntax, meaning, and rhythm of the lines are all unclear. The LXX appears to read the participles in the first line at variance from the MT, and more significantly takes קוּם as governing the following participle rather than being governed by the preceding participle. Crow argues for the retention of the MT, highlighting the apparent parallel constructions of participle followed by infinitive construct.[204] As discussed above, they together create a form of hendiadys that relates to the opening phrase. The line can therefore be seen to comprise three two-word phrases, and lends itself to being read as a para-tricolon. This is attested by Kraus who reads a tricolon with rhythm 2+2+2.[205] However, the rhythmical analysis is not completely clear-cut, since the normal vocalization of the line would twice result in consecutive stressed syllables. Sievers' approach requires the stress in the participles to be thrown back, in order to avoid a juxtaposition of stresses with the following infinitive constructs and it is interesting to note that this shift is in fact indicated by the Masoretic accentuation also.[206] The recognition of a para-tricolon is supported by the coincidence of the two minor caesurae with disjunctive accents. Goldingay prioritises the first disjunctive accent and effectively reads a 2+4 bicolon.[207] However, this is motivated by the discernment of a chiasm in the rhetorical structure of the two lines of v. 2; such a rhetorical structure may well be valid but need not dictate the colometry, which is determined principally on rhythmical grounds.

The second line in v. 2 clearly comprises two distinct phrases, the first appearing to be a continuation of the clause of the previous line and

204. Crow, *Songs of Ascents*, 66.

205. Kraus, *Psalms 60–150*, 452–53. So also Allen, *Psalms 101–50*, 233.

206. This was also the approach of Ley, cited in Cobb, *Criticism*, 95. Strictly the MT assigns no stress to מֵאַחֲרֵי due to the following *maqqeph*, but a secondary stress may be inferred from the metheg.

207. Goldingay, *Psalms*, 501–2. Goldingay does not cite a rhythmical analysis; the annotation 2+4 is used here only to illustrate how he divides the line.

the second being a separate clause. It is commonly read as a 3+3 bicolon, rhythmically equivalent to the para-tricolon of the first line.[208] There is evidence that כֵּן should read כִּי and the meaning of שֶׁנָא is obscure; but these issues would not affect the lineation of the text.[209]

Verses 3 and 4 introduce the topic of sons and the wealth and security they offer. Each of these verses is a bicolon, with rhythm 3+3 (taking the opening particle in v. 3 as an anacrusis).

In verse 5, which concludes the psalm, the rhythm and lineation are again unclear. There are lexical ambiguities, but they do not affect the colometry.[210] The verse has at least ten word-units and is too long to be a single line; nor can it reasonably form a tricolon, comprising as it does two sentences of approximately equal length. Therefore the verse is two lines, divided at the sentence break, as indicated by the accentuation. The first line of the verse is accented as a bicolon, but an unbalanced one, having 2+4 rhythm. Presumably the accentuation at this point was informed by semantic considerations above rhythmical ones, separating the nominal exclamation from the qualifying relative clause. Fokkelman responds by presenting the line as a bicolon but moving the caesura to follow מָלֵא in order to produce more "balanced" cola.[211] This produces a rhythm that does not match the syntax, creating a pause in the middle of the relative clause without any pause immediately before it. As with v. 2, it works better to read a para-tricolon, taking the line to be three phrases that together form a single thought. The exclamation is potentially syntactically complete but semantically ambiguous at each of the caesurae and so minor caesurae are appropriate. This reading does place a minor caesura coincident with a conjunctive accent, but as this is on an indicative verb followed by its direct object, this is considered acceptable, as

---

208. Loretz, *Psalmstudien*, 313, links the first four phrases of v. 2 as four cola and leaves the final clause separate as a monocolon. However, his approach is based on consonant counting and semantic considerations.

209. These are discussed by Crow, *Songs of Ascents*, 67. Barthélemy, *Critique Textuelle*, 810, favours the retention of MT. Booij, "Psalm 127," 266, explores the referent of כֵּן.

210. The final line may refer to speaking with enemies in the gate or driving back enemies from the gate. See Crow, *Songs of Ascents*, 67–68, for a discussion of the options. Dahood, *Psalms*, 225, favours "drive back" on the grounds of consistency of metaphor with the preceding lines. The lexical ambiguity of דבר may be a deliberate device of the type identified by Raabe, "Deliberate Ambiguity," 214–17.

211. Fokkelman, *Major Poems III*, 284.

discussed in the section "Psalm 122: Colometric Analysis" on pp. 87–92 (cf. 124:6, 126:2abc). The resulting enjambment is not uncommon, and the caesura is not as strong as in a bicolon or full tricolon. The line refers back to the subject of the two preceding lines that are both 3+3 and so it is appropriate that it should have equivalent rhythm. Allen supports a tripartite reading, in his terms as a 2+2+2 tricolon, noting that the two such lines occur at corresponding positions in the two halves of the psalm.[212]

In the second line of the verse, similar issues are in play, but here are complicated by the rhythmical ambiguity of the monosyllabic particles. The line cannot be read as a para-tricolon without allocating a full stress to both particles. This would be very unusual, and the line would become quite disjointed. The line should therefore be read as a bicolon, although the division remains unclear. A "balanced" division into two cola requires breaking up a subordinate clause. In this instance, the caesura would have to come after the verb, יְדַבְּרוּ. This arrangement also lends credence to the interpretation of יְדַבְּרוּ as "drive back," since it can readily be related to the earlier references to "arrows" and "guarding the city."[213] The introduction of "speaking" or "contending" at this point, without its object or modifier in the same colon, would be very difficult to relate to the preceding text. The rhythm of such a bicolon would be either 3+2 or 2+2, depending on the treatment of the particles. Since every other line in the psalm is (at least potentially) a six-stress line, it is plausible that this shorter line facilitates closure.[214]

Structural Analyses

THEMATIC ANALYSIS

Gerstenberger reads this psalm as a song of community instruction with four sections: sayings (v. 1), exhortation (v. 2), felicitation (vv. 3–4) and beatitude (v. 5).[215] Kraus made a clear distinction between vv. 1–2 and

---

212. Allen, *Psalms 101–50*, 234–35.

213. See Watson, *Classical*, 286. Cf. Ps 28:6.

214. The rhythmical regularity of the psalm is recognised by Briggs and Briggs, *Exegetical Commentary*, 457–59, in contrast to Jacquet, *Les Psaumes*, 469–73, who proposes an astonishing degree of textual emendation on the basis of a 3+2 rhythm throughout.

215. Gerstenberger, *Psalms*, 344.

vv. 3–5 based on content (protection/labor and blessing of progeny respectively), whilst urging that they be interpreted in conjunction.[216]

STROPHIC ANALYSIS

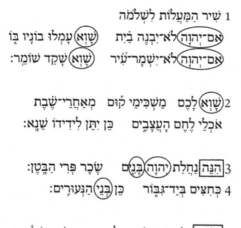

Structure: 2.2|2.2

Strophe 1 is identified by the repeated words at the beginning of each
corresponding colon. The strophe conveys the message of the psalm that
prosperity depends on Yahweh.

Strophe 2 is not clearly marked, but is identified by the change of
voice from third person to second person. The opening repetition of the
thematic word שָׁוְא provides continuity with the preceding strophe. The
psalm thus is structured according to a linear progression of thought.

Strophe 3 has an opening clearly marked with by an exclamatory
particle. As noted above, this particle is extra-metrical and strongly
marks the turning point between the two sections of the psalm. A new
topic is thus introduced and it is asserted that sons are a blessing from
Yahweh. The thematic link of dependence on Yahweh invites the reader/
listener to make a connection between the blessings of security, provision and descendents.

---

216. Kraus, *Psalms 60–150*, 453. Weiser, *The Psalms*, 764–66, concurs with the division but states that the parts are "quite unrelated." See the discussion in Estes, "Like
Arrows," 305–6.

Strophe 4 also has a clearly marked opening with the attention-grabbing key word אַשְׁרֵי. It develops the connection hinted at in strophe 3, specifically linking the blessings of sons and assuredness in the face of enemies. The psalm as a whole, and in each of its strophes, is notable for the absence of any markers of closure. However, the reference to the gate creates an allusion back to the opening statement about the city, and thus marks closure by means of an alluded inclusio.

Fokkelman, Hunter, Kissane and Terrien produce the same structure as Van der Lugt, albeit with slight variations in division of lines into cola.[217]

RHETORICO-STRUCTURAL ANALYSIS

Girard finds this psalm difficult to structure due to the relative paucity of repetitions with which to work. He suggests that the psalm is a diptych, but is unable to make any division of the sides into sections in a way that generates clear correspondences. The two sides are vv. 1–2 and vv. 3–5 such that the divine name stands at the head of each side. Girard makes a further connection between the two openings by linking בנה and בן etymologically. He may be overstating the case, but the link can be sustained simply at the level of wordplay[218] or of rhyme.[219] The first side is characterized by the repetition of שָׁוְא, the second side by the repetitions of גֶּבֶר / גִּבּוֹר and בָּנִים / בְּנֵי.[220]

Auffret offers an analysis of the themes of the psalm, noting in the second half alternating references to sons and battle terminology. These he relates thematically to the opening verse as follows:

Yahweh builds the city / provides sons:	v. 1ab	v. 3	v. 4b
Yahweh guards the city / the godly man succeeds against enemies:	v. 1cd	v. 4a	v. 5.

---

217. Fokkelman, *Psalms in Form*, 135; Hunter, *Psalms*, 210; Kissane, *Book of Psalms*, 580; Terrien, *Strophic Structure*, 828.

218. Allen, *Psalms 101–50*, 237.

219. P. D. Miller, "Psalm 127," 121, 127, 130. Miller also highlights the ambiguous reference of בַּיִת (v. 1) that incorporates both physical building and establishing a family/dynasty, thus thematically uniting the two sections of the psalm.

220. Girard, *Psaumes 3: 101–150*, 338–40.

However, Auffret, along with Girard, can find no connection to the topic of general toil in v. 2.[221] Allen does so by noting that v. 2e and v. 3 both explicitly feature divine gifts (sleep and sons respectively) and that לֶחֶם הָעֲצָבִים (v. 2d) and בְּנֵי הַנְּעוּרִים (v. 4) are parallel; and thus posits a chiastic structure for the psalm as a whole wherein reference to these two gifts are preceded and followed by expanding statements, the one negative the other positive.[222] However this structure is not clearly expounded and is dependent upon reading v. 2d as nominative absolute *casus pendens,* relating syntactically to the following clause (v. 2e) such that לֶחֶם הָעֲצָבִים is interpreted as a divine blessing rather than an illustration of futile toil. Hunter somewhat imaginatively discerns a linear structure that matches the two halves of the psalm:[223]

Building the house (v. 1ab)	Sons keeping house (v. 3)
Building the city (v. 1cd)	Sons keeping the city (v. 4)
Futility of solitary toil (v. 2)	Blessing of corporate action (v. 5)

Such interpretive analyses of themes as these fall beyond the scope of the strictly formal analytical methodology of Girard.

Summary

Although the psalm has presented challenges to interpreters, it has a clearly defined thematic and strophic structure. The rhythm is remarkably consistent. The two main topics are each developed in a canto of four lines, each with a para-tricolon in the third line and the other lines being 3+3 bicola. A rhetorical structure is more difficult to discern, but there are several aspects of association between the two halves and formal features that bind each half together. The rhetorical structure illustrated is but one possibility.

---

221. Auffret, *Etude Structurelle,* 60–61.

222. Allen, *Psalms 101–50,* 238.

223. Hunter, *Psalms,* 210.

Strophic structure	Thematic structure	Rhetorical structure	
1a 1b		1ab	
1c 1d	1–2	1cd	
2a–2b–2c			2abc
2d 2e			2de
3a 3b		3ab	
4a 4b	3–5	4ab	
5a–5b–5c			5abc
5d 5e			5de

Psalm 128

Colometric Analysis

1 שִׁיר הַמַּעֲלוֹת

הַהֹלֵךְ בִּדְרָכָיו׃   אַשְׁרֵי כָּל־יְרֵא יְהוָה

2 יְגִיעַ כַּפֶּיךָ כִּי תֹאכֵל   אַשְׁרֶיךָ וְטוֹב לָךְ׃

3 אֶשְׁתְּךָ כְּגֶפֶן פֹּרִיָּה   בְּיַרְכְּתֵי בֵיתֶךָ

בָּנֶיךָ כִּשְׁתִלֵי זֵיתִים   סָבִיב לְשֻׁלְחָנֶךָ׃

4 הִנֵּה כִי־כֵן יְבֹרַךְ גָּבֶר יְרֵא יְהוָה׃

5 יְבָרֶכְךָ יְהוָה מִצִּיּוֹן וּרְאֵה בְּטוּב יְרוּשָׁלָ͏ִם כֹּל יְמֵי חַיֶּיךָ׃

6 וּרְאֵה־בָנִים לְבָנֶיךָ שָׁלוֹם עַל־יִשְׂרָאֵל׃

This psalm resonates with the opening of the Psalter in its pronounce-
ment of the blessedness of those who fear Yahweh and walk in Yahweh's
ways. It also has some synergy with Ps 127, particularly in relation to sons
as a sign of blessing in a domestic context. Verses 1–3 consist of a series
of four bicola that expound the lot of the fortunate one as fruitfulness in
labor and in family life. Each line has 3+2 rhythm. In v. 2 the particle כִּי
is unstressed, and the final two words combine into a single-stress unit
in order to avoid consecutive stressed syllables. Verse 3 has ten stresses
and is too long to be a single bicolon. The clear bipartite structure of the
line, comprising two similarly formed comparisons, indicates that the
verse is a pair of bicola rather than a tricolon. This conclusion matches
that indicated by the accentuation and is reinforced by the regular succession of 3+2 bicola that results.

Verse 4 reverts to a non-specific statement of Yahweh's blessing that parallels v. 1; its colometry presents a number of possibilities. The opening phrase הִנֵּה כִי־כֵן is puzzling both semantically and rhythmically. It is unusual to find these three particles together, and the absence of כִי in some mss and versions leads to the hypothesis that it has been added either by "incorrect dittography"[224] or as an attempt to normalize a less common terminology.[225] The evidence is not clear-cut, and whilst the presence of this particle does not necessarily change the rhythm of the line, it does introduce ambiguity. Without it the two particles would form a single-stress unit. With all three particles this can still be the case, or הִנֵּה can considered an anacrusis, or הִנֵּה can be allocated a full separate stress. These options generate the possibilities of either a five-stress line, with or without anacrusis, or a six-stress line.

If there are five stresses, the line may be read as a 3+2 bicolon, matching the preceding lines. This is helped if the opening particle is regarded as an anacrusis, but even if not the three particles together can form a legitimate rhythmical unit with three unstressed syllables and one stress. The division of the line at גֶּבֶר ties in not only with the accentuation but in this instance with a pausal form. If there are six stresses, the division of the line at this point produces an unusual 4+2 bicolon. Fokkelman proposes an alternative 3+3 division, breaking the line after יְבֹרַךְ so that the second colon then identifies the subject of the first.[226] However, since the final phrase is an adjectival relative clause the colometry matches the syntax better if the caesura is placed between the main and relative clauses rather than breaking the main clause. A final possibility for a six-stress line is the reading of a para-tricolon, splitting the line into three two-stress units. This matches the syntax of the line, represented as a modifying phrase, a main clause and an adjectival relative clause. Semantically all three phrases are required to convey the single thought of the sentence and two equal minor caesurae are appropriate.

Each of the options outlined satisfies the constraints on syllable counts, and there is no clear means of choosing between them. A presumption that a regular metre might be sustained throughout the psalm would weigh towards a 3+2 bicolon. The possibility of an anacrusis at

224. Kraus, *Psalms 60–150*, 457.

225. Crow, *Songs of Ascents*, 73.

226. Fokkelman, *Psalms in Form*, 136. Curiously MA presents the line in this manner, despite the accentuation.

the beginning of the line would depend upon whether the line was re-garded as the conclusion of the preceding lines, or the opening of a new section of the psalm in a manner that deliberately parallels the opening of the first section, both of which interpretations are possible (see the section "Psalm 128: Structural Analyses" on pp. 138–42). In the other in-stances of הִנֵּה encountered so far, the word has been an anacrusis when highlighting a new section of the psalm (123:2; 127:3) but otherwise not (121:4). Accordingly the colometry of v. 4 is, according to the established criteria, indeterminate. The possibility of its being a para-tricolon will be explored further in the light of broader structural considerations.

Verses 5 and 6 present a number of possibilities. Together they consist of five phrases, each of two or three stresses. The syllable count for the five phrases of 9/9/6/9/6 indicates that any combination would generate an excessively long colon, and so five cola should be read. Such an approach, supported by the accentuation, offers an initial reading of tricolon and bicolon for v. 5 and v. 6 respectively.[227] However, at least three aspects of the text give cause to question this. Firstly, the apparent rhythmical regularity of the psalm, as consisting mainly of lines of 3+2 bicola, leads some to suggest that a colon has been lost after v. 5a, such that v. 5 should consist of a pair of 3+2 bicola.[228] Secondly, the repetition of וּרְאֵה in v. 5b and v. 6a is suggestive of an anaphoric opening to con-secutive lines. This observation reinforces the previous one regarding the apparent disconnection between v. 5a and the remainder of v. 5; it raises the possibility that v. 5a stands as an interjectory monocolon, although this would be a very unusual poetic feature. Fokkelman adopts this co-lometry based on syllable count, which for once shows a regular pattern, the three lines of vv. 5–6 thus having 9, 9/6 and 9/6 syllables respective-ly.[229] The conjunction at the beginning of v. 5b is curious if it stands at the beginning of a line, but can be interpreted as indicating consequence following the jussive verb of v. 5a.[230] Thirdly, the final colon, v. 6b, has no

227. Kugel, *Idea*, 5, presents v. 5 as a tricolon, whilst also commenting that it might just as well be read as a bicolon with v. 5b and v. 5c combined to form the second colon. However such a second colon would be excessively long, both in terms of words (five or six) and syllables (fifteen). Similarly, if the verse were read as a bicolon with v. 5a and v. 5b combined, this opening colon be even longer long in words (six) and syllables (eighteen).

228. Thus Kraus, *Psalms 60–150*, 457; BHS apparatus.

229. Fokkelman, *Major Poems III*, 288–89.

230. Cf. Gen 18:4; Ruth 1:9; Lam 1:22. Allen, *Psalms 101–50*, 241.

clear connection with the preceding colon, v. 6a, and is identical to the concluding benediction of 125:5c, which was determined to be a closing monocolon.[231] If v. 6b here is also a closing monocolon, the possibility presents itself that the preceding four cola (v. 5a–c, v. 6a) comprise a pair of bicola.[232] But in this case, it would seem very odd to have v. 5c at the head of a bicolon followed by v. 6a, when v. 5c relates both syntactically and semantically to v. 5b. Therefore it may be speculated that the order of the phrases has been corrupted in copying and that v. 5c has been placed before the other instance of וּרְאֵה than the one it should have been placed before.[233] An original line-form of v. 5a+ v. 5c / v. 5b+ v. 6a / v. 6b may therefore be speculated, as follows:

כֹּל יְמֵי חַיֶּיךָ׃   יְבָרֶכְךָ יְהוָה מִצִּיּוֹן

וּרְאֵה־בָנִים לְבָנֶיךָ׃   וּרְאֵה בְּטוֹב יְרוּשָׁלָ͏ִם

שָׁלוֹם עַל־יִשְׂרָאֵל׃

A similar approach was advocated by Kissane, commenting that the "metrical structure as well as the sense requires that 5c should follow 5a" and that "verses 6a and 5b are parallel."[234] The rhythm of such speculative bicola could be either 3+2, matching vv. 1–3 and allowing the *maqqeph* in v. 6a, or 3+3 and therefore equivalent to the possible para-tricolon of v. 4. In the opening cola of each line there is matching between צִיּוֹן and יְרוּשָׁלָ͏ִם, and in the following cola there is end-rhyme and a thematic link of longevity. They thus represent the most coherent presentation of vv. 5a–6a as bicola.

Appraisal of these issues involves consideration of both the status of the received text and the implications for its colometry. First, the possibility of the loss of a colon from the original form of the text is not accepted. As discussed above, the emendation of the text on metrical

---

231. See the section "Psalm 125 : Colometric analysis" on pp. 109–13.

232. Thus Beaucamp, *Le Psautier*, np; Goldingay, *Psalms*, 507.

233. Or that the incorrect instance of וּרְאֵה has followed v. 5c and the consequent duplication of v. 5b subsequently corrected erroneously.

234. Kissane, *Book of Psalms*, 583. Kissane also transposed the positions of v. 5b and v. 6a, and appended v. 6a to them so that the psalm closes with a tricolon. Jacquet, *Les Psaumes*, 480–82, proposes a similar rearrangement and additionally hypothesises a "lost" colon so that all lines are presented as bicola. Allen, *Psalms 101–50*, 241–42, also sees v. 6b as a monocolon but reads v. 5a as a monocolon and vv. 5b–6a as a tricolon. The resultant reading of monocolon-tricolon-monocolon is extraordinarily irregular and disjointed; it appears to be motivated by keeping the two anaphoric phrases in the same line but this is not necessary.

grounds alone cannot be substantiated, since no metrical theory has been fully verified; there is no textual evidence of an additional colon and a plausible colometry is apparent in this instance without the supposition of a lost colon. Secondly, the distinction between v. 5 as tricolon and v. 5 as monocolon plus bicolon is a most subtle one. A decision must rest on the degree of syntactic and semantic cohesion between the cola, since the options are equally valid from a rhythmical point of view. In this instance, the syntactic perspective of copula plus imperative indicating consequence provides a coherence to the line as a tricolon and this is the preferred option. However, this fails to address the lack of coherence in the final line of the psalm (v. 6). So thirdly, the hypothetical re-ordering of the cola can be seen to produce the most overall coherent solution to the three aspects of the text that provoke question. But to adopt such a proposal, especially without any external evidence, would be speculative, and would go against the principles of the current study that seeks to identify and analyze tripartite lines on a consistent basis. Therefore, in the present context, v. 5 is most appropriately read as a tricolon $(3+3+2)$[235], but with the awareness that it is quite possibly not as originally structured. Verse 6 is therefore read as a 3+2 bicolon.

Structural Analyses

THEMATIC ANALYSIS

Gerstenberger identifies the elements within the psalm as beatitude (v. 1–2), blessings (vv. 3–4 and vv. 5–6a) and a well-wish for Israel (v. 6b). Within these elements he notes the variation of direct address and impersonal pronouncements.[236] Kraus and Weiser each grouped vv. 1–4 and vv. 5–6 as separate sections.[237]

STROPHIC ANALYSIS

The analysis indicated here is that of Van der Lugt, and this will be discussed in detail. However, in this instance the colometry assumed by Van der Lugt differs from that deduced above, and a following discussion will address the implications arising from this difference.

235. Thus Anderson, *Psalms: Volume 2*, 869.

236. Gerstenberger, *Psalms*, 348–49.

237. Kraus, *Psalms 60–150*, 458–59; Weiser, *The Psalms*, 767.

Structure: 2.2|2.2

Strophe 1 clearly states the topic of the psalm—the happiness of those who fear Yahweh—and also introduces the 2m.s. addressee that repeats throughout the psalm. The repetition of אַשְׁרֵי in v. 2 links the two lines together, but there is no formal mark of closure.

Strophe 2 has no transition markers and so v. 3 may be thought of as a continuation of strophe 1. However, the two lines of strophe 2 clearly belong together, describing the blessings of wife and sons both in terms of fruitfulness, and a four-line strophe would be an unusual departure from the norm of two- or three-line strophes. The clear marking and structure of subsequent strophes also suggest that the psalm consists of a regular succession of two line strophes.

Strophe 3 is marked by the exclamatory particle and repeats the phrase from the opening colon thus linking the second canto with the first. The two lines of the strophe are linked by the repetition of ברך. In this structure, a colon is assumed to have been lost from v. 5; from a strophic point of view it is difficult to conceive of another reason for a departure from the regular pattern of strophes comprised of two bicola.[238] Van der Lugt regards the use of ברך with Israel as the object as a marker of closure, but the evidence for this is not great.[239]

---

238. Thus BHS apparatus; Van der Lugt, *Cantos and Strophes*, 425.

239. Van der Lugt, *Cantos and Strophes*, 556.

Strophe 4 is marked by the opening conjunction and imperative, which are also repeated in the following line, thus cohering the strophe. The reference to sons in the final line links back to the final line of the first canto. The temporal phrase in v. 5c is normally considered a marker of closure, and so is here a contra-indication. The final colon has no syntactical, and little semantic, connection with the foregoing text, but appears to have some closing function (cf.125:5c).

This analysis is an example of strophic analysis, based on recognition of transition markers and repetitions, assisting with the determination of difficult colometry. However, the result is not entirely self-evident, since it hypothesises a "lost" colon in v. 5. Therefore an alternative should be considered, in which v. 5a is linked with v. 5b–c, as deduced in the colometric analysis above. The opening of v. 4 הִנֵּה may still be read as a marker of opening a strophe, in which case with v. 5 as a tricolon the overall structure is 2.2.3. However it is noteworthy that according to Van der Lugt's principles הִנֵּה could also be a marker of closure of a higher rhetorical unit, in this case a canto comprising vv. 1–4. In this case the closing repetition of the phrase from the opening colon, יְרֵא יְהוָה, would form an inclusio around this canto. Verses 5–6 would form a second, single-strophe canto and the overall structure would be 2.3|2.

Other strophic analyses all tend to group into separate strophes vv. 1–2, the two lines of v. 3 and vv. 5–6 (with varying colometries assumed for vv. 5–6). However, the ambiguity over the place of v. 4 in the structure of the psalm is evident. Crow, Fokkelman, and Hunter connect it with the preceding verses, reading the repetition of יְרֵא יְהוָה as an inclusio.[240] Allen, Goldingay, Jacquet, Kissane, and Terrien associate it with the following verses.[241] Goldingay comments that "perhaps it constitutes an interlocking hook between the two sections, the first colon looking forward and the second backward."[242] The reasoning behind some of these analyses mixes strophic with rhetorico-critical considerations. From a purely strophic point of view, it seems most appropriate to associate v. 4 with the following verses. This produces a more balanced

---

240. Crow, *Songs of Ascents*, 72; Fokkleman 2002, 136; Hunter, *Psalms*, 213.

241. Allen, *Psalms 101–50*, 241; Goldingay, *Psalms*, 507; Jacquet, *Les Psaumes*, 481; Kissane, *Book of Psalms*, 582; Terrien, *Strophic Structure*, 831.

242. Goldingay, *Psalms*, 510–11. As such the line would fit the "inverted hinge" pattern identified by Van Dyke Parunak, "Transitional Techniques," 540–46.

overall structure rather than a two-strophe, five-line canto followed by a mere two-line canto.

RHETORICO-STRUCTURAL ANALYSIS

Girard reads in this psalm a diptych with three sections of correspondence between the sides and a linear progression, thus denoted ABC// A'B'C'. His division of the text into sections is: vv. 1–2bα, v. 2bβ, v. 3 // vv. 4–5a, v. 5bc, v. 6. The opening sections are linked by the repetition of יְרֵא יְהוָה and the idea of beatitude/blessing; the middle sections are linked by the repetition of טוֹב; and the closing sections by the repetition of בָּנֶיךָ. Note that these links can still be made without splitting v. 2 and v. 5. The first side is characterized by the theme of blessing in the home environment and in the present timeframe; the second side concerns blessing in the larger and further-reaching context of the city and of future generations.[243]

Similar observations are made by Trublet and Aletti who also note the alternating change in grammatical person: third person in v. 1 and v. 4, second person elsewhere.[244] Another similar approach was that of Boys, cited by Meynet. He focused on the alternating form of address through the psalm, and suggested a diptych (to use Girard's terminology) of two sections: v. 1, vv. 2–3 // v. 4, vv. 5–6, denoted AB//A'B'. In this scheme, each side consists of one line that speaks about the person who fears Yahweh, followed by three lines that directly address such a person and pronounce blessings upon them. The blessing is first declared, and then particularized.[245] The formal correspondences between repeated words identified by Girard are equally applicable to this scheme.

Girard also points out the more apparent structural features that tie the lines of the psalm together in pairs: אַשְׁרֵי repeated in vv. 1–2, a pair of similar comparisons in v. 3, ברך repeated in vv. 4–5a, and anaphora in vv. 5b–6.[246] These observations reinforce the strophic analyses discussed above and complement the more detailed dissection of lines that is required for his diptych analysis.

---

243. Girard, *Psaumes 3: 101–150*, 346–48.

244. Trublet and Aletti, *Approche Poétique*, 228.

245. Boys, *A Key*, 64–65, cited in Meynet, *Rhetorical Analysis*, 115–16. See also Allen, *Psalms 101–50*, 243.

246. Girard, *Psaumes 3: 101–150*, 348–49.

The ambiguity surrounding the place of v. 4 in the psalm structure is discussed by Auffret who, whilst valuing Girard's approach, also suggests that the psalm may be divided vv. 1–4/vv. 5–6. In this case v. 4 acts as a hinge, referring back to the blessings already described and introducing the following blessing.[247]

Summary

This deceptively simple psalm is particularly difficult to pin down, both in its colometry and its macrostructure. The difficulties centre on v. 4, which exhibits textual, rhythmical, and colometric ambiguities. The possibility of its functioning pivotally as both a conclusion to an opening section and an opening to a concluding section has similarities to 126:4, and this characteristic is indicated in the diagram below. The uniformity of the first four bicola is contrasted by the mixed line-forms of the concluding section of the psalm. Amongst the Psalms of Ascents it presents probably the strongest cause to believe that an original poetic form has been corrupted, either through redaction or by errors of transmission.

Strophic structure	Thematic structure	Rhetorical structure
1a 1b		1
2a 2b	1–3	2
3a 3b		
3c 3d		3
4a–4b–4c	4	4
5a 5b 5c	5–6	5
6a 6b		6

---

247. Auffret, *Etude Structurelle*, 64–66. Delitzsch, *Commentary*, 292, and Hossfeld and Zenger, *Psalmen*, 536, also read v. 4 as referring back to the preceding lines whilst respectively asserting that it opens and closes a section of the psalm.

Psalm 129

Colometric Analysis

1 שִׁיר הַמַּעֲלוֹת

רַבַּת צְרָרוּנִי מִנְּעוּרַי   יֹאמַר־נָא יִשְׂרָאֵל:

2 רַבַּת צְרָרוּנִי מִנְּעוּרַי   גַּם לֹא־יָכְלוּ לִי:

3 עַל־גַּבִּי חָרְשׁוּ חֹרְשִׁים   הֶאֱרִיכוּ [כ= לְמַעֲנוֹתָם] [ק= לְמַעֲנִיתָם]:

4 יְהוָה צַדִּיק קִצֵּץ   עֲבוֹת רְשָׁעִים:

5 יֵבֹשׁוּ וְיִסֹּגוּ אָחוֹר   כֹּל שֹׂנְאֵי צִיּוֹן:

6 יִהְיוּ כַּחֲצִיר גַּגּוֹת   שֶׁקַּדְמַת שָׁלַף יָבֵשׁ:

7 שֶׁלֹּא מִלֵּא כַפּוֹ קוֹצֵר   וְחִצְנוֹ מְעַמֵּר:

8 וְלֹא אָמְרוּ הָעֹבְרִים   בִּרְכַּת־יְהוָה אֲלֵיכֶם   בֵּרַכְנוּ אֶתְכֶם בְּשֵׁם יְהוָה:

This imprecatory psalm seeks Yahweh's action against those who have been hostile to the psalmist. Verses 1–7 each consists of a single bicolon with a rhythm of 3+2 or 3+3, except verse 4. Verse 4 is divided by the Masoretic accentuation at צַדִּיק, giving a 2+3 rhythm. Alternatively the line may be divided at קִצֵּץ, which also carries a disjunctive accent, in order to better match the other surrounding lines with a 3+2 rhythm.[248] The choice between these alternatives relates to the interpretation of the line's syntax; but there is no doubt that the line is a bicolon.[249]

The several lexical ambiguities in the psalm do not affect its colometry. In v. 3, the reference may be to either the חֹרְשִׁים (MT) or the רשעים (11QPs[a], LXX presumed *Vorlage*) with corresponding nouns in v. 3b.[250] In v. 6b the BHS apparatus proposes emendation of the text to שֶׁקֶּדֶם תִּשָׂדֶף.[251] In each case the rhythm of the alternative readings is the same, and there is no evidence for any of these lines being other than a bicolon.

Verse 8 consists of three clauses, the word count being 3/3/4 and the syllable count being 9/7/9. The combination of any two of these phrases into a single colon would result in a excessively long colon, both

248. Watson, *Classical*, 335, identifies the enjambment in this line, but does not propose how it is to be divided.

249. See the discussion of Raabe, "Deliberate Ambiguity," 222–23, on the grammatical ambiguity inherent in this line's opening phrase.

250. See Crow, *Songs of Ascents*, 77, for a discussion of the variant readings.

251. See Crow, *Songs of Ascents*, 78, for further detail.

in terms of syllable count and in relative terms when compared with the otherwise regular succession of three- and two-stress cola throughout the psalm. Conversely, the final four-word phrase could conceivably be split to form two cola.[252] However, these would be unusually short cola (five and four syllables). The established preference for not splitting a four-word colon is observed and the three clauses are judged to correspond to three cola. Whether the three cola comprise a bicolon plus monocolon or a tricolon is open to question. The three cola cohere by means of a degree of synonymy between v. 8b and v. 8c, and possibly by the subject of v. 8c being elided and referring back to the subject identified in v. 8a.

If v. 8 were a bicolon plus monocolon, the bicolon v. 8a+v. 8b would cohere with the preceding text, and v. 8c would stand apart. As a closing monocolon, v. 8c could perform a liturgical function in counterpoint to the opening of the psalm, and would make a marked contrast with the desired fate of the "wicked" that receive no such blessing. Weiser proposes such an interpretation, making a comparison with Ps 125 and suggesting that the closing monocolon would be pronounced by the priest.[253] Such a monocolon would have a different subject from the preceding line (the psalm singers/readers rather than passers-by) and a different object (the congregation rather than the "wicked"). To avoid ambiguity this change of subject and object would need to be marked in some way. A nominative absolute, אֲנַחְנוּ, might serve such a function; but no such marking is present. It seems odd to introduce a liturgical blessing that is so open to confusion with the preceding text. A formulaic blessing, such as שָׁלוֹם עַל־יִשְׂרָאֵל (Ps 125:5) or יְבָרֶכְךָ יְהוָה מִצִּיּוֹן (Ps 128:5) might be more consonant as a liturgical closing.[254] But without grammatical marking, or clearly formulaic phrasing, the identity of the subject and object of v. 8c as different from v. 8ab must be doubtful.

If v. 8 were a tricolon, then v. 8b and v. 8c would each be construed as the content of hypothetical speech.[255] This is the clearest reading of the line without resort to a supposed particular setting for the recitation of the psalm. The speech might all be supposed to be that of the passers-

---

252. The text is presented in this manner in ML and MA.

253. Weiser, *The Psalms*, 771–72. Allen, *Psalms 101–50*, 248, also supports this view, but his argument is based on his analysis of the structure of the psalm.

254. Crow, *Songs of Ascents*, 80.

255. Thus RSV, NEB, NIV, NRSV.

by. This approach leads Fokkelman to present the verse as a tricolon, regarding v. 8b and v. 8c as a "double blessing" and thus belonging together.[256] Alternatively, v. 8b alone might be regarded as speech of the passers-by, with v. 8c being the response of the harvesters, as in Ruth 2:4, such that the verse represents a hypothetical dialogue of greeting and response.[257] This reading can be nuanced by the idea of the final colon functioning as a *double-entendre*. Within the context of the psalm it is part of the hypothetical blessing (or blessing and response) that is not given, whilst at the same time for those who are reciting the psalm the words can become a blessing upon each other. Jacobson puts it thus: "By saying aloud the blessing that the fictive reapers and binders do not say to each other, the people in fact do bless each other 'in the name of the LORD.'"[258] In light of this discussion the two clauses of direct discourse in v. 8 are considered to belong together and the line is identified as a tricolon.

Structural Analyses

THEMATIC ANALYSIS

Gerstenberger reads the structure of the psalm as: complaint (vv. 1–3), affirmation of confidence (v. 4), an imprecation that comprises an evil wish (v. 5), a metaphor (vv. 6–7), and a prohibition (v. 8ab). He regards v. 8c as a concluding blessing, given by "the official liturgists leading the service," and not as part of the prohibited dialogue between reapers and passers-by.[259] Kraus simply divided the psalm between thanksgiving elements (vv. 1–4) and complaint elements (v. 5–8).[260]

---

256. Fokkelman, *Major Poems III*, 290. Similarly, Hossfeld and Zenger, *Psalmen*, 550; Dahood, *Psalms*, 230, who regards the final clause as an "emphatic repetition" of the preceding blessing.

257. Delitzsch, *Commentary*, 297; Hermann, "Psalm 129," 127. Alter, *Book of Psalms*, 453–54, Goldingay, *Psalms*, 519, and Crow, *Songs of Ascents*, 79, also discuss this reading. Anderson, *Psalms: Volume 2*, 874, regards v. 8c as integral with v. 8ab, allowing either possibility for its syntactic relationship.

258. Jacobson, *Direct Discourse*, 141. Similarly Seybold, *Die Psalmen*, 491, who adopts the colometry of bicolon plus monocolon, is open-minded on the implied speaker of the closing monocolon.

259. Gerstenberger, *Psalms*, 352–54.

260. Kraus, *Psalms 60–150*, 461–62; so also Weiser, *The Psalms*, 771, and Allen, *Psalms 101–50*, 246–47, but who read v. 8c as a priestly blessing.

STROPHIC ANALYSIS

1 שִׁיר הַמַּעֲלוֹת

(רַבַּת צְרָרוּנִי מִנְּעוּרַי)   יֹאמַר-נָא יִשְׂרָאֵל:

2 (רַבַּת צְרָרוּנִי מִנְּעוּרַי)   גַּם לֹא-יָכְלוּ לִי:

3 עַל-גַּבִּי חָרְשׁוּ חֹרְשִׁים   הֶאֱרִיכוּ [כ= לְמַעֲנוֹתָם] [ק= לְמַעֲנִיתָם]:

4 (יהוה) צַדִּיק קִצֵּץ   עֲבוֹת רְשָׁעִים:

5 יֵבֹשׁוּ וְיִסֹּגוּ אָחוֹר   כֹּל שֹׂנְאֵי צִיּוֹן:

6 יִהְיוּ כַּחֲצִיר גַּגּוֹת   שֶׁקַּדְמַת שָׁלַף יָבֵשׁ:

7 שֶׁלֹּא מִלֵּא כַפּוֹ קוֹצֵר   וְחִצְנוֹ מְעַמֵּר:

8 וְלֹא אָמְרוּ הָעֹבְרִים (בִּרְכַּת-יהוה) אֲלֵיכֶם (בֵּרַכְנוּ אֶתְכֶם) בְּשֵׁם (יהוה):

Structure: 2.2|2.2

Strophe 1 has the same structure as that of Psalm 124, with verbatim repetition of the initial colon in the two opening lines. The theme of the psalm is thus established as Israel's repeated experience of aggression. Closure of the strophe is marked by the particle גַּם.

Strophe 2 is not marked, but modifies the topic by asserting Yahweh's response to those who have oppressed Israel.

Strophe 3 is marked by the jussive force of the opening verb, and then develops the topic of the fate of "כֹּל שֹׂנְאֵי צִיּוֹן." This development continues through vv. 6–8, and with no further transition markers, nor any repetitions, the strophic division can only by hypothetical. The division into four equal two-line strophes is more plausible than an unequal division or a four-line strophe.

Strophe 4 thus comprises the final two lines of the psalm. The final line is a tricolon that appears to function as a marker of closure.

This analysis depends to a significant degree on the jussive force of the verbs in vv. 5–6, but this is interpretive and may not be the case. Allen analyzes the nature of the assertions of these verses and concludes that the verbs are imperfectives, expressing confidence in the future actions of Yahweh.[261] This ambiguity, coupled with the lack of any other

261. Allen, *Psalms 101–50*, 246–48; cf. Goldingay, *Psalms*, 515.

transition markers, results in two alternative strophic structures. Allen, Briggs, Terrien, Crow, Jacquet, and Kissane determine a structure the same as (or very similar to) Van der Lugt's.[262] But Fokkelman and Hunter read three strophes representing the assaults of the wicked (vv. 1–3), Yahweh's intervention (vv. 4–5), and the future/wished for defeat of "כֹּל שֹׂנְאֵי צִיּוֹן" (vv. 6–8).[263] While this structure is derived from thematic and rhetorical considerations rather than strophic concerns, the lack of any other transition markers means that it equally well complies with Van der Lugt's criteria if the verbs are not read as jussives.

Rhetorico-Structural Analysis

Girard comments on the lack of any significant distant repetitions that might indicate a structure for this psalm, but nevertheless offers a proposed concentric structure of the form ABCB'A' based mainly on thematic and discourse analysis. Whilst this does not strictly comply with his criteria for analysis, it makes the best possible use of the repetitions that are apparent and supplements them with appropriate thematic and syntactic analysis. The structure is as follows:[264]

vv. 1–2	Actual speech of Israel
v. 3	Agricultural metaphor for Israel's suffering
v. 4	Affirmation of confidence in Yahweh
vv. 5–7	Agricultural metaphor for enemies' suffering
v. 8	Unreal speech of enemies

In this structure vv. 1–2 are linked by anaphora and vv. 5–7 by the repetition of ישׁב and שֶׁ. Perhaps because of its place in this structure, Girard reads v. 8c as part of the hypothetical dialogue between reapers and passers-by. He also notes the repetition of ברך . . . . יְהוָה in v. 8 as an indication of the integrity of the line as a single rhetorical unit.[265]

---

262. Allen, *Psalms 101–50*, 246; Briggs and Briggs, *Exegetical Commentary*, 461; Terrien, *Strophic Structure*, 834; Crow, *Songs of Ascents*, 76; Jacquet, *Les Psaumes*, 489; Kissane, *Book of Psalms*, 584. No distinction is made here between those who regard v. 8c as integral with v. 8ab and those who read it as a separate monocolon/gloss.

263. Hunter, *Psalms*, 215; Fokkelman, *Psalms in Form*, 136.

264. Girard, *Psaumes 3: 101–150*, 352–56. Vesco, *Psautier de David*, 1216, similarly identifies v. 4 as "la pointe" of the structure, the turning point of the psalm's drama.

265. Girard, *Psaumes 3: 101–150*, 352 and 356.

Trublet and Aletti discern a similar chiastic structure based on the various designations of Israel's adversaries, as follows:[266]

vv. 1–2	"them"		
v. 3		metaphorical laborers	
v. 4			specific identification "רְשָׁעִים"
v. 5			specific identification "כֹּל שֹׂנְאֵי צִיּוֹן"
v. 6		metaphorical laborers	
v.7–8	"them"		

They comment that "the adversaries gradually appear and then disappear."[267] However, the structure is not an accurate representation since in v. 6 onwards, the adversaries are compared to a crop that withers and cannot be gathered, not to those who would do the gathering.

Van der Wal has proposed a division of the psalm into vv. 1–3, vv. 4–8b and v. 8c. He regards the only two nominal sentence constructions, each containing the divine name, in v. 4a and v. 8b as marking off the second main section. However, without any detailed analysis of the remainder of the psalm, it is not apparent why this should necessarily be an argument for these cola of similar syntax to be an inclusio for the second section as opposed to a corresponding pair that conclude the first and second sections respectively.[268] His argument for v. 8c being separate from the body of the psalm is the change of speaker to 1c.p., which does not correspond to any other aspect of the psalm. But again, this is not conclusive; the colon might still just as well be regarded as part of the hypothetical dialogue.[269]

Auffret adopts the conventional basic division of the psalm into vv. 1–4 and vv. 5–8b. He takes אמר in v. 1 and v. 8 as an inclusion for the psalm, but argues for the non-integration of v. 8c, citing Van der Wal.[270] Auffret observes some of the internal structural features of the psalm. He highlights the chiasm in vv. 5–6 (יֵבֹשׁוּ / אָחוֹר / קָדְמַת / יָבֵשׁ) and

---

266. Trublet and Aletti, *Approche Poétique*, 99–100.

267. Ibid., 99.

268. Van der Wal,"Structure of Psalm CXXIX," 366.

269. Ibid., 365.

270. Auffret, *Etude Structurelle*, 74 and 77.

the alternation of literal (vv. 1–2, v. 5, v. 8c) and metaphorical (vv. 3–4, vv. 6–8b) language.[271]

Summary

This psalm has a high degree of rhythmical regularity and is formed of two sections: the first a lament over oppression at the hands of adversaries and the second either an assertion of or a wish for Yahweh's just retribution. The overlap between the two sections can be interpreted differently from thematic, strophic, and rhetorical points of view. The one unambiguous assertion of Yahweh's action (v. 4) concludes the lament, and coheres with the opening of the following metaphor, and acts as a pivot in the rhetorical structure. The citation of direct speech in v. 1 and v. 8 forms an inclusion for the psalm as a whole, with the multifunctional final colon both rounding off the image of the second half of the psalm and performing a liturgical function that mirrors the psalm's opening.

Strophic structure			Thematic structure	Rhetorical structure	
1a	1b			1–2	
2a	2b		1–3		
3a	3b			3	
4a	4b		4		4
5a	5b		5	5	
6a	6b			6–7	
7a	7b		6–8		
8a	8b	8c		8	

271. Ibid., 74–77.

Psalm 130

Colometric Analysis

1 שִׁיר הַמַּעֲלוֹת

מִמַּעֲמַקִּים קְרָאתִיךָ יְהוָה׃   2 אֲדֹנָי שִׁמְעָה בְקוֹלִי

תִּהְיֶינָה אָזְנֶיךָ קַשֻּׁבוֹת   לְקוֹל תַּחֲנוּנָי׃

3 אִם־עֲוֹנוֹת תִּשְׁמָר־יָהּ   אֲדֹנָי מִי יַעֲמֹד׃

4 כִּי־עִמְּךָ הַסְּלִיחָה   לְמַעַן תִּוָּרֵא׃

5 קִוִּיתִי יְהוָה קִוְּתָה נַפְשִׁי   וְלִדְבָרוֹ הוֹחָלְתִּי׃

6 נַפְשִׁי לַאדֹנָי   מִשֹּׁמְרִים לַבֹּקֶר   שֹׁמְרִים לַבֹּקֶר׃

7 יַחֵל יִשְׂרָאֵל אֶל־יְהוָה   כִּי־עִם־יְהוָה הַחֶסֶד   וְהַרְבֵּה עִמּוֹ פְדוּת׃

8 וְהוּא יִפְדֶּה אֶת־יִשְׂרָאֵל   מִכֹּל עֲוֹנֹתָיו׃

This well-known and evocative psalm is the lament of an individual, concluding with an exhortation. After the superscription, v. 1 consists of just three words and is too short to be split into a bicolon. However, v. 2 is too long to be a bicolon, both in terms of words and syllables, and readily divides into three phrases. Therefore, the common practice of presenting vv. 1–2 as a pair of bicola is adopted. The first line consists of a cry to Yahweh and a request to be heard; the second line expands the request to be heard, referring back to the cry/supplication, thus creating a chiastic structure for the two lines together. The rhythm of these lines is 3+3 / 3+2.

Verses 3–4 turn to a meditation on Yahweh's forgiveness, each line being a bicolon. The rhythm of these lines is 2+2 / 2+2. At the end of v. 4, תִּוָּרֵא is translated in LXX mss variously as του νομου σου and του ὀνοματος σου. Crow comments on the common interpretation of the former as a reading of some form of תּוֹרָה and the latter as a corruption of the former. [272] However, 11QPs^a matches MT. Even if a variant text were supposed here, the rhythmical analysis would be unchanged. Of greater significance, however, is the variant colometry that appears to be adopted by LXX through vv. 4–7, along with several other textual variants.

As discussed above (in the section "Source manuscripts" on pp. 11–17) the presentation of colometry in LXX is mixed, with cola sometimes

---

272. Crow, *Songs of Ascents*, 85.

presented on separate page-lines and sometimes not. Furthermore, there is significant variation between mss.[273] Therefore the perspective of the translator on the colometry of the text is difficult to ascertain. Taking LXX[A] as the text that most closely resembles the Hebrew colometry, a *Vorlage* for vv. 4–7 can be deduced as follows:

כִּי־עִמְּךָ הַסְּלִיחָה

לְמַעַן תִּוָּרֵא   קִוִּיתִיךָ יְהוָה   קִוְּתָה נַפְשִׁי לִדְבָרְךָ

הוֹחִילָה נַפְשִׁי לַאדֹנָי   מִשֹּׁמְרִים הַבֹּקֶר עַד לָיְלָה

מִשֹּׁמְרִים הַבֹּקֶר יַחֵל יִשְׂרָאֵל אֶל־יְהוָה

כִּי־עִם־יְהוָה הַחֶסֶד   וְהַרְבֵּה עִמּוֹ פְדוּת:

The rhythmically irregular nature of this text is apparent, particularly in the orphaned monocolon of v. 4a and the excessively long monocolon representing 6c–7a, and may be taken as evidence that LXX represents a corruption, or at best a misinterpretation, of the colometry of the Hebrew. Moreover, this reconstructed *Vorlage* illustrates how the textual variants are dependent upon a variant colometry, with suffixes varied and a conjunction omitted to match the syntactic relationships implied by the colometry. Therefore, rather than assessing each variant individually, it is appropriate either to accept or to reject fully the textual and colometric variation witnessed by the LXX. [274] The pitfalls of emendation are amply illustrated by Porbúčan who significantly emends the rhythmically matching lines of vv. 5–6 on the grounds of "proportion, symmetry, and Hebrew parallelism," and ironically produces two lines that do not match rhythmically.[275] In rejecting such an approach, Tromp advocates retention of the text of MT but proposes a variant colometry without assessing the rhythmical or broader structural implications. He consequently produces an excessively long colon and relocates to the middle of a line the imperative of v. 7a that opens a new section of the psalm (see the section "Psalm 130: Strophic Analysis" on pp. 155–57).[276] In view of the less regular rhythm of a supposed LXX *Vorlage* and ab-

273. For example, in Ps 130 LXX[א] and LXX[A] present 11 and 16 "cola" respectively.

274. Kraus, *Psalms 60–150*, 465, retains the text and colometry of the MT; Crow, *Songs of Ascents*, 85–86, and Weiser, *The Psalms*, 772, typify the pick-and-mix approach. See also the studies by Sedlmeier, "Psalm 130," 474–78, and by Zenger, "Am Beispiel von Ps 129," 525–38, who concludes that LXX deliberately removes ambiguities in the Hebrew text and represents a variant theological perspective.

275. Porbúčan, "Psalm CXXX," 323.

276. Tromp, "Psalm CXXX," 102.

sence of any convincing proposals for textual emendation, this study focuses on the MT.

Verse 5 consists of three verbal clauses each having two words. The first two are strongly synonymous, using the same verb; the third expands the thought and makes it more specific. The three are equally prominent and all the criteria for reading a para-tricolon are met, the consequent minor caesurae coinciding with disjunctive accents. Verse 6 has similar characteristics but is more difficult to construe. In this line no verb is present but can be inferred in the initial colon from the preceding line.[277] "The superfluity of verbs in v. 5 continue their effect into v. 6, where there is no verb."[278] The following cola modify this elided verbal clause and have the extraordinary characteristic of verbatim repetition. Again it is appropriate for the two caesurae to be of equal weight and each coincides with a disjunctive accent. These two lines thus appear to be para-tricola, each with a 2–2–2 rhythm.[279] Amongst those who treat the lines inconsistently, it is curious that v. 5, with its three complete verbal clauses, is read as a bicolon, whilst the enigmatic nominal phrases of v. 6 are deemed to warrant a tricolon.[280]

Brief consideration may be given to the alternative reading of the lines as bicola, following the Masoretic division. This produces two un-balanced bicola with internal parallelism in each of the long cola. In v. 5 the initial colon is long, in v. 6 the following colon is long. Given the high degree of semantic and lexical overlap within these internal parallelisms, it is difficult to understand why the lines would have been written in this manner, producing rhythmical irregularities, uncoordinated with the preceding lines. Possibly the repetitions serve a rhetorical function, lengthening the lines to create a focus on the message of the lines: the length of waiting; but this function could be apparent whether the lines are read as para-tricola or as bicola.

---

277. 11QPsᵃ supplies the verb הוחלתי at the beginning of the verse. Anderson, *Psalms: Volume 2*, 877, speculates that it may have been lost from MT by haplography; but equally it may be an accretion to the scroll by dittography or as a gloss in order to make the sense explicit. It would overload the line, and the MT is here retained.

278. Goldingay, *Psalms*, 529.

279. Fokkelman, *Major Poems II*, reads both lines as tricola, highlighting the repetitions, even though he generally reads para-tricola as bicola. So also Dahood, *Psalms*, 234; Hossfeld and Zenger, *Psalmen*, 566–67.

280. Beaucamp, *Le Psautier*, np; Delitzsch, *Commentary*, 297; Seybold, *Die Psalmen*, 492; VanGemeren, "Psalms," 801.

The repetition of the phrase שֹׁמְרִים לַבֹּקֶר in v. 6 is unusual and has provoked considerable comment. It is regarded by some as dittography.[281] Kraus favors retention of the repeated phrase as "an emphatic underscoring of wistful longing"; Crow regards the repetition as "rhetorical," Dahood as suggestive of "time dragging on"; Goldingay opines that the repetition "slows the line down and makes us wait for what will come next, matching the content of the words."[282] None of these authors considers whether such effect could be achieved without verbatim repetition, in a manner that is more stylistically conventional. The use of verbatim repetition is not a normal feature of Hebrew poetry. Watson notes that in the very few instances where it does occur, it is used either to convey a sense of urgency (of address), or in the only convincing example of a phrase rather than a single word being repeated (Jer 15:2) the repetition is a necessary part of the syntax of the clause.[283] Neither urgency of address nor syntactic necessity is evident in this instance. However, the possibility that it has been deliberately used here cannot be discounted. Alter adopts a different approach, reading the first participle conventionally as a substantive, but the second participle as forming a verbal clause, such that the sense of verbatim repetition disappears.[284] This reinforces the view that there is adequate reason to keep the text intact and analyze its colometry as it stands. Especially in view of the focus of the present study on the received form of the text, vv. 5–6 are identified as para-tricola.

Verses 7–8 conclude this individual lament psalm, with an expression of hope addressed to Israel and speaking about Yahweh, rather than addressed to Yahweh. The colometry is ambiguous and some scholars have questioned the lineation.[285]

---

281. Thus BHS apparatus and Weiser, *The Psalms*, 772.

282. Kraus, *Psalms 60–150*, 465; Crow, *Songs of Ascents*, 87; Dahood, *Psalms*, 236; Goldingay, *Psalms*, 529.

283. Watson, *Classical*, 277–78.

284. Alter, *Book of Psalms*, 456.

285. A textual variant suggested by the LXX is a *yod* possibly omitted by haplography at the beginning of v. 7. The only effect would be to render the verb as jussive rather than imperative. 11QPs³ varies only in the omission of conjunctions. Kraus, *Psalms 60–150*, 465, and Weiser, *The Psalms*, 772, comment that v. 7a is missing from, or a later addition to, the Greek manuscripts; in fact this is the case for LXX˟, but not for LXXᴬ.

Sievers would probably split the text into three lines, of six, three, and five stresses respectively.[286] Gray and Robinson would focus on the semantic relationships within the text, but these allow more than one possibility.

Verse 7 has either eight or nine stresses and twenty-two syllables, and is therefore close to the upper limit of an acceptable bicolon. The line incorporates three clauses; the second and third clauses exhibit semantic and syntactic parallelism and together give reasons for the imperative opening clause. Since the line consists of three clauses, it is not possible to produce a reasonably balanced split into a bicolon. Equally, given that the three clauses are approximately equal in length, it is not possible to read a pair of bicola without producing an exceptionally short colon and/or a high degree of enjambment. Therefore the three clauses are regarded as three separate cola and the line as a tricolon with rhythm 3+3+3.[287]

Verse 8 is a common form of bicolon with a single clause split between a main verbal clause and its adverbial phrase. It has rhythm 3+2.

Crow and Fokkelman adopt a variant lineation for these two verses, reading a pair of bicola by taking v. 8 as a single colon.[288] Crow does not justify this approach, but Fokkelman does so on the basis of chiasms within the wider structure of the psalm. He reads vv. 7–8 in relation to vv. 3–4 in the following manner:

v. 3 – sins	v. 4 – forgiveness
v. 7ab – forgiveness	v. 7c/v. 8 – sins

This scheme does not quite work, since v. 7c and v. 8a are about "redemption," which is more congruous with "forgiveness" than with "sins."[289] There are other curiosities with this reading: the presence of a conjunction at the beginning of both cola in a line is clumsy and prosaic; and the resulting final colon (v. 8) is unusually and unnecessarily long (having five stresses and fourteen syllables). It seems therefore unwise to

286. Cf. Ps 7:8–9; Sievers, *Metrische Studien*, 507.

287. Or 3+2+3 if both particles with the divine name are unstressed, as suggested by the *maqqephim*. Alter, *Book of Psalms*, 455–56; Dahood, *Psalms*, 234; Hossfeld and Zenger, *Psalmen*, 567; Kraus, *Psalms 60–150*, 464, all read v. 7 as a tricolon.

288. Thus Crow, *Songs of Ascents*, 85 and Fokkelman, *Psalms in Form*, 137.

289. Fokkelman, *Major Poems II*, 297. Also, his reading of "waiting" (v. 7a) as synonymous with "fearing" (v. 4b) is tenuous.

promote an alternative colometry as the "right" solution. To do so is to unduly elevate a particular structural theory to which the text is made to fit, whilst also adopting an inconsistent approach to the Masoretic lineation.

Structural Analyses

THEMATIC ANALYSIS

Gerstenberger identifies the components of the psalm as: invocation (v. 1), plea (v. 2), confession (v. 3), affirmation of confidence (v. 4), personal prayer (vv. 5–6) and community exhortation and assurance (vv. 7–8).[290] Kraus divides the psalm into plea and confession (vv. 1–4), prayer of watchful hope (vv. 5–6) and the exhortation and promise to the community (vv. 7–8).[291] Weiser makes a connection between the personal assurance of forgiveness in v. 4 and the corporate promise of redemption in v. 8.[292]

STROPHIC ANALYSIS

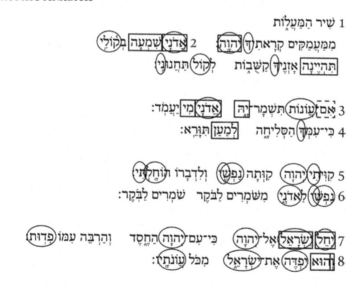

Structure: 2.2|2.2

---

290. Gerstenberger, *Psalms*, 355.

291. Kraus, *Psalms 60–150*, 466–68.

292. Weiser, *The Psalms*, 773, *contra* those who suggest that vv. 7–8 are non-original; see Allen, *Psalms 101–50*, 253, for a fuller discussion.

Strophe 1 is strongly marked in its first line with two vocatives and an imperative. The strophe makes repeated use of the 1c.s. and 2m.s. suffixes, establishing the character of the psalm as the prayer of an individual to "you/Yahweh/Lord." This strophe is a plea that the supplicant's prayer will be heard. The jussive force of the verb that begins the second line (v. 2b) is strictly a contra-indication of the opening marking function of such verb forms, but here acts in parallel with the imperative in the first line (v. 2a).

Strophe 2 is still addressed to Yahweh, but comprises a meditation on Yahweh's forgiveness rather than a supplication. Its opening is marked by the vocative and interrogative in v. 3, and to some degree by the opening protasis to which the following question forms an apodosis. Closure of the strophe is marked by the telic particle לְמַעַן. The strophe coheres well together as a rhetorical question (v. 3), an assertion that follows on from the implied answer to the question (v. 4a) and a consequence (v. 4b). This cohesion argues against the variant lineation of the LXX, in which the telic particle of v. 4b opens a new section of the psalm (as discussed in section "Psalm 130: Colometric Analysis" on pp. 150–55).

Strophe 3 is not marked, but is clearly identified by its repeated expressions of waiting. The verb קוה is used twice, and the verb יחל is introduced as a synonym and as a concatenation with the following strophe.

Strophe 4 is marked by its opening imperative, after which it is distinguished from the other strophes by the change of addressee (now "Israel") and by the change of voice from first person to third person. It makes assertions about Yahweh's steadfast mercy towards, and redemption of, Israel. The opening line is a tricolon, but this does not appear to have any structural marking function. The opening conjunction of the last line here is marking the closure of a higher structural unit rather than the opening of a strophe. Van der Lugt reads the following pronoun as a marker of closure, but it probably serves merely to give syntactical emphasis within the line. The sense of totality conveyed by the final clause, whilst not being a temporal reference, could be read as having a concluding function.

Several other strophic analyses that keep the MT intact produce the same structure.[293] A notable exception is Terrien's reading of three strophes consisting of vv. 1–3, vv. 4–6 and vv. 7–8.[294] Unfortunately no distinct rationale for this structure is offered. Kissane's strophic analysis varies from that of Van der Lugt due to emendation of the text. He adopts a colometry informed by LXX and omits v. 6c and v. 7a on the grounds of being a dittography and a later addition respectively.[295] Therefore no direct comparison can be made.

Rhetorico-Structural Analysis

The large number of repetitions within this psalm can result in very complex structural analysis.[296] Girard divides the psalm into two diptychs, each having a chiastic structure:[297]

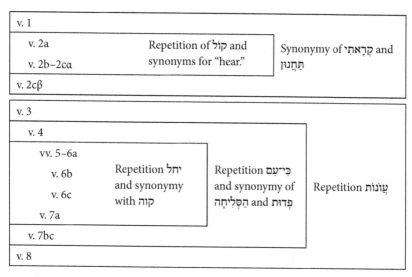

---

293. Allen, *Psalms 101–50*, 251; Anderson, *Psalms: Volume 2*, 875; Goldingay, *Psalms*, 521–22; Hunter, *Psalms*, 217; Prinsloo 2002, 455–56. Also Crow, *Songs of Ascents*, 84–85, and Fokkelman, *Psalms in Form*, 137, albeit with a variant colometry in the final strophe.

294. Terrien, *Strophic Structure*, 838.

295. Kissane, *Book of Psalms*, 586. He speculates that v. 7a has been copied from 131:3. cf. Briggs and Briggs, *Exegetical Commentary*, 466; Jacquet, *Les Psaumes*, 501.

296. Prinsloo 2002, 457–60, identifies all repetitions in detail.

297. Girard, *Psaumes 3: 101–150*, 360–62.

The two sides of the second diptych are characterized by individual concerns (vv. 3a–6b) and communal concerns (vv. 6c–8) respectively.[298]

Auffret follows the same basic structure as Girard, discerning a chiasm in vv. 3–8 based on multiple word correspondences and suggesting that v. 6bc may act as a hinge, both qualifying v. 6a and introducing v. 7a.[299] He also highlights the internal structure of pairs of lines: parallelism between v. 3 and v. 4; thematic repetition of waiting/hoping/watching for Yahweh/his word/morning in vv. 5–6; repetitions of יִשְׂרָאֵל and פדה in vv. 7–8. He also observes a contrast between Yahweh keeping/watching sins (v. 3) and the psalmist keeping/watching for morning (v. 6).[300]

Evidently more than one structure may be operative in this psalm, given its intricately woven array of matching terms. Whilst the chiastic structure of vv. 3–8 is well substantiated, a linear pattern in keeping with the conventional form-critical and strophic analyses can also be verified on rhetorico-structural grounds. The basic form is AB/A'B' and is discerned as follows:[301]

vv. 1–2	Personal prayer to Yahweh	Internal chiasm as above
vv. 3–4	Meditation on personal forgiveness	Parallel form of topic/consequences
vv. 5–6	Personal waiting for Yahweh	Rep'ns of נַפְשִׁי and thematic words
vv. 7–8	Meditation on redemption for Israel	Repetitions of יִשְׂרָאֵל and פדה

298. Ibid., 362. Trublet and Aletti, *Approche Poétique*, 100, propose a very similar structure. Marrs 1988, 88, varies slightly, reading sections as vv. 1–4a, vv. 4b–6b, vv. 6c–8.

299. Auffret, *Etude Structurelle*, 81 and 85. Weber, "Anwendung an Psalm 130," 901, suggests that v. 7a acts as the hinge.

300. Auffret, *Etude Structurelle*, 81–82.

301. Allen, *Psalms 101–50*, 254; Prinsloo, "Psalm 130," 460; Weber, "Notizen zu Psalm 130," 151–53. Schmidt, "Gott und Mensch," 241–42, produces the same structure based on the grammatical subject of discourse.

The structural connections are as follows:

vv. 1–2	vv. 5–6	Repetition of . . . יְהוָה אֲדֹנָי and high incidence of 1c.s. verbs and suffixes
vv. 3–4	vv. 7–8	Repetition of עֵינוֹת and כִּי־עַם
Repetition of יְהוָה אֲדֹנָי / יָהּ אֲדֹנָי	Repetition of יחל	

Summary

This psalm has a number of unusual textual and colometric features, and the variants amongst mss and ancient versions probably attest the difficulties that have been experienced as a result. Nevertheless, the received form of the psalm has a very clear strophic structure, with four pairs of lines that are bound together. There is some regularity of rhythm in the first half of the psalm; the focal point of the psalm consists of a pair of para-tricola that are followed by the only significant rhythmical variation: a full tricolon in v. 7.

The high number of repetitions, both verbatim and thematic, throughout the psalm result in more than one rhetorical structure being discernible. Only one is illustrated here, but rhetorico-structural features also exist that reflect and reinforce the strophic structure.

Strophic structure	Thematic structure	Rhetorical structure
1a 2a		1a 2a
2b 2c	1–4	2c 2b
3a 3b		3
4a 4b		4
5a–5b–5c	5–6	5–6a
6a–6b–6c		6bc
7a 7b 7c	7–8	7bc 7a
8a 8b		8

Psalm 131

Colometric Analysis

1 שִׁיר הַמַּעֲלוֹת לְדָוִד

יְהוָה לֹא־גָבַהּ לִבִּי   וְלֹא־רָמוּ עֵינַי

וְלֹא־הִלַּכְתִּי בִּגְדֹלוֹת   וּבְנִפְלָאוֹת מִמֶּנִּי:

2 אִם־לֹא שִׁוִּיתִי וְדוֹמַמְתִּי נַפְשִׁי   כְּגָמֻל עֲלֵי אִמּוֹ   כַּגָּמֻל עָלַי נַפְשִׁי:

3 יַחֵל יִשְׂרָאֵל אֶל־יְהוָה   מֵעַתָּה וְעַד־עוֹלָם:

This short psalm clearly expresses trust in Yahweh, although the precise meaning of some of the words used is notoriously ambiguous. It is commonly presented as two pairs of bicola, followed by an aphoristic bicolon. However, a significant minority of translators present v. 2 as a tricolon.

Verse 1 consists of three clauses, one of which divides into two phrases. The rhythmical analysis of the verse is not completely clear, since in three of the four phrases the division into word-units could legitimately be done in more than one way. Each instance of וְלֹא could either take a full stress or could be combined with the following verb; the compound word-unit וּבְנִפְלָאוֹת could either have only a single stress or could additionally carry a secondary stress in order to break up the chain of four unstressed syllables. The first phrase has three stresses and the other three have either two or three stresses. A syllable count, where there is no ambiguity, yields 7/6/8/8. From this analysis it is apparent that no two of these phrases may be combined without producing an excessively long colon.[302] Therefore four cola, comprising a pair of bicola, is the appropriate colometry for this verse. This reflects the syntactic structure of the line: in the first line two separate clauses that display semantic and syntactic parallelism form a bicolon, and their common thought is expanded in a longer clause in the following line where a po-

---

302. Although Delitzsch, *Commentary*, 301, does this, combining the first two clauses. He is probably influenced by a desire to produce matching tricolon structures for v. 1 and v. 2, each with a pair of synonymous verbs in the initial colon. Beyerlin, *Studien zum 131. Psalm*, 49–50, makes v. 1 a tricolon by combining the final two phrases, objecting to v. 1d standing as a verbless colon. He too is influenced by a desire to create a broader structural pattern, and fails to recognise that presenting v. 1cd as a bicolon is a conventional form of verbal ellipsis, as demonstrated by C. L. Miller, "Linguistic Approach," 262–65, and "Relation," 54.

tentially complete clause in the first colon is modified and expanded in the second. The rhythm is best read as 3+3 / 3+3 in order to achieve the best regularity in the succession of stressed and unstressed syllables.

Verse 2 exhibits similar rhythmical ambiguities to v. 1 but is briefer and is also rather difficult to translate, due to the ambiguities of meaning of some words and of the syntactic construction of the second half of the verse.[303] The only textual variant to contend with is וְרוֹמַמְתִּי in place of וְדוֹמַמְתִּי in some mss and represented in LXX. Unfortunately the meaning of שִׁוִּיתִי with which it forms a pair is uncertain and does not clarify the correct form of the following verb.[304] It is most likely that the variant is a misreading, since the idea of self-elevation stands at odds with the tone of humility expressed in v. 1. Although the variant has no effect rhythmically, the division into cola could potentially be influenced by whether the *waw* is read as adversative. The ambiguity over the function of the *waw* is reflected in LXX mss, where the καί of LXX^ℵ has been amended to ἀλλα by a later hand; LXX^A and other mss have ἀλλα. But reading a consistent tone of humility through the psalm, a simple conjunction, non-adversative, appears to be the more appropriate interpretation. This is reinforced by the common interpretation of the opening particles אִם־לֹא modifying both verbs, not just the first. In the second half of the verse, proposals have been made for emendation of the second instance of preposition and noun to an indicative verb form תִּגָּמֵל.[305] This proposal would have no bearing on the rhythmical analysis of the text. The syntactic structure of this part of the verse is complex, but whether it consists of a verbless comparison between two noun phrases (as MT) or of a modifying noun phrase followed by its governing verbal clause (as the possible emendation), its bipartite structure is apparent in either case.

An assessment of the colometry of v. 2 follows the same considerations as that for v. 1. The first half of the verse consists of two coordinated verbal clauses. A closer degree of connection between them is apparent than was the case in v. 1, since they may be regarded as sharing an object that is elided in the first clause. The second half of the line is

---

303. See Allen, *Psalms 101–50*, 259, and Crow, *Songs of Ascents*, 93–96.

304. See Crow, *Songs of Ascents*, 92–93, and Goldingay, *Psalms*, 536fn, for discussion of the possibilities.

305. See BHS apparatus. VanGemeren, "Psalm 131:2" carefully considered and rejected such emendation; see also Crow, *Songs of Ascents*, 93; Knowles, "Woman at Prayer," 385–86; Kraus, *Psalms 60–150*, 469 and Quell, "Struktur und Sinn," 173–75.

a single clause consisting of two phrases, however they be construed, as discussed above. One approach would therefore be to present v. 2 as a pair of bicola in order to match v. 1, and indeed this is the most common, and a legitimate, presentation. However, the relative brevity of the verse compared with v. 1 does give cause to question this approach. The stress count for the four phrases is nominally 2/2/3/3, although the three prepositions could potentially remain unstressed and the count would be reduced. The full count is that most commensurate with the treatment of v. 1 cited above. The syllable count for the four phrases is 5/6/7/7. Whilst the third and fourth phrases represent separate cola in keeping with the style of v. 1, the relative brevity of the first two phrases suggests that their combination into a single colon should be considered.[306] This produces a 4+3+3 tricolon that is in keeping with a preference not to split pairs of two-word phrases.[307] Having eleven syllables it is within the range that could legitimately either be split into two cola or remain as a single colon. Similarly the presence of a disjunctive accent on the first verb allows, but does not require, a break between cola. The decision therefore rests on more subtle considerations of the interplay between rhythmical and syntactic structures. Were the two clauses in an adversative relationship, it would probably be appropriate to separate them into two cola, the rhythmical pause introduced thereby underlining the syntactic and semantic distinction. However, this reading of the conjunction has been decided against, and the two clauses are considered to cohere in a form of verbal hendiadys, as illustrated by the sharing of the object and modifying particles.[308] Therefore there is good reason to cohere the two clauses into a single colon, allowing a reading as a tricolon with rhythm 4+3+3.[309] Since the balance of evidence is slight, this is regarded as a possibility to be explored further.

306. Jacquet, *Les Psaumes*, 512, responds to the brevity by adding נַפְשִׁי to the first phrase in order to maintain an alleged 3+2 rhythm throughout the psalm; cf. Briggs and Briggs, *Exegetical Commentary*, 467.

307. Thus Weiser, *The Psalms*, 776. Kraus, *Psalms 60–150*, 469, separates v. 2ab as a monocolon and then notes that the result is "strange." Dahood, *Psalms*, 238–39, moves אִם־לֹא from the beginning of v. 2 to the end of v. 1 (repointing to אֻמְלָא) and reads v. 2 as a tricolon on the basis that the psalm contains "nine three-beat cola." This stands at odds with his usual syllabic approach.

308. It may also be regarded as internal parallelism; B. P. Robinson, "Form and Meaning," 185.

309. Thus Alter, *Book of Psalms*, 457–58; Anderson, *Psalms: Volume 2*, 878; Delitzsch, *Commentary*, 301; Terrien, *Strophic Structure*, 842.

Structural Analyses

THEMATIC ANALYSIS

Gerstenberger sees a structure to this brief psalm that matches the verse division: confession of innocence (v. 1), affirmation of confidence (v. 2), and exhortation (v. 3).[310]

STROPHIC ANALYSIS

The analysis indicated here is that of Van der Lugt, and this will be discussed in detail. However, in this instance the colometry assumed by Van der Lugt differs from that deduced above, and a following discussion will address the implications arising from this difference.

Structure: 2.2.1

Strophe 1 is marked by the opening vocative and consists of first person address to Yahweh. The 1c.s. suffix is used four times in the strophe. The conjunction at the head of the second line is not a marker of opening, but functions together with the negative particle as a responsion to the same use in the preceding colon.

Strophe 2 is not marked, although the initial words being read as an interrogative do have some opening function. The two lines are clearly linked together by the continuity of thought and the same closing word. The address continues to be first person, with the 1c.s. suffix used five times.

---

310. Gerstenberger, *Psalms*, 359; so also Kraus, *Psalms 60–150*, 470 and Weiser, *The Psalms*, 776.

Strophe 3 is an aphoristic exhortation to always hope in Yahweh. It is distinguished by the change of voice from first person to second person, and is marked by the opening imperative. The repetition of the divine name forms an inclusio for the whole psalm, and the reference to eternity provides a clear closure to the psalm.

Amongst those who read v. 2 as a pair of bicola, most agree with this structure[311] whilst some see no separation between v. 1 and v. 2.[312] The analysis is affected little by the alternative reading proposed in this study of a v. 2 as a tricolon. Whether v. 2 then coheres with v. 1 to form a single three-line strophe or remains separate as a single-line strophe remains indeterminate due to the lack of transition markers. Terrien regards them as separate, commenting that "The strophic shortening articulates a crescendo of themes."[313] The final bicolon of v. 3 is a clearly marked separate strophe.[314]

RHETORICO-STRUCTURAL ANALYSIS

Even in this short psalm there are a good number of repetitions and wordplays that indicate rhetorical structuring. The two lines of v. 1 cohere by means of the sequence of three negative assertions; v. 2 by the repetitions of גָּמַל and נַפְשִׁי together with a wordplay between אִם and אִמּוֹ. The use of the divine name in v. 1a and v. 3a forms an inclusio.[315] Girard specifically links v. 1 and v. 2 as two sides of a diptych, since they both express personal trust in Yahweh, and regards v. 3 as being separate.[316] However, without any subdivision into smaller sections, the concept of a diptych is not particularly meaningful. The overall relationship of the three verses is AA'B.

Summary

This short psalm has a simple linear structure. The three verses each explore the theme of trust in Yahweh, who is addressed at the opening

---

311. Allen, *Psalms 101–50*, 258; Fokkelman, *Psalms in Form*, 137; Jacquet, *Les Psaumes*, 510.

312. Crow, *Songs of Ascents*, 92; Goldingay, *Psalms*, 533.

313. Terrien, *Strophic Structure*, 842.

314. *Contra* Kissane, *Book of Psalms*, 589, who whilst reading v. 2 as a tricolon regards the whole psalm as a single strophe.

315. Allen, *Psalms 101–50*, 259; Girard, *Psaumes 3: 101–150*, 367.

316. Girard, *Psaumes 3: 101–150*, 367.

of the psalm and appealed to at the end. Verses 1 and 2 relate closely to each other as personal expressions of trust in figurative terms, whilst v. 3 is an abstract exhortation. The three strophes exhibit a decreasing number of cola (4/3/2), leading the psalm to a pithy concluding statement.

Strophic structure			Thematic structure	Rhetorical structure
1a	1b		1	1a–d
1c	1d			
2a	2b	2c	2	2a–c
3a	3b		3	3

Psalm 132

Colometric Analysis

1 שִׁיר הַמַּעֲלוֹת

זְכוֹר־יְהוָה לְדָוִד   אֵת כָּל־עֻנּוֹתוֹ:

2 אֲשֶׁר נִשְׁבַּע לַיהוָה   נָדַר לַאֲבִיר יַעֲקֹב:

3 אִם־אָבֹא בְּאֹהֶל בֵּיתִי   אִם־אֶעֱלֶה עַל־עֶרֶשׂ יְצוּעָי:

4 אִם־אֶתֵּן שְׁנַת לְעֵינָי   לְעַפְעַפַּי תְּנוּמָה:

5 עַד־אֶמְצָא מָקוֹם לַיהוָה   מִשְׁכָּנוֹת לַאֲבִיר יַעֲקֹב:

6 הִנֵּה־שְׁמַעֲנוּהָ בְאֶפְרָתָה   מְצָאנוּהָ בִּשְׂדֵי־יָעַר:

7 נָבוֹאָה לְמִשְׁכְּנוֹתָיו   נִשְׁתַּחֲוֶה לַהֲדֹם רַגְלָיו:

8 קוּמָה יְהוָה לִמְנוּחָתֶךָ   אַתָּה וַאֲרוֹן עֻזֶּךָ:

9 כֹּהֲנֶיךָ יִלְבְּשׁוּ־צֶדֶק   וַחֲסִידֶיךָ יְרַנֵּנוּ:

10 בַּעֲבוּר דָּוִד עַבְדֶּךָ   אַל־תָּשֵׁב פְּנֵי מְשִׁיחֶךָ:

11 נִשְׁבַּע־יְהוָה לְדָוִד   אֱמֶת לֹא־יָשׁוּב מִמֶּנָּה

מִפְּרִי בִטְנְךָ   אָשִׁית לְכִסֵּא־לָךְ:

12 אִם־יִשְׁמְרוּ בָנֶיךָ בְּרִיתִי   וְעֵדֹתִי זוֹ אֲלַמְּדֵם

גַּם־בְּנֵיהֶם עֲדֵי־עַד   יֵשְׁבוּ לְכִסֵּא־לָךְ:

13 כִּי־בָחַר יְהוָה בְּצִיּוֹן   אִוָּהּ לְמוֹשָׁב לוֹ:

14 זֹאת־מְנוּחָתִי עֲדֵי־עַד   פֹּה־אֵשֵׁב כִּי אִוִּתִיהָ:

15 צֵידָהּ בָּרֵךְ אֲבָרֵךְ   אֶבְיוֹנֶיהָ אַשְׂבִּיעַ לָחֶם:

16 וְכֹהֲנֶיהָ אַלְבִּישׁ יֶשַׁע   וַחֲסִידֶיהָ רַנֵּן יְרַנֵּנוּ:

17 שָׁם אַצְמִיחַ קֶרֶן לְדָוִד   עָרַכְתִּי נֵר לִמְשִׁיחִי:

18 אוֹיְבָיו אַלְבִּישׁ בֹּשֶׁת   וְעָלָיו יָצִיץ נִזְרוֹ:

This psalm stands out amongst the Psalms of Ascents both by its length, being much longer than any other, and by its subject matter, being concerned with Davidic kingship and priesthood rather than any personal or familial matters. What it has in common with several other Psalms of Ascents is a concern for Jerusalem as the primary locus of worship and of Yahweh's presence.

The psalm is also distinguished by its regularity. Sixteen verses consist of a single bicolon each. Most of these bicola have a 3+3 rhythm. Verse 1 and v. 4 clearly have a rhythm of 3+2. A few other lines are ambiguous. Verse 6 and v. 14 may be either 3+3 or 3+2; v. 7 may be either 2+3 or 3+3; and v. 9 may be either 2+2 or 3+2. Lexical ambiguities are relatively few, and would not have a bearing on the division of the text into cola.

Two verses, vv. 11–12, are longer than a single bicolon can accommodate, and so warrant more detailed consideration. These two verses are closely related, ending with identical noun phrases and together reporting an oath of Yahweh.

Verse 11 reports the swearing of an oath by Yahweh, qualifies this by asserting its inviolability, and then contains the first part of the content of the oath. It has either ten or eleven stresses depending on the treatment of the closing noun phrase לְכִסֵּא־לָךְ. This may be treated as a single word-unit, or each of the words could be allocated a separate stress, with the final monosyllabic preposition/pronoun "stretched" into a disyllable in order to avoid consecutive stressed syllables.[317] Whichever option is adopted, the verse has too many stresses to be a single bicolon but is within the acceptable ranges for either a tricolon or a double bicolon.[318] The two phrases that introduce the oath have three stresses each and seven and eight syllables respectively. Therefore, these phrases each constitute a colon, the two combined being too long to be a single colon. The ambiguity in the verse therefore centres on the following verbal clause that opens the content of the oath. It has four or five stresses and twelve syllables: is it a four-word colon (such that the verse is a tricolon) or is it a bicolon (whose rhythm could be either 2+2 or 2+3)?

---

317. Cf. 122:1; Sievers, *Metrische Studien*, 226.

318. The double bicolon reading is dominant. Terrien, *Strophic Structure*, 845–47, reads an "emphatic tricolon." Crow, *Songs of Ascents*, 99, bizarrely reads a single bicolon, but the purpose of his study is exegesis rather than rhythmical analysis.

In view of the relative brevity of this line, when it is read as a bicolon, several scholars have proposed that a word has been lost from the text.[319] Some such proposals are made *metri causa* but this is not sufficient ground for textual emendation. Indeed, the rhythmical analysis of the other lines in the psalm given above indicates that the psalm is not as regular as some might like to think.[320] A syntactical argument can also be made: that the verb in this clause lacks an object.[321] However, the phrase מִפְּרִי בִטְנְךָ need not necessarily be read as a modifying phrase; rather if מִן is given a partitive sense, the phrase stands as a noun phrase and is the object of the following verb.[322] Therefore, the text should be assessed primarily as it stands, without conjectural additions.

The criteria established in this study for the assessment of potential four-word cola may be applied in this case as follows. The clause has twelve syllables and if split into two cola, they would have six syllables each. Therefore, the clause falls within the most difficult to assess range, where either option is perfectly acceptable. The extent to which the introduction of a caesura into the clause is appropriate is also ambiguous. An argument for doing so is related to the unusual word order of the clause: NPdo – V(su) – DP. The clause initial object is a focus marker, and a following caesura would reinforce the emphasis on this phrase and reflect the cognitive process of establishing the topic of the clause before moving on to the comment on that topic. Conversely an argument for not introducing a caesura is the integral nature of the clause as a four-word unit and unnecessary enjambment should be avoided. So it seems that this is a very finely balanced case indeed, and a decision will ultimately rest on broader structural considerations. The risk, therefore, is that what is found will be what is sought. Those looking for (or assuming) metrical regularity will read v. 11 as a double bicolon; those looking for tricola will read v. 11 as such. However, an assessment of v. 12 does offer some relief from such a potential pitfall.

The structure of v. 12 is quite similar to that of v. 11. It completes the content of the oath sworn by Yahweh, and consists of a protasis and

---

319. Allen, *Psalms 101–50*, 264, surveys the proposals; cf. BHS apparatus.

320. For example, Kraus, *Psalms 60–150*, 474, argues that the "meter" is 3+3 throughout, with the exception of v. 1. He proposes the addition of words to v. 9 and v. 11 to achieve this, but ignores the variation in v. 4.

321. Thus Kraus, *Psalms 60–150*, 473.

322. Thus Allen, *Psalms 101–50*, 264.

apodosis that together form a single sentence. The protasis can be construed syntactically in two ways: either as a single verbal clause with a compound and qualified object, or as two conjoined verbal clauses with subject and verb elided from the second clause. As a whole it has either five or six stresses (depending upon the treatment of זוֹ) and nineteen syllables. Therefore, it is rightly read as a bicolon, matching in its form the first half of v. 11. The apodosis in v. 12 could be read with four, five or six stresses, depending upon the treatments of the opening particle גַּם and the final phrase (as v. 11). The *maqqephim* of the Masoretic accentuation indicate only four stresses for the line, and one might question why those who have advocated the insertion of an extra word in v. 11 *metri causa* have not similarly questioned this line. Be that as it may, the number of syllables in the apodosis is fourteen and this exceeds the acceptable limit for a single colon. Therefore v. 12 is determined to be a double bicolon.

Returning to v. 11, the close connections between it and v. 12 mean that the form of v. 12 tips the balance in favor of reading v. 11 as a double bicolon. However, it is important to note that it is this local feature of the interaction between line-form and syntactic structure that influences the judgement, not a presupposition about the ideal "regularity" of the psalm as a whole. The conclusion is that this psalm consists exclusively of bicola, and therefore will not be considered any further in relation to the current exploration of the function of tricola.

Psalm 133

Colometric Analysis

1 שִׁיר הַמַּעֲלוֹת לְדָוִד

הִנֵּה מַה־טּוֹב וּמַה־נָּעִים　שֶׁבֶת אַחִים גַּם־יָחַד:

2 כַּשֶּׁמֶן הַטּוֹב עַל־הָרֹאשׁ　יֹרֵד עַל־הַזָּקָן

זְקַן־אַהֲרֹן שֶׁיֹּרֵד　עַל־פִּי מִדּוֹתָיו:

3 כְּטַל־חֶרְמוֹן שֶׁיֹּרֵד　עַל־הַרְרֵי צִיּוֹן

כִּי שָׁם צִוָּה　יְהוָה אֶת־הַבְּרָכָה　חַיִּים עַד־הָעוֹלָם:

This psalm asserts the goodness of familial unity and uses images of anointing oil, of dew and of God's blessing. The colometry of the text is generally considered to be difficult to construe, as is the interpretation of the text due to the ambiguous syntactic relationships between the different images: what is being compared to what?[323]

Verse 1 is a bicolon with rhythm 3+3. It simply states the goodness of familial unity.[324]

Verse 2 and the first half of v. 3 describe three images of things flowing down: oil of anointing, possibly Aaron's beard and the dew of Hermon. The first and third images are explicitly comparative. The semantic and syntactic similarities of these images indicate that they form a unit, but the relationships between them can be interpreted in different ways. A common interpretation is that oil of anointing and the dew of Hermon are being compared to familial unity, with Aaron's beard being a specifying expansion of the preceding reference to beard.[325] Watson takes this structure further by suggesting that a comparative particle is elided from the description of Aaron's beard and that this too is being compared to the opening image of unity.[326] In contrast, Berlin reads the two comparative particles as co-referential, such that the images of oil and dew are being compared to each other and not to the image of unity.[327] In this reading it is ambiguous as to whether שֶׁיֹּרֵד עַל־פִּי מִדּוֹתָיו refers to the oil or to the beard, but in either case the dominant image is of flowing.[328] However, the comparisons are construed, the repetition of יֹרֵד within the unit (twice with the abbreviated relative and once without[329]) and the four-fold repetition of עַל would be expected to indicate something of the structure of this unit. The second half of v. 3 makes a

---

323. There is also a significant semantic issue regarding the "impossible" image of the dew of Hermon coming down on Zion. See Braslavi, "Like the dew" and Doyle, "Metaphora Interrupta," 9.

324. Berlin, "Psalm 133," 142, believes that ישׁב יַחַד "is a technical expression meaning 'living together on undivided land holdings.'"

325. Thus Crow, *Songs of Ascents*, 107; Goldingay, *Psalms*, 563; Jacquet, *Les Psaumes*, 542; Terrien, *Strophic Structure*, 850; Allen, *Psalms 101–50*, 276; AV; NASB; ASV; NIV; NRSV. Similarly Kraus, *Psalms 60–150*, 484, reads the comparisons in relation to v. 1 but deletes the description of Aaron's beard as a digressive gloss.

326. Watson, *Traditional Techniques*, 410.

327. Berlin, "Psalm 133," 144.

328. Ibid., 144.

329. BHS apparatus suggests that all three might originally have had the abbreviated relative, the first instance being lost by haplography. Crow, *Songs of Ascents*, 107, supports this view.

separate assertion about the blessing of Yahweh that semantically and
syntactically stands apart from the preceding three images.

Turning to the colometry of the three images, the Masoretic verse
division indicates that the first half of v. 3 should be a separate line from
v. 2. This part of the text is the easiest to divide, the line having five
stresses. A variant text is attested in 11QPsᵃ which has the singular הַר
in place of the plural of MT. This potentially makes it possible to read
the line with one less stress, but the norm would still be to allocate a
full stress to the word. The MT is here retained, supported by LXX that
reads a plural. Similarly, various emendations to צִיּוֹן have been proposed
from the point of view of semantic interpretation, but these would not
have a bearing on the rhythmical analysis of the line.[330] The accentuation divides the line to form a bicolon having 3+2 rhythm, a common
line-form. Consideration may be given to splitting the line instead as a
2+3 bicolon, since placing the caesura at the boundary of the relative
clause results in less enjambment. However, the unusual 2+3 rhythm
that would result and the evidence of the accentuation weigh against
this.

Verse 2 has either nine or ten stresses, depending upon the treatment of זְקַן־אַהֲרֹן, and twenty-seven syllables. It is therefore too long to
form a single bicolon but falls within the acceptable ranges for a tricolon
or double bicolon. By far the most common reading is a double bicolon,
reflecting the overall structure of this unit of three images, with each
image therefore described in a single 3+2 bicolon. This is the colometry presented above.[331] It supports the view that the second image is
of Aaron's beard flowing down over his robes.[332] With this colometry,
the caesura in v. 2cd breaks up the relative clause, as in v. 3ab, but the
establishment of the syntactic form of the line in v. 2ab, which is then
replicated, possibly mitigates this effect in that the thematic repetition
of יֵרֵד is already anticipated and the caesurae then coincide with the
semantic pause as the hearer/reader waits to see how/where the beard/
dew will flow. Watson reconciles the colometry and syntactic structure
by placing the caesurae all immediately before the instances of (שֶׁ)יֹּרֵד

---

330. See Crow, *Songs of Ascents*, 108; Allen, *Psalms 101–50*, 277; BHS apparatus.

331. Matching presentation in BHS.

332. Watson, *Traditional Techniques*, 410; Weiser, *The Psalms*, 783; Allen, *Psalms 101–50*, 276.

creating three bicola with rhythm 3+2 / 2+3 / 2+3.[333] This is a plausible, if rhythmically unusual, colometry, and there is little to choose between these two alternatives for a presentation of three bicola.[334] However, both possibilities conflict with the accentuation, which remains to be assessed.

The accentuation appears to suggest a tripartite division of v. 2 as follows:

כַּשֶּׁמֶן הַטּוֹב עַל־הָרֹאשׁ   יֹרֵד עַל־הַזָּקָן זְקַן־אַהֲרֹן   שֶׁיֹּרֵד עַל־פִּי מִדּוֹתָיו׃

This reading as a 3+3+3 (or 3+4+3) tricolon is favored by Berlin.[335] Presenting the verse as a single line is commensurate with her syntactic interpretation of a comparison being made between the oil and the dew only, with one line describing each. In this reading the place of Aaron's beard is not particularly significant to the comparison, and it is not clear why it should be referred to so fully. Moreover, the use of the phrase עַל־הַזָּקָן זְקַן־אַהֲרֹן would be a very unusual juxtaposition of synonymous noun phrases, it being a convoluted form of זְקַן־אַהֲרֹן עַל with no apparent reason, rhythmical or otherwise, for not using this shorter form. The partial repetition does make sense when the phrase is split across two lines and the repetition can be identified both as a form of "terrace-pattern parallelism"[336] and as an "expanded repetition."[337] For these reasons, and from the point of view of the consistent unity of the larger unit of vv. 2–3ab, v. 2 is considered to be a double bicolon, not a tricolon. The accentuation probably reflects a secondary tradition that has arisen due to the complexity of the syntactic structure and has been based around reading עַל־הַזָּקָן זְקַן־אַהֲרֹן as a single phrase.

The second half of v. 3 stands apart from the comparative structure discussed above and presents a conclusion to the psalm. The line has

---

333. Watson, *Traditional Techniques*, 410.

334. Tsumura, "Sorites" adopts the same colometry as Watson but argues that the middle bicolon describes the "continual graceful movement" of the oil on the beard, not the beard itself; cf. Doyle, "Metaphora Interrupta," 10–14, and Booij, "Psalm 133," 259, who argues that a beard is static and cannot "go down."

335. Berlin, "Psalm 133," 145; also Booij, "Psalm 133," 264, and Seybold, *Die Psalmen*, 499, who tends to follow the accentuation.

336. Watson, *Classical*, 208–13.

337. Yona, "Expanded Repetition," 586–89. See the discussion of 122:4 in the section "Psalm 122 : Colometric analysis" on pp. 87–92. It is striking that these two similar constructions both occur in long verses of contentious colometry.

six stresses, and may be divided as 4+2 (as the Masoretic accentuation) or 3+3 (to more closely maintain the rhythm of preceding lines) or as a 2-2-2 para-tricolon. The word חַיִּים is omitted in 11QPsᵃ but the weight of evidence in MT, supported by LXX, is for its retention.[338] Kraus reads a tricolon, but without any justification, as does Allen who tends to follow Kraus. Dahood reads a tricolon on the basis of syllable count, resulting in a single word-unit middle colon.[339] The more common reading is as a bicolon following the accentuation.[340] However, there does appear to be a basis for reading this line as a para-tricolon. A verbal clause is supplemented by an additional noun phrase that stands in either apposition (as MT) or conjunction (as LXX) with the object noun phrase of the verbal clause. The verbal clause may be split into two two-word phrases, the initial one being a semantically ambiguous but potentially syntactically complete clause (cf. 121:8; 122:5; 124:6; 126:2abc) such that a minor caesura is appropriate after the verb. Although this coincides with a conjunctive accent, this is another instance of an indicative verb with a conjunctive accent, where the introduction of a minor caesura has been found to be acceptable (see the section "Psalm 122: Colometric Analysis" on pp. 87–92). The accentuation, which would otherwise result in the line being read as a 4+2 bicolon, is similar to other such para-tricola. Therefore the line is considered to be a para-tricolon.

Structural Analyses

THEMATIC ANALYSIS

Gerstenberger regards this psalm as an announcement of blessing, noting that in the Psalms of Ascents generally the particle הִנֵּה seems to have an instructional function. The text of the psalm divides into the exclamation (v. 1), series of metaphors (vv. 2–3b) and the hymn to Zion (v. 3cd).[341]

---

338. Crow, *Songs of Ascents*, 108; Allen, *Psalms 101–50*, 277. 11QPsᵃ also appends שלום על ישראל (cf. 125:5, 128:6) but there is no evidence of this in MT or other versions.

339. Kraus, *Psalms 60–150*, 484–85; Allen, *Psalms 101–50*, 276; Dahood, *Psalms*, 252.

340. Crow, *Songs of Ascents*, 107; Fokkelman, *Psalms in Form*, 139; Goldingay, *Psalms*, 563; Jacquet, *Les Psaumes*, 542; Terrien, *Strophic Structure*, 850; NIV; NRSV.

341. Gerstenberger, *Psalms*, 371–73.

STROPHIC ANALYSIS

This brief psalm is particularly difficult to structure, given its ambiguous colometry and lack of transition markers. The opening of the psalm is clearly marked by the exclamatory particle and emphasized use of the word טוֹב. The closing of the psalm is clearly marked by the reference to eternity.

Van der Lugt reads a structure of 2.2, but this is based upon v. 2 being a tricolon.[342] This colometry has been rejected, as discussed above. An alternative strophic structure is indicated here based upon the derived colometry, and is of the form 1.3.1.[343] Another alternative of 1.2.2 could also be hypothesized but the lack of transition markers prevents an objective appraisal. Both of these possibilities do take account of the closing force of the emphatic particle in v. 1b. A further alternative, adopted by Allen and Terrien, is 3.2, the key feature being the separation of the comparison with oil from the comparison with dew.[344] This structure appears to owe more to thematic appraisal than to analysis of formal features.

RHETORICO-STRUCTURAL ANALYSIS

Although the final line of the psalm (v. 3cde) incorporates no repeated elements, Girard links it with the opening line (v. 1) by means of the assonance between אַחִים and חַיִּים and the thematic resonance between

---

342. Van der Lugt, *Cantos and Strophes*, 425.

343. Thus Fokkelman, *Psalms in Form*, 139; Hunter, *Psalms*, 226; Jacquet, *Les Psaumes*, 542.

344. Allen, *Psalms 101–50*, 276; Terrien, *Strophic Structure*, 850.

טוֹב and בְּרָכָה. These outer lines are connected with the inner lines of comparative metaphors (vv. 2–3ab) by means of the repetition of טוֹב.[345]

The structuring of vv. 2–3ab depends on whether the triple repetition of יָרַד or the double repetition of the particle כְּ is given precedence. This question is intricately bound up with the question of syntactic interpretation: do the lines embody three similes or just two? Girard holds that there are two, and structures the lines accordingly: v. 2a/v.2bcd and v. 3aα/v.3aβ,b. In this scheme, the repetitions of יָרַד and זָקָן in v. 2bcd carry no structural significance.[346]

Auffret makes fuller use of the repetitions, whilst still maintaining that there are only two similes. He distinguishes the two descents of oil—head to beard and beard to robes—that are compared with the descent of dew, and also links these with the "descent" of Yahweh's blessing. He therefore offers the following structure for the four lines of vv. 2–3 based on word repetitions and thematic associations:

		Agent	Point of origin	Action	Point of arrival
v. 2ab	like	Oil	head	goes down	beard
v. 2cd		(oil)	beard of Aaron	goes down	robes
v. 3ab	like	Dew	Hermon	goes down	hills of Zion
v. 3cde		blessing		Yahweh commanded	"there"

The order of the elements varies in the final line, but the correspondence of the elements is apparent.[347] Such analysis as this is commensurate with Watson's syntactic interpretation, that there are three similes. Whereas the structure above assumes that the agent in v. 2cd is elided, and is the oil from the previous line, the alternative interpretation is that the comparative particle and point of origin are elided and the agent is in fact the beard of Aaron, thus:

345. Girard, *Psaumes 3: 101–150*, 383–84; cf. Trublet and Aletti, *Approche Poétique*, 266.

346. Girard, *Psaumes 3: 101–150*, 382–83.

347. Auffret, *Etude Structurelle*, 113–15.

	Agent	Point of origin	Action	Point of arrival
v. 2cd (like)	beard of Aaron	(face of Aaron)	goes down	robes

This interpretation allows the line to play a coherent part in the psalm's structure and counters the argument of Kraus,[348] and others, that v. 2cd is a historicizing gloss to be deleted. Instead it reveals a concentric structure for the five lines of the psalm as a whole, with this reference to Aaron at the centre possibly indicating a cultic setting.[349]

Summary

This short psalm has a clear thematic and rhythmical structure. Opening and closing lines of six stresses, one 3+3 bicolon and one 2-2-2 paratricolon, each make assertions about the goodness of familial unity and Yahweh's blessings. These lines sandwich three similarly-structured 3+2 bicola that connect the opening and closing assertions by means of comparative images. The three central lines are tightly knit together by verbal repetitions.

Strophic structure	Thematic structure	Rhetorical structure
1a 1b	1	1
2a 2b		2ab
2c 2d	2–3ab	2cd
3a 3b		3ab
3c–3d–3e	3cde	3cde

348. Kraus, *Psalms 60–150*, 484.

349. Allen, *Psalms 101–50*, 278; VanGemeren, "Psalms," 815.

Psalm 134

Colometric Analysis

1 שִׁיר הַמַּעֲלוֹת

הִנֵּה בָּרֲכוּ אֶת־יְהוָה   כָּל־עַבְדֵי יְהוָה   הָעֹמְדִים בְּבֵית־יְהוָה בַּלֵּילוֹת:

2 שְׂאוּ־יְדֵכֶם קֹדֶשׁ   וּבָרֲכוּ אֶת־יְהוָה:

3 יְבָרֶכְךָ יְהוָה מִצִּיּוֹן   עֹשֵׂה שָׁמַיִם וָאָרֶץ:

This short prayer describes blessings going between Yahweh and wor-shippers in the temple. Verses 1–2 consist of imperatives addressed to worshippers; v. 3 seeks a blessing on the worshippers and ascribes to Yahweh an aphoristic epithet.

Verse 1 can be read with between six and nine stresses depending upon how the words are aggregated into word-units. Clearly the line is pushing the limit of a single bicolon, as confirmed by the syllable count of twenty-four. Whilst this could in theory be read as an acceptable bico-lon (perhaps 4+4 with syllable count 13/11), the cola would seem unduly heavy in this short psalm where the remaining cola have no more than nine syllables. Such a reading is slightly more plausible if the opening particle stands in anacrusis.[350] In this case a balanced bicolon could be construed, with 4+4 stresses (without any unusually long word-units) and eleven syllables in each colon. However anacrusis is normally used to mark a disjuncture or draw attention to the opening of a section with-in a poetic text. While it is not impossible that anacrusis be used to open the poem as a whole, it is difficult to discern what function it performs. Robinson has suggested that הִנֵּה here is an example of anacrusis, "to lay especial weight on the passage which is now opening."[351] There are two problems with this interpretation: that there is no preceding material to form the backdrop to this "especial weight"; and the particle הִנֵּה of itself can serve this function, as determined by Follingstad, whether it stands in anacrusis or not.[352] The word focuses attention, and therefore has the particular nuance in this instance of reinforcing the imperative mood of

---

350. Allen, *Psalms 101–50*, 281.

351. T. H. Robinson, "Anacrusis," 38–39. This perspective has been borne out in the analysis of other instances of הִנֵּה. See comment on 128:4 in the section "Psalm 128: Colometric Analysis" on pp. 134–38.

352. Follingstad, "*Hinnēh* and Focus Function," 6, 9.

the following clause. Its semantic and syntactic contribution to the line is slight; if it is also extra-rhythmical then it is difficult to hypothesise any reason for its presence. In contrast, its presence can be taken to suggest some significance for the colometry of the psalm and it should not therefore be regarded as an anacrusis.[353]

Given that readings of the verse as bicolon and as anacrusis plus bicolon each raise doubts, the syntactic structure of the line as three phrases suggests consideration of a reading as a tricolon. The three phrases are the imperative verbal clause, a vocative noun phrase and a co-referential vocative noun phrase that expands and specifies the description of the addressees. The LXX includes an additional colon and reads בַּלֵּילוֹת with the following line. These variants suggest a *Vorlage* that could potentially have consisted of bicola throughout. Equally, since the addition creates a line identical to 135:2, it is possible that an earlier scribe might have imported the extra colon by an anamnesis.[354] The LXX possibly witnesses an alternative textual tradition; 11QPs^a supports MT. There is no strong evidence for adopting LXX over MT, and MT is maintained for the present study. Therefore v. 1 may be read as a tricolon with rhythm 3+2+3 or 3+2+4 (depending on the treatment of בְּבֵית־יְהוָה).[355] What stands out in this reading is the relative irregularity of cola in terms of syllables: 8/5/11. However, the final long colon cannot reasonably be divided, save by separating the final word and reading it with v. 2, as LXX.[356]

In view of these difficulties, and the failure to arrive at a fully satisfactory colometry, a variety of approaches has been advocated in relation to the final phrase of v. 1. Fokkelman reads it as a monocolon; but as a single noun phrase it cannot plausibly stand alone as a separate line, particularly since it clearly expands the preceding line.[357] Others have speculatively expanded it so that it becomes a bicolon by adding וּבַיָּמִים before the final word.[358] There is no ms evidence for such a reading, and the use of the plurals is not attested in comparative texts.

353. Cf. 133:1 where there is no suggestion of anacrusis, save from Robinson.

354. See Crow, *Songs of Ascents*, 121–22 for a discussion.

355. Thus Weiser, *The Psalms*, 786; Kraus, *Psalms 60–150*, 487.

356. Although Dahood, *Psalms*, 255, turns v. 1c into a bicolon, splitting the construct phrase בֵית־יְהוָה between cola. Such mismatching between colometry and syntax, that generates enjambment bordering on violent, cannot be accepted.

357. Fokkelman, *Major Poems III*, 304.

358. E.g., Jacquet, *Les Psaumes*, 552; cf. Ps 32:4; 42:4; 55:11.

In light of these various possibilities and the lack of a clearly acceptable colometry, v. 1 is identified as a possible tricolon and will be
explored further as such.

Verse 2 is a 3+2 bicolon, with the imperative to lift up hands paral-
leled by the instruction to bless Yahweh. Verse 3 is a 3+3 bicolon, seeking
Yahweh's blessings on the worshippers.

Structural Analyses

THEMATIC ANALYSIS

Gerstenberger observes in this psalm a summons to praise (vv. 1–2) and
a blessing (v. 3). He considers the opening use of הִנֵּה to be odd, in that
it is not instructional as it is in other Psalms of Ascents; here he reads it
either as reinforcement of the imperative or as arising by scribal error
(from Ps 133).[359]

STROPHIC ANALYSIS

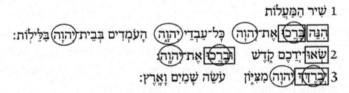

This very short psalm is remarkable for its high incidence of repetitions
and transition markers. The divine name occurs in five of the seven cola,
and the verb ברך occurs once in each of the three lines. The opening is
clearly marked by the exclamatory particle and an imperative. Verse 2
also includes two imperatives, but they function as parallels of the imperative of v. 1 rather than marking opening. The verb at the head of v. 3
has jussive meaning, which is also a marker of opening, although Van
der Lugt identifies the particular use of ברך with Israel as object as a
marker of closure, but with only slight evidence.[360]

With only three lines, it is possible to read the psalm as a single
strophe in its entirety. If a division were to be construed, it would have to
be based on the content of the lines rather than transition markers. Thus
a structure of 2.1 would be deduced, based on a two-line strophe of ex-

---

359. Gerstenberger, *Psalms*, 374–75; so also Kraus, *Psalms 60–150*, 487–88.

360. Van der Lugt, *Cantos and Strophes*, 556. cf. 128:5.

hortation to bless Yahweh, and a one-line strophe of a prayer for Yahweh to bless the worshippers.[361] However, there is no practical significance in forcing a division, and in strophic terms the psalm is best read as a three-line whole.[362]

RHETORICO-STRUCTURAL ANALYSIS

Girard divides the psalm into two parts, vv. 1–2 being a hymnic exhortation having a concentric structure and v. 3 being a ritual blessing. In vv. 1–2, he takes the temporal reference to be the central element of the structure, with the two imperative phrases flanking it, thus: v. 1abcα/ v.1cβ/v.2ab which can be denoted A/B/A. The two parts are tied together by the overall inclusio יְבָרֶכְךָ יְהוָה / בָּרֲכוּ אֶת־יְהוָה in v. 1a and v. 3a. [363]

In his structure for vv. 1–2, it is not clear why Girard separates only the temporal reference. An alternative structure may be postulated for vv. 1–2 that takes account of the two vocative forms of address and the two imperatives, thus:

v. 1a	Imperative
v. 1b	Vocative
v. 1c	Vocative
v. 2	Imperative

This structure allows clear demarcation of the different phrases in the text, as well as matching a colometric division, and distributes the four occurrences of the divine name equally between four sections. In these respects it is superior to the structure proposed by Girard.

Auffret has identified a possible chiastic structure within vv. 2–3 based on: צִיּוֹן / יְהוָה יְבָרֶכְךָ / בָּרֲכוּ אֶת־יְהוָה / קֹדֶשׁ.[364] Whilst this does not have great merit—relying on interpretive synonymy—it does further indicate the connection between v. 3 and vv. 1–2, hinting at a function for v. 2 as a hinge that relates to the lines either side of it.

361. Thus Allen, *Psalms 101–50*, 281; Crow, *Songs of Ascents*, 121; Goldingay, *Psalms*, 570; Hunter, *Psalms*, 228; Jacquet, *Les Psaumes*, 550.

362. Thus Kissane, *Book of Psalms*, 596.

363. Girard, *Psaumes 3: 101–150*, 386–88.

364. Auffret, *Etude Structurelle*, 120.

Summary

This brief psalm has a strongly liturgical tone to it. Its colometry is particularly difficult to construe and there is evidence of more than one textual tradition. The MT is best understood as a tricolon and two bicola. Although the first two lines cohere through a series of imperatives and vocatives, the third line is also closely tied to them through a network of verbal repetitions and thematic references.

Strophic structure	Thematic structure	Rhetorical structure
1a 1b 1c		1a
		1b
	1–2	1c
2a 2b		2a
		2b
3a 3b	3	3ab

Summary of Findings of Colometric Analysis

Summary Table of Findings of Colometric Analysis

Tricola	Possible tricola	Para-tricola	Possible para-tricola	Rejected tricola	Rejected para-tricola
		120:3		120:2	
		120:7			
		121:4	121:5		121:6
			121:8		
122:4			122:5		
123:4				123:2	123:2ef
	124:1				
	124:2	124:6		124:4	
125:2		125:5abc	125:1		125:3ab
			126:1		
			126:2abc		
			126:2def		
			126:3		
		127:2abc		127:2	
		127:5abc			

Tricola	Possible tricola	Para-tricola	Possible para-tricola	Rejected tricola	Rejected para-tricola
			128:4		
129:8	128:5				
130:7		130:5 130:6			
	131:2			132:11	
		133:3cde		133:2	
	134:1				

At this provisional stage of the study, a number of features are apparent from the summary table of findings. The rejection of a number of hypothesised tripartite lines provides reassurance that the analysis is not unreasonably skewed towards identifying lines as such. The tricola and para-tricola that have been identified are fairly evenly spread through the sample corpus of texts. Tricola are fewer than para-tricola, and therefore the distinction between these two line types is a particularly important one. For both line types the number of possible cases approximately equals the definite instances. However, any generalised conclusions that the detailed analysis might lead to must be tempered by the possibility that the sample corpus of texts is not necessarily truly representative of all poetic texts. Having identified these lines, a thorough appraisal of their internal syntactic and semantic characteristics will provide the basis both for clarifying the (currently) indeterminate cases and for assessing the function of each line within its poetic structural context.

4

Internal Analysis of Tricola and Para-Tricola

Basis of Analysis

Syntactic Structure

SYNTACTIC ANALYSIS WILL BE carried out according to the theories outlined in the section "Syntactic Relationships" on pp. 46–52. The surface structure of each sentence in question will be analyzed, producing a final derived phrase marker, in order to illustrate the hierarchy of constituents of which the sentence is composed. Whilst the grammatical function of each constituent is not strictly relevant to this analysis (being pertinent rather to semantic interpretation), some indication of functions will be given for ease of reference and to assist with comprehension. Information structuring will be commented on where relevant, but not incorporated into diagrams. The phrase marker representing the surface structure will enable an assessment of the extent of coincidence between syntactic pauses and colometric limits, and designation of the degree of enjambment. An appraisal of the extent to which transformations have been applied to a deep structure in order to obtain the surface structure, and comparison with surrounding lines in the light of the psalm's macro-structure, will inform the subsequent assessment of the function of each tripartite line (chapter 5 "Functions of Tricola and Para-tricola," pp. 238–53).

In order to provide a consistent basis for the production of Phrase Markers, the following Phrase Structure Rules have been postulated for Biblical Hebrew:

$$S = \{CC, VC\}$$
$$CC = NPsu + Cp (+ NP) (+ DP)$$
$$VC = NPsu + V ((+ P) + NP) (+ DP)$$
$$DP = \{D, P+NP, NP\}$$

The rules can be read as follows:

- A sentence may comprise either a copulative clause or a verbal clause. For the purposes of this exercise, nominal clauses are treated as copulative clauses in which the copula is elided.

- A copulative clause comprises a noun phrase denoting the subject, the copula and its complement, which may be either a noun phrase or an adverbial phrase or both.

- A verbal clause comprises a noun phrase denoting the subject, a verb, an optional object noun phrase, and an optional adverbial phrase. Direct object noun phrases may idiomatically incorporate a preposition, but are nevertheless regarded as noun phrases rather than adverbial phrases.

- An adverbial phrase contains an adverb, a prepositional phrase or a noun phrase that has adverbial function. An adverbial phrase may modify a whole clause or any constituent within it.

These rules represent a simplified version of the Phrase Structure rules employed by Price, and are sufficient to deal with the structures encountered in the texts under consideration.[1] They are adequate for providing a basis for the analysis of surface structure, although a thoroughly systematic appraisal would require the addition of extra rules, for example that any constituent may comprise two similar constituents in apposition or conjunction.

The rules are strictly formed to describe kernel sentences and therefore a number of differences are apparent in surface structure in view of transformations that will have been performed. In particular, the presence of particles indicating negation, interrogation or exclamation may occur within a clause or sentence, in addition to the particles indicated by the rules. Similarly, variations in word order are not formally accounted for.

1. Price, *Theory*, 36–44.

In the following analysis, these rules will be applied to the surface structure of the lines in question, in order to determine their phrase marker. For simplicity and clarity, nouns with a pronominal suffix are labelled simply as "N," without further sub-division. The phrase marker is produced so that each label at the lowest level of the marker is directly above the word on the page to which it relates. The phrase marker should therefore be read from right to left, matching the Hebrew text, even though the labels are English. Where an elided constituent is indicated, its location is based only on considerations of the clarity of the diagram and is not intended to indicate any notional word order prior to elision.

Semantic Structure

The semantic structure of the lines will be analyzed following the theory outlined in the section "Semantic relationships" on pp. 52–55. A deep structure of the text will be back-analyzed from the surface structure, and this will be presented as a set of basic propositions. The relationships between these propositions will be described and a diagram will illustrate how these relationships appear in the context of the colometry of the surface structure.

For simplicity of presentation, separate propositions for each genitive construction are omitted where the construction simply indicates possession. The illocutionary force of a proposition is annotated in cases where the proposition is not a statement, i.e., where it is a question or a command. The illocutionary category of command includes jussives and cohortatives. Given the significant amount of elision in the texts and the consequent need to supply elided components (shown bracketed) to produce grammatically correct propositions, it is necessary to render the propositions in English. However, the terms used are not intended to define or limit the semantic content of the Hebrew lexemes; they are used purely to illustrate the propositional structure. This analysis is distilled into a simplified presentation of the key relations between propositions in the line. This cannot be done perfectly due to the non-exact correspondence between cola and propositions, but does go some way toward illustrating how each of these lines is structured semantically.

The illustration of comparative relationships between propositions is particularly difficult due to the high degree of elision involved in transforming from deep structure to surface structure. Comparisons are usually expressed at the level of surface structure as a single statement, but this embodies two propositions that are being compared, e.g., "Yahweh is a rock" could be based upon a comparison between the propositions "Yahweh is strong" and "A rock is strong."[2] Therefore, both levels of structure need to be borne in mind. In addition, it is apparent that the precise point of comparison, "strength" in the example above, does not necessarily appear in the surface structure.[3] Therefore, the introduction of the point of comparison in the back-analyzed basic propositions is a subjective matter of interpretation.

Psalm 120:3

Syntactic Analysis

```
                               S
                    ┌──────────┼──────────┐
                   VC         Cj          VC
               ┌───┴───┐              ┌────┼────┐
             DPio  V(su) NPdo      DPio V(su) NPdo
            ┌──┴──┐      │        ┌─┴─┐       │
           NP     P     Pn       Pn  P       Pn
         ┌──┴──┐
        NP     Pn
      ┌──┴──┐
     Aj     N
```

לְשׁוֹן רְמִיָּה׃   יֹּסִיף לָךְ   וּמַה־   יִּתֵּן לְךָ   מַה־

The line comprises two conjoined verbal clauses that share the same subject and object. The subject of the clauses is elided and is indicated to be 3m.s. by the verb inflections. The interrogative pronouns both act as the objects of the verbs and mark the clauses as questions. An addressee is denoted initially by the 2m.s. pronoun and then by a noun phrase standing in apposition to the pronoun. This is the normal form of construction for a vocative expression.[4]

The line could be considered complete at either caesura but continues further, firstly with a parallel verb clause, and then with a vocative

---

2. See Larson, *Translation*, 246–49, for further explanation.

3. This is always the case in the use of metaphor, sometimes the case in the use of simile.

4. Waltke and O'Connor, *Syntax*, 77.

expansion of the indirect object. Therefore the enjambment is progressive in each instance.

The line has not undergone any transformations that introduce significant ambiguities. Although the subject is elided, his identity is apparent from the previous line. The attention of the reader is held to a modest degree by the delayed vocative expression identifying the addressee. The surrounding lines of the psalm are similarly unambiguous syntactically.

Semantic Analysis

- (He) will give (something) to you. [Question].
- (He) will add (something) to you. [Question].
- (You) speak haughtily.

This line consists of two equivalent propositions that are questions and a vocative epithet that describes the addressee of the questions. The agent of the action is implicit, whether the verbs are read as active forms with an elided subject, or as passive forms. The questions are addressed to an unidentified person (presumably a representative person) who is described synecdochically as "a haughty tongue." "Tongue" is a metonym for speech, and so the phrase is a means of describing a person who uses haughty speech.

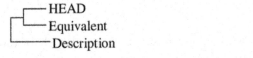

┌─── HEAD	מַה־יִּתֵּן לְךָ
├─── Equivalent	וּמַה־יֹּסִיף לָךְ
└─── Description	לָשׁוֹן רְמִיָּה:

Psalm 120:7

Syntactic Analysis

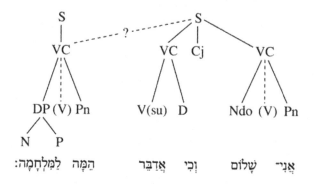

The line comprises three verbal clauses and the relationships between them are ambiguous.[5] The medial clause is often read as a temporal clause governed by the final clause, the conjunction being read as adversative. The structure preferred here is a simple coordination of the first two clauses, with the final clause forming a separate sentence.[6] As was noted above (in the section "Psalm 120: Colometric Analysis" on pp. 68–73) the absence of any clear indication of relationships between the three clauses supports the reading of the line as a para-tricolon, since a bicolon would relate the medial clause more strongly to one of the others.

The initial clause could be construed as nominal; that is, having an elided copula. However, its conjunction with the following verbal clause suggests that it is better regarded as a verbal clause with an elided verb. Similarly the final clause, creating a contrast with the first two, is most naturally read as a verbal clause with the elided verb most readily inferred as דבר. The adverbial use of כִּי adds force or distinctness to the medial clause.[7]

The initial colon could be a complete, albeit slightly ambiguous, sentence, but the second colon expands it with an additional clause. The

5. Hossfeld and Zenger, *Psalmen*, 408–9, discuss some of the possibilities.

6. Cody, "Psalm 120," 62, argues that the final clause would need an opening adversative to indicate such a structure. However, the elision of such an adversative and its implication by the colometric structure of the line can be inferred as a facet of poetic style.

7. BDB §3588.1e.

enjambment at the first caesura is therefore progressive. At the second caesura there is a clear syntactic break between sentences, and there is no enjambment.

The line has not undergone significant transformations other than the elision of verbs. Only a modest amount of additional interaction with the text is required in order to secure a syntactic interpretation. The preceding lines of the psalm have similarly straightforward syntax.

Semantic Analysis

- I (seek/support) peace.

- I speak (in support of peace).

- They (seek/support/speak in support of) war.

This line creates a clear contrast between the motives of the psalmist and of others.[8] The first proposition defines the motive of the psalmist, which by means of the elision of a verb can only be interpreted generally. This is amplified by the second proposition, which gives further information about the psalmist's pursuit of peace. These two together form a HEAD to which the third proposition provides a contrast.

┌─── HEAD	אֲנִי־שָׁלוֹם
┌┴─── Amplification	וְכִי אֲדַבֵּר
└──── Contrast	הֵמָּה לַמִּלְחָמָה:

---

8. A "unit of antithesis" identified by Krašovec, *Antithetic*, 126.

Psalm 121:4

Syntactic Analysis

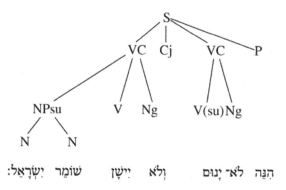

The line comprises two conjoined verbal clauses that share the same subject, which is elided in the first clause. An opening presentative particle functions syntactically as a marker of exclamation rather than declaration.[9] In the subject noun phrase, the participle is denoted as a noun rather than a verbal form since it indicates a person rather than an action.[10]

The line could be considered complete at either caesura but continues further, firstly with a parallel verb clause, and then with a noun phrase identifying the subject of the two verb clauses. Therefore the enjambment is progressive in each instance.

The line has not undergone any transformations that introduce significant ambiguities. Although the epithetic identification of the subject is delayed, his identity is apparent from the previous lines.

Semantic Analysis

- ? (See/know) that indeed,
- (He) will not slumber.
- (He) will not sleep.
- (He) guards Israel.

---

9. Waltke and O'Connor, *Syntax*, 674–75.
10. Ibid., 613.

The opening particle is presentative and indicates an exclamation rather than a statement. It could be interpreted, therefore, as having imperative force, with a verb such as "know" or "see" elided; it would therefore be an "orienter" proposition in its own right, and the remainder of the line the CONTENT. The remainder of the line consists of two equivalent propositions and a description of their subject. The identity of the subject is elided in the two equivalent propositions, suggesting that the third proposition identifies the subject. However, in the context of the psalm, the subject is already apparent from v. 2 and the use of this epithet is a description.

<table>
<tr><td>┌─── HEAD</td><td>הִנֵּה לֹא־יָנוּם</td></tr>
<tr><td>├── Equivalent</td><td>וְלֹא יִישָׁן</td></tr>
<tr><td>└── Description</td><td>שׁוֹמֵר יִשְׂרָאֵל:</td></tr>
</table>

Psalm 121:5

Syntactic Analysis

עַל־ יַד יְמִינֶךָ:   יְהוָה צִלְּךָ   יְהוָה שֹׁמְרֶךָ

The line comprises two copulative clauses, each with an elided copula, i.e., nominal clauses. The second clause is extended by an adverbial phrase. The ordering of subject followed by predicate in each clause is normal for such clauses of identification.[11] In the first clause the participle is regarded as a substantive, as in 121:4.

The first clause is complete at the first caesura and there is no enjambment. At the second caesura the second clause is potentially complete, but the final word is modified by additional information in the final colon. This final adverbial phrase can be regarded as an unmarked relative clause (i.e., with an elided relative pronoun) such that a comma would be appropriate English punctuation. Therefore the enjambment is progressive.

The line has not undergone any transformations that introduce significant ambiguities. The surrounding lines of the psalm are similarly unambiguous syntactically.

Semantic Analysis

- Yahweh is your guardian.
- Yahweh protects you.
- A shade protects you.
- The shade is on your right hand.

This line superficially makes two equivalent nominal assertions about Yahweh. However, the second is more narrowly termed than the first and should be regarded as a specific instance of the generic first proposition, rather than an equivalent. A further and more important distinction between the two assertions regards their use of language. The first can be interpreted literally. While an anthropomorphism is not strictly literal (equating Yahweh to a human "guardian"), the assertion can be regarded as literal in that Yahweh is "one who guards you." In contrast, there is no literal sense in which Yahweh is a "shade," and the word is being used metaphorically.[12] Therefore, the assertion is making a comparison between an aspect of Yahweh and a certain aspect of a shade, the context dictating that this is its protective aspect. This simple nominal assertion thereby embodies two distinct propositions, stated above, that

11. Ibid., 130–31.

12. Alter, *Book of Psalms*, 438, highlights this as virtually the only figurative language in the psalm.

are being compared. This comparison is a specific example of the preceding generic assertion about Yahweh's being a guardian. A separate descriptive proposition follows. This is usually taken as a description of the "shade" to which Yahweh is compared, as illustrated in the diagram below. An alternative interpretation is that the description qualifies both of the preceding propositions, as in 120:3 and 121:4.

Psalm 121:8

Syntactic Analysis

The line is a single verbal clause. The two infinitive constructs have a nominal function and may be interpreted as gerunds.[13] The word order of the line is curious in respect of the fronting of the subject noun of the clause. In the previous line (v. 7), יְהוָה was fronted as an argument focus marker, resuming יְהוָה as the topic of the text and the agent of protection after the digression into the potential sources of harm in v. 6. In this line (v. 8) יְהוָה carries over as the topic from the preceding line (v. 7). The line has predicate focus, with a topic–comment structure, and a verb–subject–object word order would be expected.[14] Therefore, it is likely that the subject has been fronted in this line as a poetic device, to create an anaphora, rather than due to information structuring.

13. Waltke and O'Connor, *Syntax*, 601.
14. Lunn, *Word-Order*, 37–43.

At the first caesura, the verbal clause is potentially syntactically complete, but is clearly semantically incomplete without the identification of an object. Once completed by the following object noun phrase, no punctuation would be appropriate at the caesura and so the enjambment is integral (cf. 122:5; 124:6; 126:2abc). Such semantic dependency possibly lies behind the Masoretic joining of the verb to the following noun by a *maqqeph*. At the second caesura the clause is potentially complete, but is supplemented by the adverbial phrase in the final colon, and the enjambment is therefore progressive.

Other than the relocation of the subject noun to clause-initial position, the line has not undergone any significant transformations, as is the case in the preceding line.

Semantic Analysis

- Yahweh guards (you) continually.

- You go.

- You come.

The HEAD proposition in this line asserts Yahweh's guarding. This is expanded by a pair of embedded propositions stating the circumstances in which this happens. To state that "Yahweh guards your going" means that "Yahweh guards you" when "you go." The two circumstances are mutually exclusive, and together form a merism to imply "all of your travelling." The adverbial phrase of the HEAD proposition expresses a hendiadys and asserts the continuing timelessness of Yahweh's guarding.

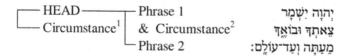

HEAD	Phrase 1	יְהוָה יִשְׁמָר
Circumstance[1]	& Circumstance[2]	צֵאתְךָ וּבוֹאֶךָ
	Phrase 2	מֵעַתָּה וְעַד־עוֹלָם:

Psalm 122:4

Syntactic Analysis

שֶׁשָׁם עָלוּ שְׁבָטִים   שִׁבְטֵי־יָהּ עֵדוּת לְיִשְׂרָאֵל   לְהֹדוֹת לְשֵׁם יְהוָה:

The syntax of this line is, in part, very ambiguous, as is reflected in the difficulties in assessing its colometry. A simple verbal clause is modified by two adverbial phrases. The first simply uses the relative pronoun, referring back to the subject of the previous line (v. 3), as a *casus pendens,* which is immediately resumed by an adverb. The second adverbial phrase is based around an infinitive construct. Since this infinitive governs a prepositional phrase, it is best construed as a verb, such that the verbal clause that it predicates stands as a constituent noun phrase governed by the preceding preposition לְ.[15] The preposition and constituent noun phrase together form the adverbial phrase that stands in the place of a subordinate clause. The infinitival verbal clause has no explicit subject; this is naturally inferred to be the same as that of the main verbal clause to which it is subordinate (cf. 124:2; 126:1, 2cde, 3).

The ambiguity in the line concerns the relationship of the medial noun phrase to the rest of the line. Three possibilities are indicated approximately in the diagram. One possibility is that the phrase relates to the final adverbial phrase, suggesting a nominal clause consisting of these two phrases: "It is an ordinance for Israel to give thanks to the

---

15. Waltke and O'Connor, *Syntax,* 600.

name of Yahweh." This interpretation implies a separation from the main verbal clause, and is best represented colometrically by reading the verse as two bicola. A second possibility is that the phrase relates to the entire verbal clause as a parenthetical comment embedded within it: "There go up tribes, the tribes of Yah (as is decreed for Israel), to give thanks to the name of Yahweh." The introduction of a mid-sentence unmarked parenthetical comment is very unusual. The third possibility is that the phrase relates to the immediately preceding noun phrase, in apposition: "There go up tribes, the tribes of Yah, the testimony of Israel, to give thanks to the name of Yahweh." This interpretation is best represented colometrically by reading the verse as a tricolon, and supports the alternative textual witness of 11QPs[a] of עדת for עֵדוּת. The rhythmical analysis of the line has demonstrated its identity as a tricolon, and so this third possibility for its syntactic structure (and consequent semantic structure) is adopted here.

At each caesura the main verbal clause is potentially complete but is supplemented by the following colon. Therefore the enjambment is progressive in each case.

Based on the deduced syntactic structure, the line has not undergone any significant transformations. However, the lack of marking of syntactic relationships of the medial noun phrase has generated ambiguity, and it may be the case that the colometry of the line has a role as a marker of syntactic structure. Surrounding lines are straightforward syntactically.

Semantic Analysis

- Tribes go up there.
- The tribes are of Yah.
- (The tribes) are a testimony/congegation for/of Israel.
- (Tribes) praise Yahweh's name.

This ambiguous line has been analyzed semantically in accordance with the conclusion of the colometric and syntactic analyses above.[16] The HEAD proposition states the means (going up there) and the final

---

16. See the sections "Psalm 122: Colometric Analysis" on pp. 87–92 and "Psalm 122:4: Syntactic Analysis" on pp. 194–95.

proposition states the purpose (praising Yahweh's name). Two intervening propositions identify and describe the tribes that are the subject of the two main propositions.

```
┌─ MEANS ──┬── HEAD              שָׁשָׁם עָלוּ שְׁבָטִים
│          └── Ident. & Desc.   שִׁבְטֵי־יָהּ עֵדוּת לְיִשְׂרָאֵל
│
└─ Purpose                      לְהֹדוֹת לְשֵׁם יְהוָה:
```

Psalm 122:5

Syntactic Analysis

כִּי שָׁמָּה יָשְׁבוּ   כִסְאוֹת לְמִשְׁפָּט   כִּסְאוֹת לְבֵית דָּוִד:

The line comprises a conjunction and a verbal clause, the subject of which is expressed in apposed noun phrases. The adverb is placed at the beginning of the sentence as a topic marker.

The assessment of enjambment in this line is particularly difficult. At the first caesura, the verbal clause is in theory potentially syntactically complete, although it would be semantically ambiguous due to the non-identification of the grammatical subject. Once the clause is recognised as incomplete at this point, it not appropriate to construe any significant syntactic pause at the caesura, such that the enjambment is integral. This accords with the placing of a conjunctive accent on יָשְׁבוּ in the MT.[17] At the second caesura there is no ambiguity: the clause is

17. Cf. 121:8.

potentially complete but supplemented with additional information and the enjambment is progressive.

Other than the relocation of the adverb to clause-initial position, the line has not undergone any significant transformations. The surrounding lines have a similarly simple surface structure.

Semantic Analysis

- In that place, thrones are established.
- Thrones are of/for justice.[18]
- Thrones are of/for David's house.

This line can be read as a proposition regarding the locus of thrones together with two propositions describing the thrones. The two descriptions are juxtaposed without any logical connection, and appear to have equal prominence. It would be possible to read some equivalence between these two descriptions, but this would depend upon a particular interpretation of the significance of ascribing the thrones to "David's house."[19] An alternative postulation would be that the ascription to "David's house" identifies rather than describes the thrones. However, the ambiguity of the specific referents means that this cannot be certain.

```
HEAD ──┬─ Phrase 1                       כִּי שָׁמָּה יָשְׁבוּ
        └─ Phr.2 & Desc:──┬─HEAD¹        כִּסְאוֹת לְמִשְׁפָּט
                          └─HEAD²        כִּסְאוֹת לְבֵית דָּוִיד:
```

---

18. Strictly the abstract noun "justice" represents a separate proposition "(Someone) makes judgements."

19. "House" is probably used metonymically for "dynasty."

Psalm 123:4

Syntactic Analysis

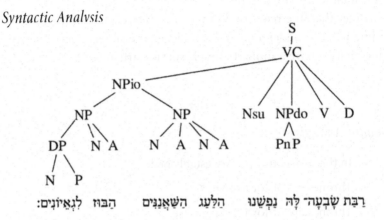

רַבַּת שָׂבְעָה־ לָּהּ נַפְשֵׁנוּ   הַלַּעַג הַשַּׁאֲנַנִּים   הַבּוּז לִגְאֵיוֹנִים:

The line comprises a single verbal clause, the indirect object of which is expanded as two noun phrases in apposition. Canonical word order of verb–subject–object is observed.

The initial colon potentially represents a syntactically complete clause and is then expanded by identification of the indirect object. This in turn is further expanded by the noun phrase in the final colon, so that the enjambment at each caesura is progressive.[20]

The line has not undergone any significant transformations. The pair of indirect object noun phrases indicates that two separate clauses at a deeper level have been combined, and this is readily understood from the surface structure.

Semantic Analysis

- We are fully sated with (others') scorn.[21]

- The scorn is of those who are at ease.

- (We are fully sated with others') contempt.

- The contempt is of those who are proud.

20. Dobbs-Allsopp, "Enjambing Line (Part 1)," 228–29, refers to this construction as "appositional enjambment" and notes that it can be difficult to distinguish from verb gapping.

21. Reading "our souls" as a synecdoche for "us" and simplifying the reference to "scorn," which as an abstract noun strictly requires a further proposition.

The syntactic structure of this line is very similar to that of 122:5. However, the semantic structure may be different. Whilst the surface structure is a single clause regarding satiation with two equivalent descriptions of the content (as described above), at a deep level it consists of two equivalent propositions regarding satiation each with an accompanying identification, as outlined in the propositions above. The greater part of the equivalent proposition has been elided to produce the surface structure.

Psalm 124:1

Syntactic Analysis

:לוּלֵי יְהוָה שֶׁהָיָה לָנוּ יֹאמַר־נָא יִשְׂרָאֵל

The line comprises a verbal clause in the precative mood, inviting speech. The constituent noun clause that forms the invited speech is an incomplete sentence, comprising the protasis of an irreal condition but no apodosis. Indeed even as a protasis it is an incomplete clause, comprising merely a noun (presumed to be a grammatical subject) and a qualifying relative clause but no predicate. The qualifying relative clause is copulative, as indicated in the diagram. It might be possible to read the relative idiomatically such that the copulative clause is not a relative clause qualifying the noun but constitutes the predicate of the protasis. Nevertheless, the sentence would still be incomplete without an apodosis.

The first two words of the line cannot form a complete clause and must be continued. The presence of a relative clause straight after implies a syntactic pause at the caesura and so the enjambment is periodic (cf. in English the commas that bracket a dependent relative clause). Similarly, at the second caesura the protasis is still incomplete and must be continued, and the enjambment is also periodic. Note, however, that the continuation is not as expected, in either the continuation of the protasis clause or the addition of an apodosis, but is in fact a governing verbal clause that reinterprets the syntactic function of the foregoing material.

The line has undergone a significant transformation of word order that departs from the canonical word order. The consequence is that the syntactic relations between clauses need to be reinterpreted as the line proceeds: the opening (incomplete) clause turns out to be not a protasis governed by an apodosis but a constituent noun clause governed by a verbal clause. In this way the attention of the reader/hearer of the psalm is engaged at its outset.

Semantic Analysis
See the section "Psalm 124:2: Semantic Analysis" on p. 202.

Psalm 124:2

Syntactic Analysis

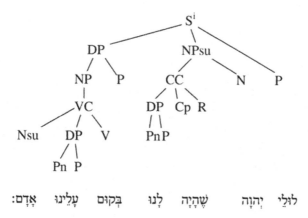

לוּלֵי יְהוָה שֶׁהָיָה לָנוּ בְּקוּם עָלֵינוּ אָדָם:

The first two cola have the identical structure to 124:1. The third colon is an adverbial phrase that specifies the circumstances of the syntactically incomplete and irreal protasis. This adverbial phrase is based around the infinitive construct קוּם, which could be construed as a noun in the sense of a gerund.[22] However, since it governs a prepositional phrase, it is best construed as a verb, such that the verbal clause it predicates stands as a noun phrase with the preposition בְּ to form the adverbial phrase.[23] An apodosis is still awaited.

The enjambment at both caesurae is periodic, for the same reasons as discussed for 124:1. As in that instance, the continuation after the pause at the second caesura is not as expected, being (in effect) a subordinate clause modifying the incomplete protasis rather than a completion of the protasis or an apodosis. This ongoing non-completion results in periodic enjambment at the end of the line as well as at its caesurae.

The line has not undergone any transformations that introduce significant ambiguities. However, attention is held by the anticipation of an apodosis.

22. Waltke and O'Connor, *Syntax*, 613.

23. Ibid., 600; cf.122:4; 126:1.

Semantic Analysis

- If Yahweh were not with us.
- Israel will say. [Command]
- If Yahweh were not with us.
- People rose up against us.

The propositions in these lines are straightforward but the relationships between them quite complex. The opening two cola, repeated in each line, could be treated as two separate propositions, but effectively function here as a single proposition that expresses a contrary-to-fact condition. The relationship between this proposition and the following colon is different in the two lines. In v. 1 it represents a CONTENT of suggested speech, whereas in v. 2 it is the HEAD proposition that is then associated with a circumstance. The whole of v. 2 then functions in the larger structure as a statement of contrary-to-fact condition, with the following verses expressing the CONSEQUENCE.

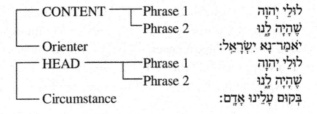

Psalm 124:6

Syntactic Analysis

```
                              S
                              |
                             CC
                          ⌐--'--⌐
                      NPsu  (Cp)  Aj
                     ⌐--'          \
                   VC              N
               ⌐---'  /  \
            NPio    V-o  Ng R
           /  \
         DP    N
        /  \
       N    P
```

בָּרוּךְ יְהֹוָה   שֶׁלֹּא נְתָנָנוּ   טֶרֶף לְשִׁנֵּיהֶם׃

The initial colon is a nominal clause (construed here as a copulative clause with elided copula) in the precative mood, expressing the wish that Yahweh may be the-one-being-blessed.[24] In this context, the opening passive participle is essentially adjectival.[25] The following two cola comprise a dependent relative clause that is verbal and that qualifies the subject of the initial clause (Yahweh).

Enjambment at the first caesura is clearly progressive, since the first colon could stand as a complete sentence in its own right, but further material is then added to it. At the second caesura, in the middle of the relative clause, the classification of enjambment is influenced by semantic as well as syntactic features (cf. 121:8; 122:5). Although the relative clause is in theory potentially syntactically complete at this point (having a subject, verb and object), it would fall short of providing any clear meaning. The addition of the final phrase completes the clause as a syntactic and semantic entity, and so the enjambment should be considered integral.

---

24. Ibid., 133–34.

25. However, in such a construction the participle does have some verbal quality. See Waltke and O'Connor, *Syntax*, 623–24.

The line has not undergone any transformations that introduce significant ambiguities. The surrounding lines of the psalm are similarly unambiguous syntactically.

Semantic Analysis

- (Someone) bless Yahweh. [Command]

- He did not give us (to someone).

- (We were) prey for them.[26]

This line opens with a phrase of imperative force, which stands as a RESULT, and follows with the commensurate reason. Superficially it appears that the following cola constitute a description of Yahweh, and relate only to the identity of Yahweh rather than the assertion that Yahweh be blessed. However, the broader context of the psalm implies that the reported action of Yahweh is the reason for the blessing.

```
┌── RESULT                          בָּרוּךְ יְהוָה
└── Reason ──┬── Phrase 1           שֶׁלֹּא נְתָנָנוּ
             └── Phrase 2           טֶרֶף לְשִׁנֵּיהֶם:
```

Psalm 125:1

Syntactic Analysis

```
        VC              VC                    CC
       /  \            /  \                 /  |  \
   V(su)  DP       V(su)  Ng          DP  (Cp)   NPsu
         /  \                        /  \          |
        N    P                     NP    P         V      A
                                  /  \           /  \
                                 N    N        DP    V(su)
                                              /  \
                                             N    P
```

לְעוֹלָם יֵשֵׁב: כְּהַר־צִיּוֹן לֹא־יִמּוֹט   הַבֹּטְחִים בַּיהוָה

---

26. Simplifying the notion of "their teeth" that stands synecdochically for "them" and highlights their potential identity as eaters of prey.

The line comprises three independent clauses, one copulative and two verbal. They are joined paratactically and any relations between them must be inferred. The two verbal clauses may reasonably be conjoined under a single node, but their relation to the copulative clause is ambiguous. They might be independent and share the same subject, although the singular verbs would then not be in agreement with the plural opening participle; more likely therefore they constitute relative clauses qualifying הַר־צִיּוֹן.[27] It is possible that the ambiguity is a deliberate device that develops the comparison made in the copulative clause. The subject noun phrase of the copulative clause is itself a verbal clause, the participle being essentially verbal in character since it focuses on the action of trusting and governs a prepositional phrase.[28]

The opening noun phrase cannot form a clause, nor would any punctuation be expected after it. The enjambment at the first caesura is therefore integral. The second caesura occurs between the two verbal clauses, each of which can stand as a complete independent sentence. However, allowing for the possibility of these clauses being read as conjoined, the enjambment here is progressive.

The line has possibly undergone a transformation that elided a relative pronoun and/or a conjunction. The resulting ambiguity creates tension and holds attention at the outset of this psalm. Note also the possibility that הַר־צִיּוֹן does double-duty as the complement of the opening nominal clause and the subject of the verbal clauses.

Semantic Analysis

- Some people trust in Yahweh.
- (Nobody/nothing) will shake those people.
- Those people will abide forever.
- (Nobody/nothing) will shake Mount Zion.
- Mount Zion will abide forever.

In this line two equivalent points of comparison are made between certain people and Mount Zion. The full diagramming of the semantic structure of the comparisons requires the propositions to be re-written

27. Hossfeld and Zenger, *Psalmen*, 487, note that both options are legitimate.
28. Waltke and O'Connor, *Syntax*, 615–16.

in the form given above. [29] However, the simplified diagram below gives a reasonable indication of the structure. The two points of comparison are not being shaken and abiding forever. The people who are the subject of the comparison are described as those who trust Yahweh.

┌─ Description	הַבֹּטְחִים בַּיהוָה
├─ HEAD & Comparison	כְּהַר־צִיּוֹן לֹא־יִמּוֹט
└─ Equivalent	לְעוֹלָם יֵשֵׁב

Psalm 125:2

Syntactic Analysis

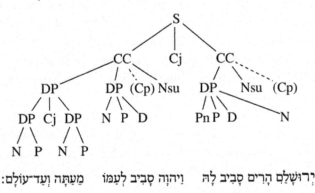

יְרוּשָׁלַ͏ִם הָרִים סָבִיב לָהּ   וַיהוָה סָבִיב לְעַמּוֹ   מֵעַתָּה וְעַד־עוֹלָם:

The line comprises two conjoined nominal clauses. The first clause opens with a nominal absolute, creating a *casus pendens* that is resumed by a pronoun at the end of the clause. This nominative absolute acts as a focus marker for the first clause, resolving any ambiguity regarding the topic of the discourse that remains from the previous line (see analysis of 125:1). The second clause includes two adverbial phrases the first of which matches that of the first clause.

At the first caesura the initial clause is complete but is supplemented by the second clause. At the second caesura, the second clause is potentially complete, but then is expanded by an additional adverbial phrase. Therefore, the enjambment in both instances is progressive.

---

29. See Larson, *Translation*, 246–49, for an explanation of the semantic structure of comparisons.

The transformation that has introduced the nominative absolute at the beginning of the line both resolves the ambiguity introduced in the previous line and sustains the attention of the reader/hearer until the *casus pendens* is resumed. However, the remainder of the line has not been complicated by any transformations and has straightforward syntax, as have the following lines.

Semantic Analysis

- Hills (are) (always) surrounding Jerusalem.
- Yahweh (is) always surrounding his people.

The structure of this line is similar to that of 125:1, but the HEAD and comparison propositions are inverted, and the comparison is made more explicit by the repetition of the adverb. The use of "hills" as the comparative image in both lines creates a semantic link between them, such that the topic of strength/stability, explicit in the first comparison (לֹא־יִמּוֹט v. 1), is also implicit in the second comparison (v. 2). The topic of permanence is explicit in both comparisons. The continuous nature of the HEAD proposition is stated using the same aphorism as 121:8.

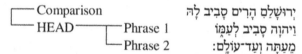

Psalm 125:5abc

Syntactic Analysis

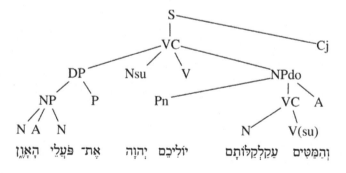

The line consists of a single verbal clause, the object of which is introduced in clause-initial position as a *casus pendens*, which is resumed by a pronominal suffix to the verb. An adverbial phrase completes the line. The initial object noun phrase is formed of a verbal clause, with the participle having an essentially verbal character (cf. 125:1).

At the first caesura, a syntactic pause is apparent that approximates to that between a subordinate clause and a following main clause. The enjambment is therefore periodic. At the second caesura the main verbal clause is potentially complete and the enjambment is progressive.

The line has undergone a word-order transformation that introduces the object of the clause as a *casus pendens*. This creates some ambiguity over the grammatical function of the phrase in the main clause and so heightens attention (cf. 125:2). The preceding lines in the psalm have not undergone any significant transformations, and so the effect in this line is an attention-grabbing close to the psalm.

Semantic Analysis

- (People) make their ways crooked.
- Yahweh leads away (people) with (other people).
- (Other people) do iniquity.

The head proposition in this line states that Yahweh leads people away. An initial proposition describes these people as those who make their ways crooked, and a following proposition describes those people with whom they will be lead away.

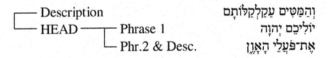

Psalm 126:1

Syntactic Analysis

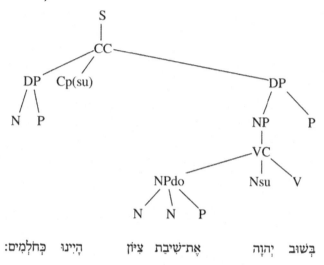

The line comprises a copulative clause modified by a circumstantial adverbial phrase. The adverbial phrase is formed around a preposition and infinitive construct in the same manner as 122:4 and 124:2, and stands in place of a subordinate clause.[30]

The initial colon cannot form a complete clause, but could potentially form a complete substitute for a subordinate clause. In actual fact the first two cola together form the circumstantial phrase without syntactic pause and so the enjambment at the first caesura is integral. However the potential of the first colon to stand alone creates the possibility of experiencing the enjambment at this point as periodic. At the second caesura, the circumstantial phrase is clearly complete, and the enjambment is periodic.

The transformation that has placed the circumstantial phrase in the clause initial position creates some tension, but not unusually so, and the overall syntax of the line is straightforward, as is that of the following lines.

---

30. Waltke and O'Connor, *Syntax*, 600.

Semantic Analysis

- Yahweh restored the fortunes of Zion.[31]

- We are (happy).

- (People) dreaming (are happy).

The topic of the comparison in this line is not manifest, and has been adduced here from the context of the following verses. The HEAD proposition may be taken simply as "We were dreamers," with the preceding cola defining the circumstance. On a wider level, this line acts as the referent for אָז in each of the following lines, and so the one circumstance is subordinate to a sequence of three HEAD propositions.

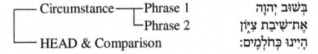

Psalm 126:2abc

Syntactic Analysis

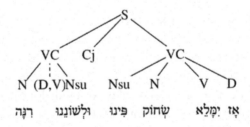

The line comprises two conjoined verbal clauses. The clauses share the same verb and adverb, which are elided from the second clause.

At the first caesura, the adverb and verb alone cannot form a meaningful clause without an identifiable subject and there is no syntactic pause after the verb, so the enjambment is integral.[32] At the second cae-

---

31. Textual variants invite alternative translations, but the role of the clause as circumstantial is not in doubt.

32. Cf. 121:8; 122:5; 124:6.

sura, a completed clause is supplemented with an additional clause, and the enjambment is progressive.

The line has not undergone any transformations that introduce significant ambiguities. The elision of verb and adverb in the second clause is a common feature of poetry and requires relatively little interpretive effort to decode.

Semantic Analysis

- Then laughter filled our mouths.
- (Then) shouts of joy (filled) our tongues.

The opening temporal particle refers to the preceding line as a circumstantial proposition (see the section "Psalm 126:1: Semantic Analysis" on p. 210). The remainder of the line consists of a HEAD proposition and an equivalent. The verb is elided from the equivalent, making it shorter.[33]

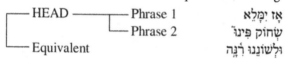

33. If translation of the text were at stake, a more careful rendering of the propositions may be required since the language is figurative. However, for the purposes of analyzing the structure of the relationships in the line, a literal rendering is sufficient.

Psalm 126:2def

Syntactic Analysis

אָז יֹאמְרוּ בַגּוֹיִם הִגְדִּיל יְהוָה לַעֲשׂוֹת עִם־אֵלֶּה׃

The line comprises a verbal clause citing direct speech. The constituent noun phrase representing the speech is itself a verbal clause with an embedded infinitival verbal clause standing in the place of a subordinate clause. The structure of the infinitive construction is similar to that discussed for 122:4 (cf. also 124:2; 126:1, 3). Its subject is not explicit but is inferred from the main clause.

The initial caesura clearly falls at a syntactic pause in the main verbal clause (the beginning of the direct speech) and the enjambment is periodic. Within the speech, the infinitive construct עֲשׂוֹת is understood as a verbal complement to the main verb הִגְדִּיל and so at the caesura the clause is incomplete and does not have a syntactic pause; the enjambment is therefore integral.

The line has not undergone any transformations that introduce significant ambiguities.

Semantic Analysis

See the section "Psalm 126:3: Semantic Analysis" on pp. 213–14.

Psalm 126:3

Syntactic Analysis

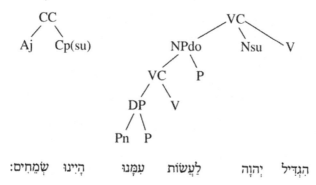

The line comprises a verbal clause that repeats as an assertion the content of the direct speech of the previous line (126:2def) and a separate copulative clause. Any conjoining of the clauses would have to be inferred. The closing participle, as the predicate of the copulative clause, is primarily adjectival (cf. 124:6).

At the first caesura the enjambment is integral, as in 126:2def. The second caesura falls between the two clauses and there is no enjambment.

The line has not undergone any transformations that introduce significant ambiguities. Following lines are similarly straightforward.

Semantic Analysis

- The nations said that,
- Yahweh did great things for these (people).
- Yahweh did great things for us.
- We (are/were) rejoicing.

The opening temporal particle, by reference to the preceding lines, can be regarded as a circumstantial proposition (see the section "Psalm 126:1: Semantic Analysis" on p. 210). The phrase that is repeated in these two lines has two different relationships to its counterparts. Firstly it is the CONTENT of speech; secondly it is the reason for the RESULT of rejoicing.

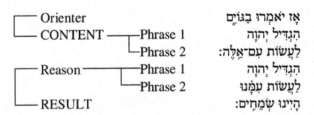

Psalm 127:2abc

Syntactic Analysis

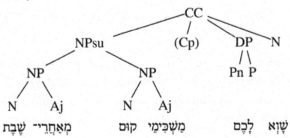

The line comprises a single nominal clause and is read, therefore, as a copulative clause with an elided copula. The subject of the clause is formed of two apposed noun phrases, each comprising a participle and an infinitive construct. The participles are substantives that function here as adjectives.[34] The infinitive constructs do not govern any other word or phrase and are construed as nouns in the manner of a gerund.[35] The word order of predicate–subject is normal for such nominal clauses of classification.[36]

At the first caesura the clause is necessarily incomplete and the enjambment is integral. At the second caesura, the clause is potentially complete but is supplemented by additional material and the enjambment is progressive.

The line has not undergone any transformations that introduce significant ambiguities. Surrounding lines are similarly straightforward.

---

34. Waltke and O'Connor, *Syntax*, 613.

35. Ibid., 600.

36. Ibid., 132.

Semantic Analysis

- It is in vain that . . .
- You rise up early.
- You go late to rest.

This line comprises two propositions concerning rising (too) early and retiring (too) late, introduced by an evaluative orienter. The two have equal prominence, and although a chronological sequence could be inferred, this is not necessarily implied. Rather the pair form a hendiadys expressing the concept "being up too long."

Psalm 127:5abc

Syntactic Analysis

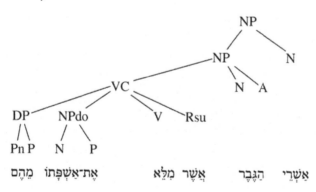

The line is a nominal exclamation, one of the constituents of which is expanded by a verbal relative clause. It adopts the common idiomatic usage of אַשְׁרֵי, "a petrified plural noun found only in construct phrases."[37]

At the first caesura the exclamation is clearly incomplete, but a syntactic pause is evident prior to the relative clause. The enjambment is therefore periodic. At the second caesura the relative clause is incom-

37. Ibid., 681.

plete and there is no syntactic pause after the verb, so the enjambment is integral.

The line has not undergone any transformations that introduce significant ambiguities. Surrounding lines are similarly straightforward.

Semantic Analysis

- (A warrior is happy.)
- (His) quiver is full (of arrows).
- A man is happy.
- He has (a "full complement") of sons.

Superficially it appears that this line simply identifies a man who is asserted to be happy. However, the broader context of the psalm implies that the description of the man's fullness is the reason for his happiness.[38] In fact, the line embodies a complex comparison between a warrior with a quiver full of arrows and a man with a "full complement" of sons. In each case the man's happiness is the result of the "fullness." In the preceding line (v. 4), a comparison is explicitly drawn between arrows and sons. In this line, the final 3m.p. pronoun must refer back to the subject of the previous line, which was "sons," and so the description of the man's "quiver" being full of them indicates that the metaphor is being continued.[39]

In order to detail the comparison in full, as attempted in the propositional presentation above, a reason and result are required on both sides. However, the line as written contains only one result and one reason, with some elements from both sides of the comparison included but everything else elided, the elided text being shown bracketed above. The simplified structure of the line is indicated below, but the full structure, based around the propositions in English, is also shown in order to indicate the structure of the comparison.

38. Cf. 124:6.

39. Delitzsch, *Commentary*, 290, simply suggests that "quiver" is a metaphor for "house"; but the point of comparison in this metaphor would not be apparent. The comparison is more complex, as detailed here.

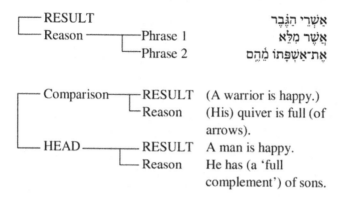

Psalm 128:4

Syntactic Analysis

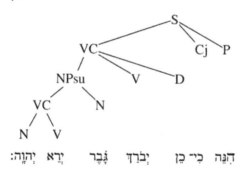

The line is a single verbal clause introduced by a presentative particle and a conjunction (cf. 121:4). Although the combination of particles is very unusual, the syntax of the line is simple. The participle has a verbal character and creates the equivalent of a dependent relative clause qualifying the subject noun of the main clause.[40]

At the first caesura there is no syntactic pause and the enjambment is integral. At the second caesura the verbal clause is potentially complete, but is supplemented by material in the following colon, and the enjambment is progressive.

The line has not undergone any transformations that introduce significant ambiguities. The surrounding lines of the psalm are similarly unambiguous syntactically.

40. Waltke and O'Connor, *Syntax*, 621.

Semantic Analysis

- (See/know that) indeed[41]

- (Someone) will bless a man in this/that way.

- The man reveres Yahweh.

This line is based around a simple proposition stating that a man will be blessed. A following proposition describes the man. An adverb alludes to the manner of the blessing, but the referent of the particle כֵן is ambiguous. It could be either the preceding or the following lines of the psalm, depending upon how the structure of the psalm is construed, and these would form manner propositions for this line's HEAD.

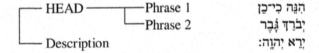

Psalm 128:5

Syntactic Analysis

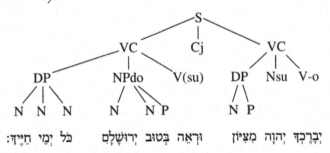

The line comprises two conjoined verbal clauses in the precative mood,[42] each incorporating an adverbial phrase.

At the first caesura the first clause is complete and the enjambment is progressive. At the second caesura the second clause is potentially

---

41. Cf. 121:4

42. Although the verb in the second clause is formally an imperative. See the discussion in the section "Psalm 128 : Colometric analysis" on pp. 134–38.

complete, although a modifying phrase is added, and the enjambment is also progressive.

The line has not undergone any transformations that introduce significant ambiguities. Surrounding lines are similarly straightforward.

Semantic Analysis

- Yahweh will bless you from Zion. [Command]

- See/enjoy goodness in/for Jerusalem. [Command]

- You will be living (many) days.

The semantic structure of this line is somewhat ambiguous, and the diagram represents but one possibility. There are clearly two distinct propositions, each having a jussive force. These are followed by an adverbial phrase, which has been construed here as a separate proposition referring to the addressee's living. There is no explicit logical connection between the first two, and they are of equal prominence, as indicated. An alternative interpretation would be to read the second proposition as an equivalent of the first, but there is not quite sufficient clear semantic overlap between the propositions to state this definitively. Similarly, the final circumstantial proposition may be part of the second HEAD proposition only; or it could relate to both HEAD propositions, contributing to a greater sense of equivalence between the two.

HEAD[1] — יְבָרֶכְךָ יְהוָה מִצִּיּוֹן
HEAD[2] — וּרְאֵה בְּטוּב יְרוּשָׁלָ͏ם
Circumstance — כֹּל יְמֵי חַיֶּיךָ:

Psalm 129:8

Syntactic Analysis

וְלֹא אָמְרוּ הָעֹבְרִים בִּרְכַּת־יְהוָה אֲלֵיכֶם בֵּרַכְנוּ אֶתְכֶם בְּשֵׁם יְהוָה׃

The line comprises two verbal clauses with no explicit connections between them. The first is conjoined to preceding material and cites direct speech that is presented as a copulative clause with elided copula. The second clause has a subject identified only by the verb inflection: 1c.p. As discussed above (in the section "Psalm 129: Colometric Analysis" on pp. 143–45), it could possibly be read as a paratactic extension of the direct speech of the first clause. The participle forming the subject of the first clause is used here as a substantive (cf. 121:4, 5).

The first caesura coincides with the introduction of speech and the enjambment is periodic. The second caesura comes between the two apparently independent clauses and there is no enjambment. If the second clause is read as an extension of the speech, then the enjambment is progressive.

The transformation that has elided the explicit identification of the subject of the final clause has introduced significant ambiguity into that clause and with it the ambiguity over the relationship between these two clauses. This is rather puzzling in that it appears to have the very opposite effect of closure but results in an open ending to the psalm.

Semantic Analysis

- People pass by.
- (People) do not say that,
- Yahweh will bless you. [Command]
- We bless you in Yahweh's name.

The semantic structure of this line is indeterminate, and the two principal alternatives have been diagrammed below. The initial colon is clearly an orienter, introducing speech that follows in the second colon. However, the relationship of the third colon is ambiguous. It appears to convey further content of speech, but has no explicit orienter. It could be a continuation of the same speech, a separate speech within the same dialogue (i.e., a response from those spoken to), or a speech with a different dialogical reference altogether. If the third colon is read as separate speech content, it is the elision of an orienter for this speech that creates the ambiguity.

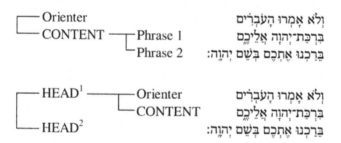

Psalm 130:5

Syntactic Analysis

The line comprises three verbal clauses, the second and third being conjoined. In the first and third clauses the subject is elided, but being 1c.s., as indicated by the verb inflection, can only be the psalmist and is therefore not ambiguous.

The first caesura occurs between clauses and there is no enjambment. The second caesura coincides with the conjunction between clauses, and the enjambment is progressive.

The line has not undergone any transformations that introduce significant ambiguities. The departure from canonical word order in the third clause requires only minimal interaction to understand. Preceding lines are similarly straightforward. See the section "Psalm 130:6: Syntactic Analysis" on pp. 223–24 for following lines.

Semantic Analysis

- I wait for Yahweh.
- I wait.[43]
- I hope in his word.

The three propositions in this line are closely related semantically. The first two are equivalents of each other. The third proposition could possibly be read as an additional HEAD that is conjoined to the others, i.e., as a proposition of equal prominence that is not logically or chronologically related to the others. However, in view of the semantic over-

---

43. Reading "my soul" as a synecdoche for "me."

lap between the verbs קוה and יחל, and matching between their objects יְהוָה and דְּבָרוֹ, the thematic unity of the line is best treated by regarding the third proposition as a specific example of the previous generic propositions.

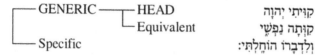

Psalm 130:6

Syntactic Analysis

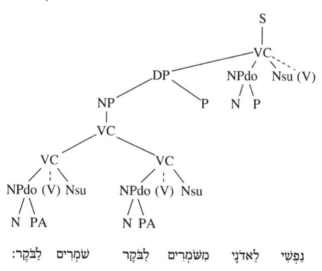

This line is syntactically complex, but can be read as a single verbal clause with an elided verb. The action described by the elided verb is modified by comparison to another verbal clause, which also has an elided verb and which is repeated. In the latter clauses, the participles are substantives (cf. 121:4, 5; 129:8).

At each caesura, the overarching verbal clause is potentially complete, and the enjambment is progressive.

The transformations that have elided the verbs in this line, presumably inviting an inference from the previous line, require a significantly greater degree of reader/listener interaction than is the case in the psalm up to this line.

Semantic Analysis

- I (wait) for the Lord.[44]
- Watchmen (wait) for morning.
- Watchmen (wait) for morning.

The lack of verbs in the three propositions of this line necessitates reference to the previous line for interpolation of an elided verb. Given the thematic unity of the preceding line, this is regarded as "wait." Thus this line makes a comparison between two descriptions of waiting, with the second description being repeated verbatim.

```
┌── HEAD                              נַפְשִׁי לַאדֹנָי
└── Comparison ──┬─HEAD              מִשֹּׁמְרִים לַבֹּקֶר
                 └─Equivalent        שֹׁמְרִים לַבֹּקֶר׃
```

Psalm 130:7

Syntactic Analysis

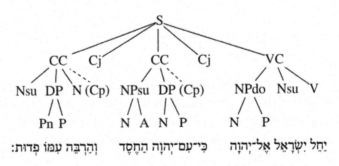

The line comprises a verbal clause in the imperative mood and two copulative clauses with elided copulae. The three clauses are conjoined. The

---

44. Reading "my soul" as a synecdoche for "me."

first conjunction implies a logical relation between clauses, the second not. In the final clause, the *hiphil* infinitive absolute of רבה is used nominally and has an accusative function as part of the clause predicate.[45]

Each caesura coincides with a conjunction between clauses and the enjambment is progressive.

The line has not undergone any transformations that introduce significant ambiguities. The constituent order in the nominal clauses is as would be expected (cf. 127:2abc).

Semantic Analysis

- Israel hopes in Yahweh. [Command]
- Yahweh has faithful love.
- Yahweh redeems in many (times/ways).

The opening proposition in this line has the illocutionary force of a command, and stands as a RESULT, with the remainder of the line giving the reason. The reason is expressed in two conjoined propositions, which are of equal prominence and sufficiently distinct not to be regarded as equivalents.

```
┌─── RESULT                              יַחֵל יִשְׂרָאֵל אֶל־יְהוָה
└─── Reason ───┬─── HEAD¹                כִּי־עִם־יְהוָה הַחֶסֶד
               └─── HEAD²                וְהַרְבֵּה עִמּוֹ פְדוּת׃
```

---

45. Waltke and O'Connor, *Syntax*, 592.

Psalm 131:2

Syntactic Analysis

This complex line comprises two distinct sentences, the structure of the second of which can be interpreted in two alternative ways. The first sentence consists of two conjoined verbal clauses. In both clauses the subject is elided, but being 1c.s., as indicated by the verb inflection, can only be the psalmist and is therefore not ambiguous. The opening particle marks the sentence as a question, rather than its more common usage as a marker of a conditional clause.[46] This particle functions in conjunction with the negative particles to create a rhetorical question with an implied positive answer. The two verbal clauses share the same subject (elided in both), the negative particle (elided in the second clause) and the same object (elided in the first clause).

46. Ibid., 316.

The second sentence has at its heart a copulative clause with a subject נַפְשִׁי, an elided copula and a complement that is a comparative adverbial phrase (כַּגָּמֻל עָלָי). The relationship between this adverbial phrase and the comparative adverbial phrase that opens the sentence is ambiguous. The first possibility illustrated above is that the two are independent and form apposed adverbial phrases that together form the complement of the clause. Such a syntactic structure would be represented in English by: "My soul (is) like a weaned child upon me (and) like a weaned child upon his mother." The second possibility is that the opening comparative adverbial clause functions in the manner of a nominative absolute, qualifying the word גָּמֻל in the following phrase and being resumed by it. In this case the preposition כְּ is also repeated in order to indicate the common reference of the two phrases. This syntactic structure is more difficult to represent in a single sentence, but could be rendered in English by: "My soul (is) like a weaned child (i.e., a weaned child upon his mother) upon me." The sentence is an example of a surface structure that could have been derived from more than one deep structure, and there can be no definitive means of resolving the inherent ambiguity.

The first caesura occurs between the two sentences and there is no enjambment. The second caesura comes at the end of the first comparative adverbial phrase of the second sentence. This phrase cannot form a complete clause, but is followed by a syntactic pause, and so the enjambment is periodic.

The transformations that have elided common elements in the two clauses of the first sentence are commonplace and require little effort to decode. However, the complexity and ambiguity of the second sentence requires a reasonable level of interaction with the text, retaining the content of the initial phrase and waiting to see how it is resumed in, and relates to, the rest of the sentence. It is the only sentence in this very short psalm that requires such interaction.

Semantic Analysis

- I have calmed myself. [Question]
- I have quieted myself. [Question]
- A weaned child (is quiet) with its mother.
- I (am quiet) with myself.

The initial colon comprises two equivalent propositions. The remaining two cola represent one proposition each that together form a comparison. There is no relationship of dependency between the initial pair of propositions and the following comparison; they are simply juxtaposed as conjoined HEAD propositions of equal prominence.

```
┌─ HEAD¹ ──── HEAD & Equiv. אִם־לֹא שִׁוִּיתִי וְדוֹמַמְתִּי נַפְשִׁי
└─ HEAD² ──┬─ Comparison              כְּגָמֻל עֲלֵי אִמּוֹ
           └─ HEAD               כַּגָּמֻל עָלַי נַפְשִׁי:
```

Psalm 133:3cde

Syntactic Analysis

כִּי שָׁם צִוָּה יְהוָה אֶת־הַבְּרָכָה   חַיִּים עַד־הָעוֹלָם:

The line is a single verbal clause introduced by a conjunction. The object of the clause is compound, with two noun phrases in apposition.

At the first caesura, the clause is potentially syntactically complete, but would be semantically very ambiguous without the subject and object of the verb being identified. The enjambment is therefore considered to be integral (cf. 121:8). At the second caesura the clause is potentially complete but is supplemented by the extra noun phrase, and so the enjambment is progressive.

The line has not undergone any transformations that introduce significant ambiguities, and therefore contrasts with the the preceding line and its ambiguous syntactic structure.

Semantic Analysis

- Yahweh ordained blessing there.
- The blessing is ongoing life.

This simple line has a HEAD proposition split into two phrases. It is followed by a description of the object of that proposition. Strictly the description embodies two state propositions.

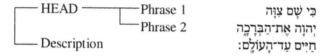

Psalm 134:1

Syntactic Analysis

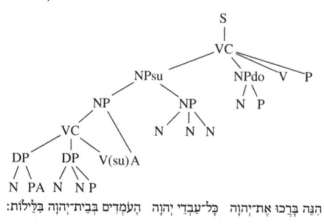

The line comprises a single verbal clause in the imperative mood, the vocative subject of which is detailed in a noun phrase and a dependent relative clause formed by a participle (cf. 128:4). An opening presentative particle stands as a marker of exclamation, reinforcing the imperative mood (cf. 121:4).

The first colon could potentially form a complete imperative verbal clause, without the explicit identification of the addressees. The following clauses add supplementary identifying material and the enjambment at each caesura is progressive.

The line has not undergone any transformations that introduce significant ambiguities. Following lines are similarly straightforward.

Semantic Analysis

- (People) bless Yahweh. [Command]
- People serve Yahweh.
- People stand in the temple at night.

In this line an imperative summons to "bless Yahweh" is repeated with two vocative descriptions of the addressees.[47] The two vocative descriptions function to highlight the status and the circumstances of the addressees respectively.

```
┌─ HEAD                              הִנֵּה בָּרֲכוּ אֶת־יְהוָה
└─ Description ─┬─ HEAD¹            כָּל־עַבְדֵי יְהוָה
               └─ HEAD²   הָעֹמְדִים בְּבֵית־יְהוָה בַּלֵּילוֹת:
```

Summary and Discussion of Syntax

Summary of Enjambment

A notional enjambment "value" has been calculated for each tripartite line by assigning values of 0, 1, 2, and 3 to the four degrees of enjambment—none, progressive, periodic and integral—respectively. The value for each line is the sum of the values of the degrees of enjambment at its two caesurae.

47. Cf. 122:5.

Summary Table of Analysis of Enjambment

	Value	None	Prog.	Per.	Int.		Value	None	Prog.	Per.	Int.
Tricola						Possible tricola					
122:4	2		✓✓			124:1	4			✓✓	
123:4	2		✓✓			124:2	4			✓✓	
125:2	2		✓✓			128:5	2		✓✓		
129:8	2	✓		✓		131:2	2	✓		✓	
130:7	2		✓✓			134:1	2		✓✓		
Average	2.0					Average	2.8				
Para-tricola						Possible para-tricola					
120:3	2		✓✓			121:5	1	✓	✓		
120:7	1	✓	✓			121:8	4		✓		✓
121:4	2		✓			122:5	4		✓		✓
124:6	4		✓		✓	125:1	4		✓		✓
125:5abc	3		✓	✓		126:1	5			✓	✓
127:2abc	4		✓		✓	126:2abc	4		✓		✓
127:5abc	5			✓	✓	126:2def	5			✓	✓
130:5	1	✓	✓			126:3	3	✓			✓
130:6	2		✓			128:4	4		✓		✓
133:3cde	4		✓	✓							
Average	2.8					Average	3.8				

Two points are of immediate interest. Firstly, the average degree of enjambment in definitively identified tricola and para-tricola is less than in the uncertain cases. This reflects the fact that the greater the degree of enjambment, the more reason there is to question the colometry that gives rise to it. Secondly, the average degree of enjambment in para-tricola (whether definite or possible) is greater than in tricola. This reflects the constriction of para-tricola to cola of two word-units each, thereby limiting the possibilities for matching clause and colon, in contrast to the greater flexibility afforded by a full tricolon.

The degree of enjambment that might be expected in a line merits further consideration. The inevitable difficulty of always matching clause and colon, and the stilted effect that would result, means that an instance of progressive or periodic enjambment is to be expected in many lines. Therefore, lines that have been analyzed as having a particularly low degree of enjambment are worthy of re-examination. Conversely, lines that have been assessed as having a particularly high degree of enjambment should rightly have their colometry reappraised in case the text has unreasonably been chopped into cola. The threshold for a noteworthy low score can be seen from the table to be anything less than two, since a score of two is evident for a significant number of lines, including definite tricola and para-tricola. A score of less than two equates to having only one instance of progressive enjambment or no enjambment at all. A questionably high degree of enjambment is not so much a matter of overall score but identifiable by the presence of any integral enjambment. This non-coincidence of rhythmical pause and syntactic pause requires careful justification, whereas the other types of enjambment may reasonably be expected to occur from time to time.

Only three lines have a notably low degree of enjambment. In 120:7 and 130:5 the line consists of three distinct clauses, two of which are conjoined. In 121:5 the line consists of two terse clauses, one of which is supplemented by an adverbial phrase. In each case, therefore, the broken, staccato rhythm of the line is inherent in its syntactic structure and the proposed colometry simply matches this.

There are twelve lines that have been assessed as having an integral enjambment, based upon the proposed colometry. Notably all of these are para-tricola, whether definite or possible, which again indicates that the greater flexibility of a full tricolon allows integral enjambment to be avoided in a way that the constriction of the para-tricolon does not. The issues lying behind the presence of integral enjambment vary from line to line and may be categorised as indicated in the following table:

Classification of Lines with Integral Enjambment

	Semantic interaction	Rhythmical interaction	Verbal idiom	Nominal clause
121:8	✓			
122:5	✓			
124:6	✓			
125:1				✓
126:1	✓	✓		
126:2abc	✓	✓		
126:2def			✓	
126:3			✓	
127:2abc				✓
127:5abc	✓	✓		
128:4		✓		
133:3cde	✓	✓		

Semantic Interaction

The integral enjambment arises in these cases where a caesura splits a verbal clause. In 126:1 the caesura follows a colon comprising a preposition, infinitive construct and noun subject. The colon potentially forms a complete adverbial phrase. In the other six instances the caesura follows an indicative finite verb, three of which are preceded by an adverb, two by the relative pronoun and one by the verb's subject noun. One of these verbs also incorporates a pronominal object suffix. In each case, from a purely syntactic view the clause is potentially complete at the caesura. However, the clause is semantically ambiguous without the addition of the following colon. In these cases, rather than reading an integral enjambment, it is more appropriate to recognise a transformation that has rendered the text into colometric form and in so doing has introduced a rhythmical pause at a point that is syntactically legitimate but which necessitates a greater level of interaction to facilitate semantic decoding. It would be apparent from a rhythmical point of view that the line could not be complete at the caesura in question, and so an engaging tension is created between the potential for syntactic completeness, suggested by the caesura, and the actual semantic incompleteness, reinforced by the anticipation of the following colon/cola. This tension forms an alternative to parallelism in binding the cola together, as explored by Dobbs-Allsopp (see the section "The Problem with 'Parallelism'" on pp. 39–42).[48]

Rhythmical Interaction

In these cases there is flexibility in the accentuation of the text. The phrases כִּי שָׁם צִוָּה יְהוָה and בְּשׁוּב, אָז יִמָּלֵא, אֲשֶׁר מָלֵא, הִנֵּה כִּי־כֵן (126:1; 126:2abc; 127:5; 128:4; 133:3cde respectively) can each carry either one stress or two, depending on how the overall structure of the line is construed. The reading of a caesura following each such phrase is contingent upon it having two stresses, so that from a rhythmical point of view a pause is tolerable. Reading the phrase with only a single stress (preceded by three unstressed syllables in each case) would create a stronger forward impetus and a following caesura would seem inappropriate. So the tension that has been created by a semantically incomplete phrase (but potentially syntactically complete in the verbal cases) is supported by an accentuation that, as it were, slows down the presentation of the clause by assigning a full stress to each word.

---

48. Dobbs-Allsopp, "Enjambing Line (Part 1)," 237–38.

Verbal Idiom

In these lines the idiom of using the infinitive construct עֲשׂוֹת as a complement to the main verb הִגְדִּיל (in 126:2def and 126:3) results in a clause that stands out as unusually long in its context. In order to achieve a reasonably consistent rhythm the clause must be split, particularly in view of its repetition in adjacent lines but in differing positions within the line. Although by reading the clause as an idiomatic whole the result of the caesura is an integral enjambment, the location of the caesura at least allows the possibility of reading the following colon as a subordinate purpose clause, in which case the degree of enjambment is reduced. Such syntactic ambiguity between verbal complements and subordinate purpose clauses is attested by Waltke and O'Connor: "The line of demarcation between the purpose infinitive clause and the complementary infinitive is somewhat blurred."[49]

Nominal Clause

It is quite striking that the only two remaining instances of integral enjambment both occur within nominal clauses. In both instances the caesura separates the subject of the clause from the predicate and so creates a rhythmic representation of the syntactic structure of the clause.

Summary and Discussion of Semantics

The following table summarises in schematic form the key relationships between the simplified propositions identified in each line. The "/" symbol indicates the caesurae in each line; "p.1" and "p.2" denote the parts of a proposition that is split between cola. Where nested relationships exist, that is two of the cola relate together to the third, those two cola have been bracketed together.

---

49. Waltke and O'Connor, *Syntax*, 607.

Summary Table of Semantic Relationships

Tricola	Possible tricola
122:4 (MEANS/Ident.&Desc.)/Purpose 123:4 (HEAD p.1/p.2)/Equivalent 125:2 Comparison/(HEAD p.1/p.2) 129:8 Orienter/(CONTENT p.1/p.2) or (Orienter/CONTENT)/HEAD 130:7 RESULT/(Reason[1]/Reason[2])	124:1 (CONTENT p.1/p.2)/Orienter 124:2 (HEAD p.1/p.2)/Circumstance 128:5 HEAD[1]/HEAD[2]/Circumstance 131:2 (HEAD&Equiv.)/(Comparison/HEAD) 134:1 HEAD/(Description[1]/Description[2])
Para-tricola	**Possible Para-tricola**
120:3 (HEAD/Equivalent)/Description 120:7 (HEAD/Amplification)/Contrast 121:4 (HEAD/Equivalent)/Description 124:6 RESULT/(Reason p.1/p.2) 125:5abc Description/HEAD/Description 127:2abc Orienter/(CONTENT[1]/CONTENT[2]) 127:5abc RESULT/(Reason p.1/p.2) 130:5 (GENERIC/Equivalent)/Specific 130:6 HEAD/(Comparison/Equiv) 133:3cde (HEAD p.1/p.2)/Description	121:5 GENERIC/Specifics & Comp./Desc. 121:8 HEAD p.1/Circum.[1] & [2]/HEAD p.2 122:5 HEAD/Description[1]/Description[2] 125:1 Description /HEAD & Comp./Equiv. 126:1 (Circumst. p.1/p.2)/HEAD & Comp. 126:2abc (HEAD p.1/p.2)/Equivalent 126:2def Orienter/(CONTENT p.1/p.2) 126:3 (Reason p.1/p.2)/RESULT 128:4 (HEAD p.1/p.2)/Description

The next table simply presents the incidence of each type of tripartite line according to the number of simplified propositions of which they consist.

Table of Incidence of Lines by Number of Simplified Propositions

	2	3	4		2	3	4
Tricola	✓✓	✓✓	✓	Possible tricola	✓✓	✓✓	✓
Para-tricola	✓✓✓	✓✓✓✓✓✓		Possible para-tricola	✓✓✓✓	✓✓✓	✓✓

The data presented in the tables do not indicate any clear distinction between tricola and para-tricola, nor any clear characteristic for all tripartite lines.

A range of semantic structures is evident. In the twenty nine lines under consideration, it is more common for two cola to relate together to the third in a nested relationship. In other words, one of the cola cannot relate to either of the other two individually but relates to them as a pair. This occurs in twenty four lines. In the other five lines, the relationships between cola are independent of each other. The reason for half of these nested relationships is the splitting of a proposition between cola. This occurs in twelve lines. The range of nested and non-nested lines, and the incidence of propositions split between cola, are not significantly different for tricola than for para-tricola.

The number of simplified propositions per line is predominantly two or three, as might be expected. A similar proportion of the para-tricola have three or more simplified propositions as do the tricola.

It is difficult to draw significant conclusions from the numbers of simplified propositions per line due to the way in which some simple syntactical constructions necessarily embody more than one proposition. As has already been highlighted, a simple comparative statement embodies two propositions, and even a single word can represent an entire proposition, e.g., the infinitives construct in 121:8. It is such features as these that tend to account for lines embodying a higher number of propositions. Whilst a higher number of propositions may be required in order to accurately model the semantic structure of the line, it does not necessarily indicate a greater conceptual complexity. Indeed, in the case of 121:8 the two infinitives construct form a hendiadys and so require two propositions in order to accurately represent a single nominal concept: "all your travelling." And in 121:5 the two statements about Yahweh—יְהוָה שֹׁמְרֶךָ and יְהוָה צִלְּךָ—are conceptually parallel, yet one uses literal language and requires only one proposition whereas the other uses metaphorical language and requires two. In light of such factors, the number of simplified propositions per line is not considered to be a characterizing factor either of tripartite lines in general or of tricola or para-tricola in particular.

It is interesting to note that the two tricola that stand out due to embodying four simplified propositions are the two lines whose colometry is most difficult to establish and which are each commonly presented as a pair of bicola. This possibly indicates a tendency to allow semantic structure to influence the assessment of colometry, whereas the foregoing discussion suggests that it is a less significant factor than rhythmical and syntactic considerations.

Very few of the tripartite lines fit a simplistic pattern of three synonymous cola. Equally, a characterization of two synonymous cola and one that adds an extra dimension is not consistently borne out by the evidence. While some lines have this type of structure, others do not. In lines where two of the cola are more closely related and the third carries a distinction, it is more commonly because the two together form a single semantic proposition that is split between cola than because of a variance in the degree of synonymy between cola. This is as much the case for full tricola as it is for para-tricola.

Therefore, the semantic analysis of tripartite lines does not indicate any consistent characterization of them nor any clear distinction between tricola and para-tricola.

5

Functions of Tricola and Para-Tricola

General

THE FOREGOING APPRAISAL OF the structure of each psalm (chapter 3 "Colometric and Structural Analysis of the Psalms of Ascents") and of the structure of each tripartite line (chapter 4 "Internal Analysis of Tricola and Para-Tricola") provides the data for an assessment of the function of each of those lines. Where the identity of a line as tripartite was only previously regarded as a possibility, this assessment will clarify whether a tripartite line-form is the appropriate reading of the line or not.

Many authors working in the field of poetic analysis have adopted a convention of denoting the structure of a line, or lines, according to the relationships between cola. For example, a tricolon may be denoted as AA'B to imply that the second colon is a restatement of the first and the third is distinct. Such characterizations of a line can be misleadingly simplistic. Relationships between cola can include semantics, syntax, word order, and other poetic features, and these distinct domains are all too readily conflated in a simplified analysis. In order to respect the multi-faceted and complex relationships between cola, as expounded in the preceding chapters, simple denotations of tripartite lines will not generally be offered. However, in some specific cases, a denotation of the semantic structure will be offered. This will follow the convention of the present study by denoting each colon by a lower-case letter, not upper-case. These denotations of semantic relationships within a line will provide a convenient reference for the aggregation of the assessment of functions of individual lines into more generalised conclusions regarding the character and function of tripartite lines, which will follow in the final chapter (chapter 6 "Conclusions").

Psalm 120

Psalm 120 contains no tricola and two para-tricola: v. 3 and v. 7. It exhibits a relatively high degree of rhythmical regularity, with two five-stress lines followed by five six-stress lines. The two para-tricola bracket the set of six-stress lines.

Verse 3 uses a tripartite line-form in order to express two synonymous phrases and supplement them with a vocative expression that relates to them both. As such it bears out the common observation (albeit of tricola, see the section "Previous Tricolon Studies" on pp. 3–8) of a third colon that adds an extra dimension to the line such that it may be characterized as having a structure aaʼb. The syntax and semantic structure of the line are both simple. The placing of the vocative phrase at the end of the line creates some tension as the identity of the addressee is delayed, thereby holding the attention of the hearer/reader. The line opens a strophe but its tripartite structure is not strongly related to a marking function in the structure of the psalm.

Verse 7 has several similar features. The syntax and semantic structure of each clause are quite simple, although the elision of verbs engages the hearer/reader. The first two phrases reinforce each other and the third provides a contrast, the contrast being all the more prominent for having followed a pair of amplifying phrases rather than just one. The structure of the line could possibly be characterized as aa$^+$a$^-$. These features are not unrelated: it is the elision of the verbs that make the phrases sufficiently short for the line to be divided into three rather than two, and therefore to emphasise the contrast. Although the line closes the psalm, it is the sense of emphatic contrast that contributes to the closure, rather than the tripartite structure of itself.[1] However, the structure does have a slight closing function in conjunction with v. 3 in that they together bracket a rhythmically coherent section of the psalm.

---

1. Krašovec, *Antithetic*, 75, notes that a single antithetic parallelism may occupy in a key position in a psalm, functioning as a summary. Wyckoff, "Closure," 107–9, notes that the closure here is also effected by the variation in syntax: noun clauses rather than verbal clauses.

Psalm 121

Psalm 121 contains no tricola and three para-tricola: v. 4 which is definitely so, v. 5 and v. 8 possibly so. In this case the para-tricola are interspersed with five-stress lines. Their distribution is such that three consecutive strophes each comprise a para-tricolon and a 3+2 bicolon. It is possible that vv. 4–5 form a seam at the centre of the psalm, whilst v. 5 and v. 8 together bracket the second half of the psalm. The lack of transition markers in this psalm means that this role of the para-tricola may be more significant.

The structure of v. 4 is very similar to that of 120:3, with two synonymous verbal phrases and then a description, here of the subject rather than the addressee. Again the delayed identification holds attention, but less so than in 120:3 since the subject of the verbs can already be inferred from vv. 2–3. The tripartite structure arises from deliberately keeping the verbal phrases terse in order to allow space within the line for the extra dimension of the epithet in the third colon. The tripartite structure of the line of itself does not have a marking function in the structure of the psalm.

Similar observations apply to v. 5, where the use of the para-tricolon is a device to accommodate text that would otherwise produce a rhythmical aberration where none is intended. The identity of the line as a para-tricolon is contingent on reading the third colon as qualifying the other two, in contrast to the common interpretation of it qualifying only the second colon. In view of the structure of similar lines, and the rhythmical regularity that results from the preceding line having this structure, it is postulated that the third colon should in fact be regarded as qualifying both the preceding phrases. The line is confirmed as a para-tricolon, but will not form the basis of a characterization of para-tricola, since this would create a circular argument.

Verse 8 varies from the para-tricola considered so far in that it consists of a single clause. Nevertheless it is still the case that the third colon adds an extra dimension to the other two, which would be syntactically and semantically complete without it. Since the final phrase expresses totality (time-wise) it strongly reinforces, both in form and content, the message of totality expressed in the merism of the middle colon. The sense of totality creates closure for the psalm, and this is reinforced therefore by the tripartite structure of the line. The senses of totality and closure would be apparent if the line were read as a bicolon, but the additional brief caesura gives a little extra focus to the middle colon and thereby also to the reinforcement of it by the closing phrase. In light of these observations, the line is confirmed as a para-tricolon, since this line-form better reflects the syntactic structure and rhetorical function of the line than would a bicolon.

Psalm 122

Psalm 122 contains one tricolon, v. 4, and one possible para-tricolon, v. 5. It is potentially significant that these occur together in the strophe at the heart of the psalm, eulogizing Jerusalem.

Verse 4 is syntactically, and consequently semantically, ambiguous. Of itself it does not exhibit any clear structure or feature that would explain its nature as a tripartite line, although the colometry and syntactic structure potentially inform each other. This could possibly be explained by textual corruption: it has been noted that the text of 11QPs[a] offers the reading most commensurate with a tricolon. When presented as a tricolon, it is apparent that the first and third cola together would form an acceptable, and contextually meaningful, bicolon. So why has the middle colon been introduced? It slows down the whole line and creates significant ambiguity. The explanation may lie in the place of the line at the heart of the psalm and the phenomenon of "paired tricola" identified by Van Grol (see the section "Previous tricolon studies" on pp. 3–8). Adoption of his schema would be based on the observation that v. 4a could just as well be read as a third colon to v. 3 as an introduction to v. 4.[2] It syntactically matches v. 3b, providing an additional marked dependent relative clause qualifying the subject from v. 3a.[3] The essential condition that "the central colon has to be in balance with the surrounding cola" is met. The suggestion is, therefore, that vv. 3–4 should be read together as a unit, with v. 4a acting as the pivot that relates to both preceding and following cola, thus binding the lines together. The subsidiary characteristic of such paired lines, that there be matching between the preceding and following cola, is not clearly met in this instance, but it is possible to infer some thematic resonance between the idea of a city

---

2. Van Grol, "Paired Tricola," 57, did not identify these lines as paired tricola, but that would have been precluded by his following the colometry of BHS, which presents v. 4 as a double bicolon.

3. Hossfeld and Zenger, *Psalmen*, 453.

being "bound together as one" and the tribes of Yah constituting Israel as a unity. Indeed, the phenomenon of "paired tricola," with two lines being tightly bound together, is probably used here as a structural form that deliberately reflects the subject matter of the text. Together with the following line, they constitute a strophe forming the "core" of the psalm.[4] Reading v. 4a as a separate pivotal colon within the "paired tricola" supports the division of the remainder of the line into two cola, not three, such that the colometry is a marker of the syntactic structure of the line.

In the light of this discussion, it seems appropriate that v. 5 should also be a tripartite line, being bound together with the paired tricola of vv. 3–4 in the core of the psalm. Since the first two cola together form a single clause, and the third colon adds an (approximately) synonymous phrase, the line might naturally be expected to take the form of a bicolon. However, the initial colon of a bicolon would stand out rhythmically as the only four-stress colon in the psalm. It may therefore be that the line is presented as tripartite in order to achieve greater rhythmical regularity and to complete the core of tripartite lines. It possibly also functions a structural marker of the end of the strophe, but this is difficult to substantiate given that the preceding line is also a tricolon. The variations possible in the stress allocation in the line means that it could reasonably be construed as a para-tricolon or a full tricolon. The evidence for any one line-form is not particularly strong, but the balance lies with a tripartite rather than bipartite form in view of its placement. The residual ambiguity, however, means that the features of this line should not inform the generalised characterization of tripartite lines.

Psalm 123

Psalm 123 contains just one tricolon, its final line, v. 4. The structure of the line is very similar to that of 122:5. The first and second cola together form a complete clause, and the third colon adds a phrase broadly synonymous to the second. A designation of the structure of the line could take the form $a^1a^2a^{2'}$. As with 122:5, the line length is just within the range of an acceptable bicolon, but in this case a bicolon would combine the second and third cola rather than the first and second. The syntactic and semantic structures of the line do not suggest any reason for its form as a tricolon. The main purpose of the line being tripartite, therefore, is

---

4. Van Grol, "Paired Tricola," 69.

to facilitate the introduction of the two synonymous phrases that are rhythmically too long to constitute a single colon. In addition, the introduction of a caesura between them adds emphasis, lending each phrase slightly greater weight. In fact this sense of emphatic recapitulation is matched by the initial colon, which re-expresses the sentiment of v. 3b. This emphasis, together with the sense of completeness expressed in the line (in terms of satiation) combine to create closure for the psalm. The fact that this is the only tripartite line in the psalm indicates a function of marking a significant juncture in the psalm structure, in this case closure.[5]

The possibility of this line and the preceding line together being "paired tricola" warrants some consideration. As with 122:3–4, the essential condition is met. Verse 4a could be read as a concluding colon to v. 3, forming a semantic parallel with v. 3b, and an emphatic repetition of the reason for the prayer for mercy in v. 3a, which itself contains an emphatic repetition.[6] However, there is little clear matching between the outer cola of the "pair," other than the repetition of the key word בּוּז. Perhaps for this reason Van Grol did not identify these lines as "paired tricola." Nevertheless, structural characteristics are apparent: the lines together form a strophe and this is the final strophe of the psalm that certainly fits his description of an "expanded conclusion." Therefore the function of the tricolon of v. 4, in providing emphasis and conclusion that together contribute to closure is enhanced by its interaction with the preceding line, and the pivotal role of v. 4a within the pair.

Psalm 124

Psalm 124 contains two possible tricola, vv. 1–2, and one para-tricolon, v. 6. The opening lines function together to form a (probable) liturgical opening to the psalm, whilst v. 6 marks a significant turning point at its centre.

A tripartite line-form for vv. 1–2 does not have a prosodic function, since the lines could equally legitimately be read as bicola. The rhythmical regularity of the following three lines has been noted, and it is possible to accent these lines in a commensurate fashion (see the section

---

5. Alter, *Book of Psalms*, 442.

6. Delitzsch, *Commentary*, 274, commented on the step-parallelism between v. 3b and v. 4a, suggesting an increasing intensity from the abstract רַב "much" to the concrete רַבַּת "a great measure."

"Psalm 124: Colometric Analysis" on pp. 102–5). Nor can any marking function of these lines within the structure of the psalm be discerned. The lines function syntactically and semantically to facilitate the liturgical recitation of the psalm and to express the circumstances with which it is concerned. This is in no way influenced by the internal division of the lines, given that their syntactic structure is respected by either a tripartite or bipartite division. The line has a transformed constituent order that engages attention and facilitates liturgical use, but this also is not related to its internal division. The principal effect of the tripartite structure is to highlight the detailed syntactic structure in the first half of the lines, where a dependent relative clause qualifies the main subject, Yahweh. Coupled with the introduction of a caesura immediately after that name, greater attention is thereby focused on Yahweh. However, within v. 2 (which is the principal line of the pair and informs the analysis of v. 1) there is a contrast expressed in two word pairs: יְהוָה and אָדָם, and לָנוּ and עָלֵינוּ. From a rhetorical point of view, therefore, a balance might be expected between the two sides of the contrast, each containing the respective members of the two word pairs, rather than splitting one side of the contrast and not the other. This reflects the semantic analysis of the line that represents it in terms of just two basic propositions. The syntactic analysis of these lines also found them to have a greater degree of enjambment, when read as tricola, than any other tricola identified in the study. Given, then, that the evidence for a tripartite structure is so slight, it is concluded that these lines cannot be relied upon to cast any light on the character and function of tripartite lines and, at least for the purposes of the present study, are best regarded as bicola.

The para-tricolon of v. 6 is a single sentence in two clauses. As with all para-tricola it could form a legitimate bicolon, but rhythmically the text divides better into three two-stress phrases. The unity of the line is assisted by the enjambment at the second caesura that indicates that the line is not complete at that point. The para-tricolon form also allows the terse exclamation בָּרוּךְ יְהוָה to assume the significance of a complete colon without creating an unbalanced line. There is no syntactic parallelism between the three phrases, but semantically the two clauses express a result and a reason. The line lies within a succession of bicola, and therefore stands out as a variation from that line-form. The structural analysis of the psalm has illustrated that the line comes at a significant juncture. The opening exclamation both marks this juncture and acts as a pivot for the whole psalm. The use of a para-tricolon therefore enhances the structural significance of the line both by the variation in line-form marking it out as in some way distinct and allowing the key expression to assume a complete colon whilst maintaining rhythmical regularity and balance. However, it is not the line-form of itself that achieves that structural marking function.

Psalm 125

Psalm 125 contains a tricolon, v. 2, and two para-tricola: v. 5 which is definitely so and v. 1 possibly so. The other lines are all 3+2 bicola.

In relation to v. 1, the difficulties of determining colometry and the ambiguities of the syntactic structure have been discussed (in the sections "Psalm 125: Colometric Analysis" on pp. 109–13 and "Psalm 125:1: Syntactic Analysis" on pp. 204–5). The effect of the ambiguous syntax is to create tension and thereby hold attention as the line progresses. Although the tripartite line-form does not map exactly onto the syntactic structure of the line, it does reflect the semantic structure with a central colon expressing the key comparison and the surrounding cola describing the subject and adding an equivalent comparison. This structure also matches the information structure of the line, with the cola corresponding to its topic and two comments respectively. In this line-form it is apparent that the line could be complete after the second colon; the addition of extra material adds complexity and richness to the image. However, since the subject of the third colon is not explicit, the line closes with some residual ambiguity, which creates a forward impetus to the next line. It is concluded that this line should indeed be read as a para-tricolon.

The opening *casus pendens* of v. 2 can be regarded as immediately resolving the ambiguity residual from v. 1. The line expresses a simple comparison in two cola and then adds to this image by means of a modifying phrase in the third colon. This final phrase both emphasises the point of the comparison and links in with the semantic field of permanence that was introduced in v. 1. Together with the repetition of הַר, this binds the first two lines together, and the reference to eternity effects the closing of the strophe. Van Grol cited 125:1–2 as an example of "paired tricola" (his only one within the Psalms of Ascents) but did not give details.[7] Whilst the two lines clearly interact, it is difficult to discern how v. 2a could act as a concluding colon to v. 1. The assertion that hills are surrounding Jerusalem has no obvious syntactic or semantic relationship to the comparison between those trusting in Yahweh and Mount Zion. The interaction between the two lines is not, therefore, based around v. 2a acting as a pivot. Rather the interaction is based on the correspondence of each line making a comparison and of the use of a repeated word and repeated semantic domain. This correspondence is reinforced by both lines having a tripartite structure. Although v. 1 is being read as a para-tricolon, rather than a full tricolon, it is close to being a tricolon and shares many of the characteristics of a tricolon. This is an illustration of the dual character of the para-tricolon, a line-form which matches bicola rhythmically but tricola colometrically. In this particular instance it is the synergy of the para-tricolon with another tricolon that comes to the fore and contributes to the correspondences that allow the two lines together to form a bound opening strophe to the psalm.[8] The simpler syntactic structure of v. 2, and its resolution of the ambiguities in v. 1, contribute to a closure of this strophe.

The para-tricolon of v. 5 is a single-clause sentence, the syntax of which is complicated by the *casus pendens* of the opening colon. Until this is resumed, the case function in the sentence of this noun phrase is not known, and this ambiguity heightens attention after the syntactically simple preceding lines.[9] In addition, the use of an alternative line-form ties in with the contrast in subject matter from the immediately preceding line. The line has three phrases and the para-tricolon line-form is used to facilitate the expression of this such that the colometry mirrors the syntactic structure. The verbal core of the clause occupies the central colon giving the line symmetry; it is flanked by descriptions of two groups of people, and semantic parallelism is apparent between these two. Although the line closes the psalm, this cannot necessarily be related to its form as a para-tricolon in itself. However, in conjunction with the tripartite opening lines, it possibly forms a line-form-based inclusio for the psalm as a whole. This reinforces the topically contrastive

7. Van Grol, "Paired Tricola," 57.

8. Cf. 122:3–5.

9. Curiously, Greenstein suggested that a syntactically simple line after a succession of complex lines generates closure, but here we find the opposite arrangement. Perhaps this is because the ambiguity is only temporary and is resolved in the second colon.

inclusio developed by the only two participles in the psalm: הַבֹּטְחִים and הַמַּטִּים at the heads of v. 1 and v. 5 respectively.

Psalm 126

The first four lines of Psalm 126, which comprise its first half, can all be read as para-tricola. As such they appear to form an integrated section with consistent line-form.

Verse 1 has a bipartite syntactic and semantic structure, but the division into three cola allows these to be rhythmically balanced. The opening circumstantial subordinate clause sets the scene for the psalm, and the introduction of a minor caesura after יְהוָה gives a slightly greater prominence to the name than it would have if it were mid-colon. This befits the principal topic of the psalm being Yahweh's salvation. There is no parallelism between the three cola, other than rhythmical, but they aggregate to express a single thought.

Verse 2abc has a similar structure to that of 122:5.[10] A complete clause is expressed in the first two cola, and the third colon adds a parallel expression for half of the clause, thereby representing a complete parallel clause but with common elements elided. The two synonymous clauses are conjoined but a bipartite line-form would be rhythmically unbalanced. Instead the para-tricolon line-form has been used with the two synonymous phrases kept equally terse in order to achieve rhythmical regularity in a similar fashion to the way a ballast variant is often used in a bipartite line in order to compensate for an elided element.[11]

Verse 2def contains the reporting of speech and its content, such that again a bipartite structure might be considered appropriate. However, this also would produce an unbalanced line, in a manner that would be exacerbated if the same pattern were followed in v. 3. The tripartite division of the text therefore allows rhythmical regularity without undue disruption of the line's syntactic or semantic structure. As in v. 1, it also introduces a minor caesura after יְהוָה, and maintains the sense of focus on the action of Yahweh. The features of v. 3 are similar. In both lines there is no synonymy or contrast between cola, nor is there any interaction between lines. Rather the para-tricolon form allows each line to

---

10. Cf. also 123:4.

11. See Watson, *Classical*, 343–48 on ballast variants.

express a narrative flow of thoughts in a rhythmically regular manner, whilst also emphasizing the name "Yahweh."

None of these lines has a function in the overall structure of the psalm that is related to its form as a tripartite line, but together they form a rhythmically coherent section that is marked out by the common line-form, which is thereby confirmed as an appropriate reading for these lines.

Psalm 127

Psalm 127 includes two lines that have been identified as para-tricola: v. 2abc and v. 5abc. All other lines in the psalm are 3+3 bicola, except the final line which is rhythmically shorter.

Verse 2abc naturally divides into three phrases that together form a single copulative clause. The second and third phrases together form a hendiadys and relate equally to the opening phrase, which is the complement of the clause.[12] The use of a tripartite structure for the line offers rhythmical balance and a match between colometry and semantic structure. As a para-tricolon the line matches the surrounding lines rhythmically, but also stands out as distinct and therefore possibly indicates a focal point for the first half of the psalm. The line opens a strophe but is not strongly marked as such, so the variant line-form possibly contributes a structural function in this instance. The shorter opening colon of a para-tricolon, compared with a 3+3 bicolon, gives the hearer/reader an early indication that the line-form is different, thereby enabling the variant line-form to act as a marker of opening. This stands in contrast to the nature of a full tricolon that, with its distinction coming at the end of the line, can mark closure but not opening.[13]

Verse 5abc expresses a single thought without any significant matching between cola. Again the principal reason for the para-tricolon line-form is to achieve rhythmical balance within the line. Equal prominence is given to the key assertion of the opening colon (cf. 124:6), to the concept of fullness by the caesura after מָלֵא and to the completion of the image by reference back to the preceding line. All three aspects of the line are important, given its complex comparative semantic structure, and a bipartite line-form would not be able to make this quite so appar-

---

12. Cf. 122:5; 126:2abc.

13. As discussed in the review of the works of Korpel and de Moor and of Van der Lugt in the section "Strophic approaches" on pp. 56–60.

ent. As with v. 2abc the line opens a strophe, but in this case the opening is more clearly marked and the use of the variant line-form follows this rather than contributing to it. However, it is also noteworthy that this line comes at the same point in the second half of the psalm as that line did in the first half, again possibly indicating a focal point. And so the two para-tricola together contribute to indicating the overall structure of the psalm.

Psalm 128

Psalm 128 contains one possible para-tricolon, v. 4, and one possible tricolon, v. 5. These follow a set of four 3+2 bicola.

Verse 4 presents a syntactically and semantically simple assertion, the text of which readily divides into three phrases. There is no synonymy or contrast between cola; they simply aggregate to express the assertion. The core of the assertion takes the central colon and is flanked by introductory particles/adverb and by a subordinate participial clause describing the subject of the main clause (cf.125:5abc). The para-tricolon line-form thereby allows symmetry and rhythmical balance that could not be achieved by a bipartite line-form. In the analysis of the structure of the psalm, it is unclear whether this line refers back to the previous lines or forward to the following. It is possible that it is deliberately ambiguous, and acts as both a focal point in the psalm and a pivot (cf. 124:6). The variation in line-form helps to mark it out as a focus, and the symmetry of the para-tricolon may reflect a pivotal function. The character of the line as a para-tricolon is therefore confirmed.

The possible tricolon of v. 5 contains two clauses that exhibit thematic synonymy and a third phrase that adds to them by qualifying them both and extending their scope. Its structure could be denoted aa'b. It is very difficult to discern a particular function for this line-form. There is no prosodic reason, since the text could just as well be expressed in bicola, as has been demonstrated (see the section "Psalm 128: Colometric Analysis" on pp. 134–38). Similarly the syntactic and semantic structures are not dependent upon the lineation. The line is not occupying a significant juncture in the psalm that requires marking. The use of the extra colon possibly functions to emphasise the timelessness of Yahweh's blessing, but this effect is diminished by the anti-climactic following line. If the two lines functioned together as "paired tricola" to form a tightly-knit conclusion to the psalm, a rhetorical function would be clearer, but this does not seem to be the case since a hypothetical tricolon 5c–6a–6b would be syntactically disjointed, with no clear coherence between cola.

The lack of a clearly identifiable function for v. 5 as a tricolon suggests that this is not an appropriate reading. The most coherent reading for the text as received appears to be as a monocolon plus bicolon; the possibility remains that the text and/or colometry of vv. 5–6 is not as originally intended.

Psalm 129

Psalm 129 consists of bicola throughout except for its closing line, the tricolon of v. 8. This line introduces speech in its first colon and includes two separate clauses of speech, the relationship between the two (*viz.* the speaker of the second clause) being ambiguous. If the speech is intended to represent dialogue between reapers and passers-by, the tricolon can be seen to have two functions. As a tripartite line it facilitates the introduction of speech and the two sides of the dialogue in a single line. Additionally, the repetition of blessing achieves a sense of emphatic closure to the psalm, given that this is its last line. If, however, the second clause of speech is read as unrelated to the first, the function is more difficult to discern. It is probably related to the liturgical use of the psalm, as indicated by its opening (cf. Ps 124, which has the same opening format, and which also closes with an aphorism not directly connected to the preceding lines). As the analysis above suggested (see the section "Psalm 129" on pp. 143–49) the ambiguity might be a deliberate device to mobilise both of these readings and consequent functions simultaneously.

Psalm 130

Psalm 130 includes two para-tricola, vv. 5–6, and one tricolon, v. 7. The other lines of the psalm are bicola, but there is no regular rhythm.

Verse 5 consists of three separate clauses and so naturally forms a tripartite line. There is strong synonymy between the three, and between the first two particularly so. The form of the line could be denoted aaʹaʺ. Either of the first two cola could have been omitted to form a legitimate 2+2 synonymous bicolon. However, an approximate repetition has been incorporated in order to lengthen the line in a manner that reflects its content: the length of waiting. Very similar considerations apply to v. 6, where it is the second and third cola that are almost identical. In this case a verb is elided from the initial colon in order create the three short cola of the para-tricolon line-form.[14] The two lines together form a strophe and the same line-form of para-tricolon has been used to contribute to the identity of this strophe as well as to interact with its content. While the surface syntactic structure of v. 5 is very simple, v. 6 has significant elision such that a greater degree of interaction is required to secure its interpretation. The colometric similarity of these lines, and variant degrees of transformation represented in their surface syntactic structures, suggest that the para-tricolon line-form is not related to any particular degree or type of transformation of surface syntactic structure.

Verse 7 also consists of three clauses, but these are longer and form a full tricolon. The line comes at a significant juncture in the psalm, but this is marked by the line's opening imperative and change of person (a rousing exhortation contrasting the repetitive self-focused meditation on waiting), not by its line-form. The semantic structure of the line follows its colometric and syntactic structure, consisting of a result and two reasons that have some synonymy and relate equally to the reason. This structure could be denoted abb'. The use of the tricolon, allowing the provision of two reasons rather then just one, is an emphatic device that reinforces the rousing impact of the line's opening imperative. The tripartite line-form also reflects the preceding lines such that the double reason for hope is a counterpoint to the pair of doubled expressions of waiting. The same hope continues to be expressed in v. 8, and the two lines can be seen to interact as "paired tricola." The final colon of v. 7 can form an introduction to v. 8, as is indeed seen in some presentations of the text that revise the colometry of MT.[15] With v. 7c acting as a pivot in this pair, some matching can be observed between the preceding and following cola: the repetition of יִשְׂרָאֵל in v. 7a and v. 8a and the contrasting pair חֶסֶד (v. 7b) and עֲוֹנֹת (v. 8b). Therefore the tricolon of v. 7 functions together with v. 8 to form an emphatic conclusion to the psalm and to provide a rhythmical line-form that supports the thematic counterpoint to the preceding lines.

14. Weber, "Anwendung an Psalm 130," 902fn, refers to the line's consequent "rhythmical parallelism."

15. E.g., Fokkelman, *Psalms in Form*, 137, who presents vv. 7–8 as a pair of bicola with the whole of v. 8 as the final colon.

Psalm 131

Psalm 131 includes a possible tricolon, v. 2. It consists of two separate sentences. The initial colon comprises a pair of verbal clauses; the other two cola from a comparative nominal clause. There is no syntactic connection between the sentences; semantically they are two of a set of four that convey the same image of quiet trust in different ways. The syntactic structure of the comparison in this line requires greater interaction to understand than do any of the other clauses in the psalm. However, this is not related to the colometry in which it is presented. Therefore there does not appear to be any feature of the internal structure of the line that explains its form as a tricolon. In the context of the structure of the psalm, it is possible that a tricolon is being used as a marker of closure, to conclude the set of four images. It cannot reasonably be interpreted as a pair with the preceding line, v. 1cd, since that line more clearly corresponds with the opening line, v. 1ab than with v. 2.

The evidence for a tricolon from a functional point of view is therefore quite weak, and it is evident that the common reading of v. 2 as a pair of bicola remains legitimate. Indeed, from a point of view of semantic structure the double-bicolon reading is supported by the observation that each of the first four lines (1ab, 1cd, 2a [as a bicolon], 2cd) would consist of a pair of propositions. The first three pairs would be equivalent and the last pair comparative, the change of semantic relationship marking the closure of the set.

There is little to choose between reading v. 2 as a tricolon and reading it as a double-bicolon. Without sufficient clear evidence for the function of a tripartite line-form, it is concluded that reading a tricolon is legitimate but cannot contribute to the basis of characterizing tricola.

Psalm 133

Psalm 133 concludes with a para-tricolon, v. 3cde. This line is a single clause, the object of which is developed by a fuller description. It could potentially be presented as a bicolon, but due to the introduction of an adverb before the verb, better rhythmical balance is achieved by reading a para-tricolon. The line does not interact with any others and there is no simple relationship between the cola in the line; although the final colon develops the preceding word that is only part of the central colon. Therefore, the line is best considered as a unity, with the tripartite structure used for purely prosodic reasons. Since all the other lines in the psalm are bicola, the variant line-form indicates a juncture in the psalm, which is in fact closure as marked by the reference to eternity. The simpler syntax of the line's surface structure, compared with the preceding lines, contributes to a closing function but this is not related to the line's tripartite structure.

Psalm 134

Psalm 134 opens with a possible tricolon, v. 1. This line contains an imperative verb phrase followed by two descriptions of those to whom it is addressed. Its structure may therefore be denoted abb'. Verse 2 consists of two imperative phrases that are broadly synonymous with v. 1a. Together these clearly form a unit, but it is not at all apparent why there is an odd number of cola. The same thoughts could just as well be expressed in four or six cola, allowing a set of bicola. Equally, in such a short psalm it is not possible to ascribe any structural function to the tricolon of v. 1. The most plausible explanation (aside from textual corruption) is that vv. 1–2 together form "paired tricola" and it is curious that Van Grol did not identify them as such.[16] The final colon of v. 1 can function as an introductory colon to v. 2, and as the longest of the five cola forms appropriately forms a pivot for the unit. Not only that, but there is strong correspondence between the outermost cola (v. 1a and v. 2b) such that the evidence here for "paired tricola" is the strongest of all the instances found in the Psalms of Ascents. Therefore the character of v. 1 as a tricolon is confirmed and vv. 1–2 act together as "paired tricola" to form the core of this psalm's summons to praise, with a separate line (v. 3) wishing a reciprocal blessing from Yahweh and closing the psalm with an aphoristic epithet.[17]

16. This may be because BHS apparently presents v. 1 as bicolon plus monocolon.
17. Cf. Pss 121, 124, 125, 128, and 131 which all conclude with an aphoristic phrase.

6

Conclusions

Summary of Basis of Study

THIS STUDY SET OUT to perform a methodologically transparent appraisal of the function of tripartite lines in Biblical Hebrew poetry. Previous studies had postulated various theories about the form or structure or function of tripartite lines, but none had been comprehensive and the results did not agree (see the section "Previous Tricolon Studies" on pp. 3–8). One of the reasons for that was the inconsistent (and often non-explicit) basis upon which the colometry and lineation of the text was determined. For the present study, a review of the principal contenders among the many theories of colometry determined that an accentual analysis is the most robust and appropriate basis for determining colometry (see the section "Theories concerning the Form of a Colon: Reviews and Summary" on pp. 37–39). The rhythmical analysis of Sievers was adopted on the basis of its thoroughness and its influence on subsequent works (see the section "Accentual Metre" on pp. 23–29). The MT was taken as the primary data (see the section "Source Manuscripts" on pp. 11–17) and its colometry determined in light of its accentuation, Sievers' rhythmical analysis, and Fokkelman's observations regarding the normal range of colon length (see the section "Other Appraches" on pp. 32–37). Studies of the typical relationships between cola in a line have also informed the process (see the section "The Nature of 'Parallelsim'" on pp. 42–44) and specific criteria have been established in order to resolve ambiguities on a consistent basis (see the sections "The Problem of Four-Word Cola" on pp. 44–46 and "Basis of Analysis: Colometry" on pp. 66–67). A preference for regularity and balance between cola (however that be assessed) was noted as a common feature of most theorists.

A careful reading of Sievers' original study has given rise to a previously little-regarded nuance in the identification of tripartite lines. The commonly designated tricolon line-form consists of three cola that are similar in length to those of a bicolon, such that a tricolon is a significantly longer line than a bicolon. But there is a distinct tripartite line-form in which the cola are shorter, having two stresses each, such that the overall line length is the same as a typical six-stress bicolon. The caesurae in this line-form are briefer such that the unity of the line is stronger and the disjunction between cola lesser, when compared to a tricolon. This distinct line-form, which is colometrically tripartite but rhythmically equivalent to a bicolon, has been dubbed a para-tricolon. Therefore, the need to respect and to investigate the implications of this difference between tricola and para-tricola has been fundamental to this study.

Having identified tripartite lines, their place and function within the structure of the psalm has been assessed. Structural analysis of psalms has distinguished between strophic structure and rhetorical structure. Strophic structure is based on prosodic concerns and textual transition markers, following the theory of Van der Lugt (see the section "Strophic Approaches" on pp. 56–60). Rhetorical structure is based on patterns of repetitions and correspondences between lexemes, following the practice of Girard (see the section "Rhetorico-Structural Approaches" on pp. 61–65). Multiple levels of structure have been found to co-exist. In addition, the syntactic and semantic structures of tripartite lines have been analyzed following principles derived from generative grammar (see the section "Syntactic and Semantic Realtionships" on pp. 46–55).

Findings of Study

In the Psalms of Ascents, a greater incidence of para-tricola has been found than of tricola. This fact highlights the need to take careful account of the differences between these two line-forms, especially by those involved in studies of colometry. Para-tricola have dual characteristics, being colometrically equivalent to tricola but rhythmically equivalent to bicola. Their context and usage highlights these dual aspects to different degrees, such that a simplistic characterization (such as Watson's "staccato tricolon") will often be misleading. The failure to distinguish carefully between these two types of tripartite line-form explains in part the inconsistent results of previous tricolon studies.

There is no simple means of characterizing tripartite lines beyond their fundamental identity as comprising three cola. Both tricola and para-tricola exhibit a range of semantic structures. Lines with three synonymous cola, lines with two synonymous cola and a distinct colon, lines with nested relationships and lines without are all attested (see the section "Summary and Discussion of Semantics" on pp. 234–37). The tricolon is just as flexible a line-form as the bicolon as far as semantic structure is concerned (in fact more so given the extra colon), and any normalizing characterization should be resisted. The same applies to para-tricola, which have the additional possibility of three phrases that together create a semantic unity with no relationships of equivalence, contrast or subordination between them at all. This possibility is not in evidence for the full tricolon.

Similarly the syntactic structures of tripartite lines vary widely. Most consist of two or three clauses, but the nature of these and their dis-position between cola does not follow a consistent pattern. Para-tricola present the additional possibility of a single clause split between its three short cola. The degree of enjambment in a tricolon is consistently found to be low, the flexibility of the greater line length allowing good match-ing between clause structure and colometry. By contrast the relative inflexibility of the para-tricolon often results in a greater degree of en-jambment. Where this is particularly apparent, an interaction is evident between syntax, semantic structure, and accentuation of the line, such that the reader/hearer is drawn in to experiencing the line as a semantic and syntactic unity but with rhythmical balance and regularity (see the section "Summary and Discussion of Syntax" on pp. 230–34). This re-flects the finding of Dobbs-Allsopp that one of the most obvious effects of enjambment is to provide a sense of forward movement, thus binding together enjambed cola and acting as an alternative to parallelism.[1]

No general evidence has been found of tripartite structure being related to an unusual degree of transformation of the surface syntactic structure of a line. Most tripartite lines found have a simple syntactic structure that in some cases offers a contrast to preceding lines and con-tributes to closure (125:2; 130:7; 133:3cde). In some lines a more com-

1. Dobbs-Allsopp, "Enjambing Line (Part 2)," 371.

plex surface structure is used in order to engage attention, but this is not necessarily related to a tripartite line-form (125:1; 125:5abc; 130:6).

The functions of tricola vary and incorporate rhetorical and structural aspects. By means of their internal syntactic and semantic structures, they can express emphasis (123:4) and climax (130:7). By means of their greater length (compared with bicola) they can mark closure (123:4), sometimes in conjunction with their semantic content (125:2). However, they have not been found to mark opening,[2] and it is postulated in this study that they cannot. In one instance the length of a tricolon and lack of marking of its internal structure has possibly been used as a device to allow ambiguous voicing that relates to its liturgical use (129:8). Tricola can also have a structural marking function by matching or interacting with other tripartite lines (130:7). The interaction of lines takes on a particular form in the incidence of "paired tricola" as identified by Van Grol. Here a tricolon coheres with a bicolon in an integrated unit that forms a reinforced opening (134:1–2), core (122:3–4), or conclusion (130:7–8) to a psalm. This phenomenon is particular to full tricola and could not be achieved by a para-tricolon.

The functions of para-tricola also vary, but less so than those of tricola. The predominant purpose of a para-tricolon is to present text in a rhythmically regular manner, with balanced cola, where this would not be possible in a bicolon (e.g., 121:4, 5). Its use sometimes represents an alternative to the technique of using a ballast variant in the second half of a bicolon. The colometry of a para-tricolon sometimes exactly matches its syntactic structure (120:7; 130:5), sometimes its semantic structure (127:2abc), but often neither. The internal structure of the line and the relationships between its cola are rarely of significance, although the tripartite form can be used, for example, to heighten a contrast (120:7). Much more commonly the para-tricolon does not perform a function of itself, but the variation in line-form from bicola supports and assists in locating a function that is achieved by other means. That function could be rhetorical (e.g., contrast [125:5abc] or focus [127:5abc]) or structural (e.g., pivot [124:6; 128:4] or closure [121:8; 133:3cde]). Similarly, a psalm structure may be indicated in part by a distribution of para-tricola within it (126:1–3; 130:5–6), but a single para-tricolon generally does not act alone in marking a structural juncture in the way that tricolon can. A possible exception to this general rule is the para-tricolon as a marker

2. I.e., a new section (strophe or stanza) within the body of a psalm.

of opening (127:2abc, 5abc) but the evidence for this is slight. As well as interacting with other para-tricola, a para-tricolon can also cohere with or match a tricolon as an indicator of structure (125:1 and possibly 122:5). In doing so the tripartite aspect of its character is emphasised, whereas more commonly it is the rhythmical equivalence to a bicolon that takes precedence.

Scope for Further Study

The study has been based on a limited corpus (the Psalms of Ascents) and further study is required to substantiate the current conclusions, which must be considered provisional. An extension of the study to cover the entire Psalter could be followed by study of Biblical Hebrew poetry outside the book of Psalms.

An ongoing re-appraisal of the criteria used to determine colometry will need to proceed alongside the analysis. The study of poetic texts that are more diverse in their style, for example in their line lengths and structures, will provide a broader grounding for general conclusions regarding the functions of tripartite lines, and should further confirm the crucial distinctions between tricola and para-tricola.

The conclusions arrived at in this study are dependent upon the particular theories of poetic structure that were selected and the way in which these were applied to the sample texts. The application of theory has been as consistent and explicit as possible and others may wish to re-appraise the content and conclusions of the study by varying its analytic framework. Would, for example, the proponents of syllabic metre find similar results? But for those who persist along the accentual approach so ably charted by Sievers, the nuanced appreciation of tripartite lines, distinguishing tricola and para-tricola, merits careful attention.

Glossary

Anapaest   In Classical metrical verse, a *foot* comprising two short syllables and one long syllable. In general verse, two unstressed syllables followed by a stressed syllable.

Bicolon   A *line* of poetry consisting of two *cola*.

Colometry   The division of a poetic text into cola; also known as stichometry.

Colon   (plural *cola*) The basic unit of Hebrew poetry, typically a phrase of three words; also known as stich, hemistich, verset (Alter), line (Watson, Weiser, Sievers).

Foot   The basic division of metrical verse, having a fixed length defined as certain number(s) and type(s) of syllables; usually a single word or part of a word, occasionally two parts of adjacent words.

Iamb(us)   In Classical metrical verse, a *foot* comprising one short syllable and one long syllable. In general verse, an unstressed syllable followed by a stressed syllable.

Line   A set of *cola* (most commonly two), or a single *colon*, usually making up a semantically coherent unity; also known as verse, strophe (Watson), period (Sievers).

Metre   The regular and predictable pattern of sound in a poetic text: in Classical metrical verse, the regular variation of short and long syllables according to a prescribed pattern; alternatively, the regular variation of stressed and unstressed syllables or the overall distribution of syllables between lines or cola.

259

Monocolon	A *line* of poetry consisting of one *colon*.
Page-line	A line of a manuscript; the physical space occupied by text, irrespective of any poetic division.
Rhythm	The descriptive characteristic of a poetic text in terms of the pattern of recurrence of stressed syllables.
Stanza	In a longer poem, a group of two or three *strophes* marking out a major division within the structure of the poem; also known as canto, canticle.
Strophe	A group of two or three *lines* constituting a section of a poem; also known as stanza.
Tricolon	A *line* of poetry consisting of three *cola*.
Verse	This term is reserved to refer to the versification of the MT. It has no direct relevance to considerations of poetic structure. A verse commonly consists of a single *line* of poetry, but this need not necessarily be the case.

Bibliography

Alden, R. L. "Chiastic Psalms: A Study in the Mechanics of Semitic Poetry in Psalms 1–50." *JETS* 17 (1974) 11–28.

———. "Chiastic Psalms (III): A Study in the Mechanics of Semitic Poetry in Psalms 101–150." *JETS* 21 (1978) 199–210.

Alonso-Schökel, L. *A Manual of Hebrew Poetics*. Rome: Editrice Pontificio Istituto Biblico, 1988.

Allen, L. C. *Psalms 101–50*. WBC21. Rev. ed. Dallas: Word, 2002.

Alter, R. *The Art of Biblical Poetry*. Edinburgh: T. & T. Clark, 1985.

———. *The Book of Psalms: A Translation with Commentary*. London: Norton, 2007.

Anderson, A. A. *The Book of Psalms: Volume 2, Psalms 73–150*. NCB. London: Oliphants, 1972.

Auffret, P. *Là Montent les Tribus: Etude Structurelle de la Collection des Psaumes des Montées, d'Ex 15, 1–18 et des Rapports entre Eux*. BZAW 289. Berlin: de Gruyter, 1999.

Barker, D. G. "Voices for the Pilgrimage: A Study in the Psalms of Ascent." *ET* 116 (2005) 109–16.

Barthélemy, D. *Critique Textuelle de l'Ancien Testament: Tome 4. Psaumes*. OBO 50/4. Fribourg: Academic Press, 2005.

Beaucamp, E. *Le Psautier: Ps 73–150*. Paris: Gabalda, 1979.

Beekman, J. and J. Callow. *Translating the Word of God: With Scripture and Topical Indexes*. Grand Rapids: Zondervan, 1974.

Berlin, A. *The Dynamics of Biblical Parallelism*. Revised and expanded ed. Grand Rapids: Eerdmans, 2008.

———. "On the Interpretation of Psalm 133." In *Directions in Biblical Hebrew Poetry*, JSOTSup 40, edited by E. R. Follis, 141–48. Sheffield, UK: JSOT, 1987.

Beyerlin, W. *We are like Dreamers: Studies in Psalm 126*. Translated by D. Livingstone. Edinburgh: T. & T. Clark, 1982.

———. *Wider die Hybris des Geistes: Studien zum 131. Psalm*. SBS 108. Stuttgart: Katholisches Bibelwerk, 1982.

Boys, T. *A Key to the Book of Psalms*. London: Seeley, 1825.

Booij, Th. "Psalm 127, 2b: A Return to Martin Luther." *Bib* 81 (2000) 262–68.

———. "Psalm 133: 'Behold, How Good and Pleasant.'" *Bib* 83 (2002) 258–67.

———. "Psalm CXXII 4: Text and Meaning." *VT* 51 (2001) 262–66.

Bovon, F. "French Structuralism and Biblical Exegesis." In *Structural Analysis and Biblical Exegesis: Interpretational Essays*, PTMS 3, translated by A. M. Johnson Jr., 4–20. Pittsburgh, PA: Pickwick, 1974.

Braslavi, J. "'Like the dew of Hermon, that cometh down upon the mountains of Zion' (Psalm 133:3)." *Beth Mikra* 49 (1972) 143–45.

Briggs, C. A., and E. G. Briggs. *A Critical and Exegetical Commentary on the Book of Psalms, Vol. II.* ICC. Edinburgh: T. & T. Clark, 1907.

Ceresko, A. R. "The Function of Chiasmus in Hebrew Poetry." *CBQ* 40 (1978) 1–10.

———. "Psalm 121: A Prayer of a Warrior?" *Bib* 70 (1989) 496–510.

Childs, B. S. *Introduction to the Old Testament as Scripture.* London: SCM, 1979.

Chomsky, N. *Syntactic Structures.* The Hague: Mouton, 1957.

———. *Topics in the Theory of Generative Grammar.* The Hague: Mouton, 1966).

Christiansen, D. "Logoprosodic Analysis of the Hebrew Scriptures." 2002. No pages. Online: http://www.bibal.net/04/proso/proso.html.

Clines, D. J. A. "The Parallelism of Greater Precision: Notes from Isaiah 40 for a Theory of Hebrew Poetry." In *Directions in Biblical Hebrew Poetry,* JSOTSup 40, edited by E. R. Follis, 77–100. Sheffield, UK: JSOT, 1987.

Cloete, W. T. W. "The Colometry of Hebrew Verse." *JNSL* 15 (1989) 15–29.

———. *Versification and Syntax in Jeremiah 2–25: Syntactical Constraints in Hebrew Colometry.* SBLDS 117. Atlanta: Scholars, 1989.

Cobb, W. H. *A Criticism of Systems of Hebrew Metre: An Elementary Treatise.* Oxford: Clarendon, 1905.

Cody, A. "Psalm 120 (119), 7." In *Ein Gott, Eine Offenbarung: Beiträge zur Biblischen Exegese, Theologie und Spiritualität. Festschrift für Notker Füglister OSB zum 60. Geburtstag,* edited by F. V. Reiterer, 51–64. Würzburg, Germany: Echter, 1991.

Collins, T. *Line-Forms in Hebrew Poetry: A Grammatical Approach to the Stylistic Study of the Hebrew Prophets.* Rome: Biblical Institute, 1978.

Creach, J. F. D. "Psalm 121." *Int* 50 (1996) 47–51.

Crow, L. D. *The Songs of Ascents (Psalms 120–134): Their Place in Israelite History and Religion.* SBLDS 148. Atlanta: Scholars, 1996.

Culler, J. *Structuralist Poetics: Structuralism, Linguistics and the Study of Literature.* London: Routledge, 1975.

Culley, R. C. "Metrical Analysis of Classical Hebrew Poetry." In *Essays on the Ancient Semitic World,* edited by J. M. Wevers and D. B. Redford, 12–28. Toronto: Toronto University Press, 1970.

Dahood, M. "A New Metrical Pattern in Biblical Poetry." *CBQ* 29 (1967) 574–79.

———. *Psalms III: 101–150.* AB 17A. Garden City, NY: Doubleday, 1970.

Delitzsch, F. *Biblical Commentary on the Psalms: Vol. 3.* Translated by D. Eaton. London: Hodder & Stoughton, 1889.

De Hoop, R. "The Colometry of Hebrew Verse and the Masoretic Accents: Evaluation of a Recent Approach. (Part 1)." *JNSL* 26.1 (2000) 47–73.

Deurloo, K. "Gedächtnis des Exils. (Psalm 120–134)." *CV* 34 (1992) 5–14.

Dobbs-Allsopp, F. W. "The Enjambing Line in Lamentations: A Taxonomy. (Part 1)" *ZAW* 113 (2001) 219–39.

———. "The Enjambing Line in Lamentations: A Taxonomy. (Part 2)" *ZAW* 113 (2001) 370–85.

Donner, H. "Psalm 122." In *Text and Context: Old Testament and Semitic Studies for F. C. Fensham,* JSOTSup 48, edited by W. Claassen, 81–91. Sheffield, UK: JSOT, 1988.

Doyle, B. "Metaphora Interrupta: Psalm 133." *ETL* 77 (2001) 5–22.

Eissfeldt, O. "Psalm 121." In *Stat Crux Dum Volvitur Orbis: eine Festschrift für Landesbischof D. Hanns Lilje Abt zu Loccum zum sechzigsten Geburtstag am 20. August 1959,* edited by G. Hoffman and K. H. Rengstorf, 9–14. Berlin: Lutherisches, 1959.

Estes, D. J. "Like Arrows in the Hand of a Warrior. (Psalm CXXVII)" *VT* 41 (1991) 304–11.

Fleming, D. E. "Psalm 127: Sleep for the Fearful, and Security in Sons." *ZAW* 107 (1995) 435–44.

Flint, P. W. *The Dead Sea Scrolls and the Book of Psalms.* STDJ 17. Leiden: Brill, 1997.

———. "Variant Readings of the Dead Sea Psalms Scrolls against the MT and the Septuagint Psalter." In *Der Septuaginta-Psalter und seine Tochterübersetzungen: Symposium in Göttingen 1997,* edited by A. Aejmelaeus and U. Quast, 337–65. Göttingen: Vandenhoech and Ruprecht, 2000.

Fohrer, G. "Über den Kurzvers." *ZAW* 25 (1954) 199–236.

Fokkelman, J. P. *Major Poems of the Hebrew Bible: At the Interface of Hermeneutics and Structural Analysis. Vol. I: Ex.15, Deut.32 and Job 3.* Assen: Van Gorcum, 1998.

———. *Major Poems of the Hebrew Bible: At the Interface of Hermeneutics and Structural Analysis. Vol. II: 85 Psalms and Job 4–14.* Assen: Van Gorcum, 2000.

———. *Major Poems of the Hebrew Bible: At the Interface of Hermeneutics and Structural Analysis. Vol. III: The Remaining 65 Psalms.* Assen: Van Gorcum, 2003.

———. *The Psalms in Form: The Hebrew Psalter in its Poetic Shape.* Leiden: Deo, 2002.

———. *Reading Biblical Poetry: An introductory guide.* London: Westminster John Knox, 2001.

Follingstad, C. M. "*Hinnēh* and Focus Function with Application to Tyap." *JTT* 7.3 (1995) 1–24.

Freedman, D. N. "Another Look at Biblical Hebrew Poetry." In *Directions in Biblical Hebrew Poetry,* JSOTSup 40, edited by E. R. Follis, 11–28. Sheffield, UK: JSOT, 1987.

———. *Pottery, Poetry and Prophecy: Studies in Early Hebrew Poetry.* Winona Lake, IN: Eisenbrauns, 1980.

Gerstenberger, E. S. *Psalms, Part 2, and Lamentations.* FOTL XV. Grand Rapids: Eerdmans, 2001.

Gillingham, S. E. *The Poems and Psalms of the Hebrew Bible.* Oxford: Oxford University Press, 1994.

Girard, M. *Les Psaumes: Analyse Structurelle et Interprétation.* Recherches nouvelle série-2. Montréal: Bellarmin, 1984.

———. *Les Psaumes Redécouverts: De la Structure au Sens. Vol. 1:1–50.* 2nd ed. Québec: Bellarmin, 1996.

———. *Les Psaumes Redécouverts: De la Structure au Sens. Vol. 3:101–150.* Québec: Bellarmin, 1994.

Goldingay, J. *Psalms Volume 3: Psalms 90–150.* BCOT Wisdom and Psalms. Grand Rapids: Baker Academic, 2008.

Goulder, M. D. *The Psalms of the Return (Book V, Psalms 107–150): Studies in the Psalter, IV.* JSOTSup 258. Sheffield, UK: Sheffield Academic, 1998.

Gray, G. B. *The Forms of Hebrew Poetry.* Jersey City, NJ: Ktav, 1972.

Greenstein, E. L. "How Does Parallelism Mean?" In *A Sense of Text: The Art of Language in the Study of Biblical Literature,* JQRSup, 41–70. Winona Lake, IN: Eisenbrauns, 1983.

Grinder, J. T., and S. H. Elgin. *Guide to Transformational Grammar: History, Theory, Practice.* New York: Holt, Rinehart, and Winston, 1973.

Grossberg, D. *Centripetal and Centrifugal Structures in Biblical Poetry.* SBLMS 39. Atlanta: Scholars, 1989.

Gunkel, H. *The Psalms: A Form-Critical Introduction.* Translated by T. M. Horner. 1930. Philadelphia: Fortress, 1967.

Gunkel, H., and J. Begrich. *Introduction to Psalms: The Genres of the Religious Lyric of Israel.* Translated by J. D. Nogalski. 1933. Reprint. Macon, GA: Mercer University Press, 1998.

Hermann, W. "Psalm 129." In *Von Gott Reden: Beiträge zur Theologie und Exegese des Alten Testaments. Festschrift für Siegfried Wagner zum 65. Geburtstag,* edited by D. Vieweger and E.-J. Waschke, 123–32. Neukirchen-Vluyn: Neukirchener, 1995.

Hobbins, J. F. "Annotated Bibliography." 2007. No pages. Online: http://ancient hebrewpoetry.typepad.com/ancienthebrewpoetry/files/annotatedbibliography .pdf.

———. "Meter in Ancient Hebrew Poetry: A History of Modern Research." 2005. No pages. Online: http://ancienthebrewpoetry.typepad.com/ancienthebrewpoetry/ files/meterinancienthebrewpoetryahistoryofmodernresearch.pdf.

———. "Regularities in Ancient Hebrew Verse: A New Model." *ZAW* 119 (2007) 564–85.

Holladay, W. L. "Hebrew Verse Structure Revisited (I): Which Words "Count?" *JBL* 118 (1999) 19–32.

———. "Hebrew Verse Structure Revisited (II): Conjoint Cola and Further Suggestions." *JBL* 118 (1999) 401–16.

Hossfeld, F-L., and E. Zenger. *Psalmen 101–150.* HThKAT. Freiburg: Herder, 2008.

Hunter, A. G. *Psalms.* London: Routledge, 1999.

Jacobson, R. A. *'Many are Saying': The Function of Direct Discourse in the Hebrew Psalter.* JSOTSup 397. London: T. & T. Clark, 2004.

Jacquet, L. *Les Psaumes et le Cœur de l'Homme: Etude Textuelle, Littéraire et Doctrinale; Psaumes 101–150.* Gembloux: Duculot, 1979.

Jobes, K. H., and M. Silva. *Invitation to the Septuagint.* Grand Rapids: Baker Academic, 2000.

Kaddari, M. Z. "A Semantic Approach to Biblical Parallelism." *JJS* 24 (1973) 167–75.

Keel, O. "Psalm 127: Ein Lobpreis auf Den, der Schlaf und Kinder Gibt." In *Ein Gott, Eine Offenbarung: Beiträge zur Biblischen Exegese, Theologie und Spiritualität. Festschrift für Notker Füglister OSB zum 60. Geburtstag,* edited by F. V. Reiterer, 155–64. Würzburg, Germany: Echter, 1991.

Keet, C. C. *A Study of the Psalms of Ascents: A Critical and Exegetical Commentary upon Psalms CXX–CXXXIV.* London: Mitre, 1969.

Kirk, G. S. "Studies in some Technical Aspects of Homeric Style: II. Verse-Structure and Sentence-Structure in Homer." In *Homeric Studies,* YCS 20, edited by G. S. Kirk and A. Parry, 105–52. New Haven, CT: Yale University Press, 1966.

Kissane, E. J. *The Book of Psalms: Translated from a Critically Revised Hebrew Text.* Dublin: Richview, 1964.

Knowles, M. D. "A Woman at Prayer: A Critical Note on Psalm 131:2b." *JBL* 125 (2006) 385–89.

Korpel, M. C. A., and J. C. de Moor. "Fundamentals of Ugaritic and Hebrew Poetry." In *The Structural Analysis of Biblical and Canaanite Poetry,* JSOTSup 74, edited by W. Van der Meer and J. C. de Moor, 1–61. Sheffield, UK: Sheffield Academic, 1988.

Kosmala, H. "Form and Structure in Ancient Hebrew Poetry." *VT* 14 (1964) 423–45.

———. "Form and Structure in Ancient Hebrew Poetry (continued)." *VT* 14 (1966) 152–80.

Kraft, C. F. "Some Further Observations concerning the Strophic Structure of Hebrew Poetry." In *A Stubborn Faith: Papers on Old Testament and Related Subjects*

Presented to Honor William Andrew Irwin, edited by E. C. Hobbs, 62–89. Dallas: Southern Methodist University Press, 1956.

Krašovec, J. *Antithetic Structure in Biblical Hebrew Poetry.* VTSup 35. Leiden: Brill, 1984.

Kraus, H.-J. *Psalms 1–59: A Continental Commentary.* Translated by H. C. Oswald. Minneapolis: Fortress, 1993.

———. *Psalms 60–150: A Continental Commentary.* Translated by H. C. Oswald. Minneapolis: Fortress, 1993.

———. *Theology of the Psalms* Minneapolis: Fortress, 1992.

Kugel, J. L. *The Idea of Biblical Poetry: Parallelism and its History.* Baltimore: John Hopkins University Press, 1981.

Labuschagne, C. "General Introduction to Logotechnical Analysis." 2006. Online: http://www.labuschagne.nl/aspects.pdf.

———. "Significant Compositional Techniques in the Psalms: Evidence for the Use of Number as an Organizing Principle." *VT* 59 (2009) 583–605.

Lake, K., and H. Lake. *Codex Sinaiticus: The Old Testament.* Oxford: Clarendon, 1922.

Lambrecht, K. *Information Structure and Sentence Form: Topic, Focus and the Mental Representations of Discourse Referents.* Cambridge: Cambridge University Press, 1994.

Larson, M. L. *Meaning-Based Translation: A Guide to Cross-language Equivalence.* Lanham, MD; University Press of America, 1984.

Leatherman, D. W. "An Analysis of Four Current Theories of Hebrew Verse Structure." PhD diss., McGill University, Montreal, 1998.

Levine, N. "Vertical Poetics: Interlinear Phonological Parallelism in Psalms." *JNSL* 29 (2003) 65–82.

Loretz, O. *Psalmstudien: Kolometrie, Strophik und Theologie ausgewählter Psalmen.* BZAW 309. Berlin: de Gruyter, 2002.

Loretz, O., and I. Kottsieper, I. *Colometry in Ugaritic and Biblical Poetry: Introduction, Illustrations and Topical Bibliography.* Altenberge, Germany: CIS, 1987.

Lowth, R. *Lectures on the Sacred Poetry of the Hebrews.* London: Tegg, 1839.

Lund, N. W. *Chiasmus in the New Testament: A Study in Formgeschichte.* Chapel Hill, NC: University of North Carolina Press, 1942.

———. "Chiasmus in the Psalms." *AJSL* 49 (1933) 281–312.

Lunn, N. P. "The Last Words of Jacob and Joseph: A Rhetorico-Structural Analysis of Genesis 49:29–33 and 50:24–26." *Tyndale Bulletin* 59.2 (2008) 161–79.

———. *Word-Order Variation in Biblical Hebrew Poetry: Differentiating Pragmatics and Poetics.* Milton Keynes, UK: Paternoster, 2006.

Mandolfo, C. *God in the Dock: Dialogic Tension in the Psalms of Lament.* JSOTSup 357. Sheffield, UK: Sheffield Academic, 2002.

Mannati, M. "Les Psaumes Graduels constituent-ils un Genre Littéraire Distinct à[set grave over a] l'Intérieur du Psautier Biblique?" *Sem* 29 (1979) 85–100.

Maré, L. P. "Some Remarks on Yahweh's Protection against Mythological Powers in Psalm 121." In *Psalms and Mythology*, edited by D. J. Human, 170–80. London: T. & T. Clark, 2007.

Marrs, R. R. "A Cry from the Depths. (Ps 130)" *ZAW* 100 (1988) 81–90.

———. "Psalm 122, 3.4: A New Reading." *Bib* 68 (1987) 106–93.

Meynet, R. *Rhetorical Analysis: An Introduction to Biblical Rhetoric.* JSOTSup 256. Sheffield, UK: Sheffield Academic, 1998.

Miller, C. L. "A Linguistic Approach to Ellipsis in Biblical Poetry: (Or, What to Do When Exegesis of What is There Depends on What Isn't)." *BBR* 13 (2003) 251–70.

———. "The Relation of Coordination to Verb Gapping in Biblical Poetry." *JSOT* 32 (2007) 41–60.

Miller, P. D. "Psalm 127—The House that Yahweh Builds." *JSOT* 7.22 (1982) 119–32.

———. "Synonymous-Sequential Parallelism in the Psalms." *Bib* 61 (1980) 256–60.

Mowinckel, S. *The Psalms in Israel's Worship: Vol. II.* Translated by D. R. Ap-Thomas. Oxford: Blackwell, 1962.

———. *Real and Apparent Tricola in Hebrew Psalm Poetry.* Avhandlinger utgitt av Det Norske Videnskaps-Akademi i Oslo II. Historisk-Filosofisk Klasse 1957 No. 2. Oslo: Aschehoug, 1957.

Norton, G. J. "A Diplomatic Edition of the Psalter?" In *Sôfer Mahîr: Essays in Honour of Adrian Schenker Offered by the Editors of Biblia Hebraica Quinta*, VTSup 110, edited by Y. A. P. Goldman et al., 193–205. Leiden: Brill, 2006.

O'Connor, M. *Hebrew Verse Structure.* Winona Lake, IN: Eisenbrauns, 1980.

Petersen, D. L., and K. H. Richards. *Interpreting Hebrew Poetry.* Minneapolis: Fortress, 1992.

Pietersma, A. "The Present State of the Critical Text of the Greek Psalter." In *Der Septuaginta-Psalter und seine Tochterübersetzungen: Symposium in Göttingen 1997*, edited by A. Aejmelaeus and U. Quast, 12–32. Göttingen: Vandenhoech and Ruprecht, 2000.

Porúbčan, Š. "Psalm CXXX 5–6." *VT* 9 (1959) 322–23.

Price, J. D. *A Theory for Bible Translation: An Optimal Equivalence Model.* Lewiston, NY: Mellen, 2007.

Prinsloo, G. T. M. "Analysing Old Testament Poetry: An Experiment in Methodology with Reference to Psalm 126." *OTE* 5 (1992) 225–51.

———. "Historical Reality and Mythological Metaphor in Psalm 124." In *Psalms and Mythology*, edited by D. J. Human, 181–203. London: T. & T. Clark, 2007.

———. "Psalm 130: Poetic Patterns and Social Significance." *OTE* 15 (2002) 453–69.

———. "The Role of Space in the שירי המעלות (Psalms 120–134)." *Bib* 86 (2005) 457–77.

Quell, V. G. "Struktur und Sinn des Psalms 131." In *Das Ferne und Nahe Wort: Festschrift Leonhard Rost zur Vollendung seines 70. Lebensjahres*, BZAW 105, edited by F. Maass, 173–85. Berlin: de Gruyter, 1967.

Raabe, P. R. "Deliberate Ambiguity in the Psalter." *JBL* 110 (1991) 213–27.

———. *Psalm Structures: A Study of Psalms with Refrains.* JSOTSup 104. Sheffield, UK: Sheffield Academic, 1990.

Revell, E. J. "The Accents: Hierarchy and Meaning." In *Method in Unit Delimitation*, Pericope 6, edited by M. C. A. Korpel et al., 61–91. Leiden: Brill, 2007.

———. *Biblical Text with Palestinian Pointing and Their Accents.* SBLMasS 4. Missoula, MT: Scholars, 1977.

———. "Pausal Forms and the Structure of Biblical Poetry." *VT* 31 (1981) 186–99.

———. "Pausal Forms in Biblical Hebrew: Their Function, Origin and Significance." *JSS* 25 (1980) 165–79.

Richter, H-F. "Von den Bergen kommt keine Hilfe. Zu Psalm 121." *ZAW* 116 (2004) 406–8.

Robinson, B. P. "Form and Meaning in Psalm 131." *Bib* 79 (1998) 180–97.

Robinson, T. H. "Anacrusis in Hebrew Poetry." In *Werden und Wesen des Alten Testaments*, BZAW 66, edited by P. Volz et al., 37–40. Berlin: Töpelmann, 1936.

———. *The Poetry of the Old Testament.* London: Duckworth, 1947.

———. Review of *Real and Apparent*, by Sigmund Mowinckel. *JTS* 11:1 (1960) 122–24.

Ruwet, N. *An Introduction to Generative Grammar.* North-Holland Linguistic Series 7. Translated by N. S. H. Smith. Amsterdam: North-Holland, 1973.

Ryken, L. *Words of Delight: A Literary Introduction to the Bible.* Grand Rapids: Baker, 1992.

Sanders, J. A. *The Dead Sea Psalms Scroll.* Ithaca, NY: Cornell University Press, 1967.

———. *The Psalms Scroll of Qumrân Cave 11 (11QPsa).* DJD IV. Oxford: Clarendon, 1965.

Sanders, P. "The Colometric Layout of Psalms 1 to 14 in the Aleppo Codex." In *Studies in Scriptural Unit Division*, Pericope 3, edited by M. C. A. Korpel and J. M. Oesch, 226–57. Assen: Van Gorcum, 2002.

———. "Pausal Forms and the Delimitation of Cola in Biblical Hebrew Poetry." In *Unit Delimitation in Biblical Hebrew and Northwest Semitic Literature*, Pericope 4, edited by M. C. A. Korpel and J. M. Oesch, 264–78. Assen: Van Gorcum, 2003.

Schmidt, H. "Gott und Mensch in Ps 130." *TZ* 22 (1966) 241–53.

Schmitt, A. "Zum literarischen und theologischen Profil von Ps 121." *BN* 97 (1999) 55–84.

Scholes, R. *Structuralism in Literature: An Introduction.* New Haven, CT: Yale University Press, 1974.

Scott, W. R. *A Simplified Guide to BHS: Critical Apparatus, Masora, Accents, Unusual Letter & Other Markings.* 3rd ed. N. Richland Hills, TX: Bibal, 1995.

Sedlmeier, F. "'Bei dir, da ist die Vergebung, damit du gefürchtet wurdest.' Überlegungen zu Psalm 130." *Bib* 73 (1992) 473–95.

Segert, S. "Vorarbeiten zur Hebräischen Metrik." *ArOr* 21 (1953) 481–52.

Seybold, K. "Anmerkungen zum *parallelismus membrorum* in der Hebräischen Poesie." In *Parallelismus Membrorum*, OBO 224, edited by A. Wagner, 105–14. Fribourg: Academic Press, 2007.

———. *Poetik der Psalmen.* Stuttgart: Kohlhammer, 2003.

———. *Die Psalmen.* Handbuch zum Alten Testament I/15. Tübingen: Mohr, 1996.

———. "Die Redaktion der Wallfahrtspsalmen." *ZAW* 91 (1979) 247–68.

———. *Die Wallfahrtspsalmen: Studien zur Entstehungsgeschichte von Psalm 120–134.* BThSt 3. Neukirchen-Vluyn: Neukirchener, 1978.

Sievers, E. *Metrische Studien: I.Studien zur Hebräischen Metrik.* Leipzig: Teubner, 1901.

Skehan, P. W. "Gleanings from Psalm Texts from Qumrân." In *Mélanges Bibliques et Orientaux en l'honneur be M. Henri Cazelles*, AOAT 212, edited by A. Caquot and M. Delcor, 439–52. Neukirchen-Vluyn: Neukirchener, 1981.

Stuart, D. K. *Studies in Early Hebrew Meter.* Harvard Semitic Monograph Series 13. Missoula, MT: Scholars, 1976.

Sturrock, J. *Structuralism.* 2nd ed. London: Fontana, 1993.

Terrien, S. *The Psalms: Strophic Structure and Theological Commentary.* Grand Rapids: Eerdmans, 2003.

Tov, E. "Special Layout of Poetical Units in the Texts from the Judean Desert." In *Give Ear to My Words: Psalms and other Poetry in and around the Hebrew Bible: Essays in Honour of Professor N. A. van Uchelen*, edited by J. W. Dyk, 115–28. Amsterdam: Societas Hebraica Amstelodamensis, 1996.

———. *Textual Criticism of the Hebrew Bible.* 2nd rev. ed. Minneapolis: Fortress, 2001.

Tromp, J. "The Text of Psalm CXXX 5–6." *VT* 39 (1989) 100–103.

Trublet, J., and J.-N. Aletti. *Approche Poétique et Théologique des Psaumes: Analyses et Méthodes*. Paris: Cerf, 1983.

Tsumura, D. T. "Sorites in Psalm 133, 2–3a." *Bib* 61 (1980) 416–17.

———. "Vertical Grammar of Parallelism in Hebrew Poetry." *JBL* 128 (2009) 167–81.

Ulrich, E. "The Dead Sea Scrolls and their Implications for an Edition of the Septuagint Psalter." In *Der Septuaginta-Psalter und seine Tochterübersetzungen: Symposium in Göttingen 1997*, edited by A. Aejmelaeus and U. Quast, 323–36. Göttingen: Vandenhoech and Ruprecht, 2000.

Ulrich, E. et al. *Qumran Cave 4 XI: Psalms to Chronicles*. DJD XVI. Oxford: Clarendon, 2000.

Vance, D. R. *The Question of Meter in Biblical Hebrew Poetry*. Studies in Bible and Early Christianity 46. Lampeter, UK: Mellen, 2001.

Van der Lingen, A. "BW'–YṢ' ("To go out and to come in") as a Military Term." *VT* 42 (1992) 59–66.

Van der Lugt, P. *Cantos and Strophes in Biblical Hebrew Poetry: With Special Reference to the First Book of the Psalter*. Oudtestamentische Studiën 53. Leiden: Brill, 2006.

Van der Wal, A. J. O. "The Structure of Psalm CXXIX." *VT* 38 (1988) 364–67.

Van Dyke Parunak, H. "Transitional Techniques in the Bible." *JBL* 102 (1983) 525–48.

VanGemeren, W.A. "Psalm 131:2—*kegamul*: The Problems of Meaning and Metaphor." *HS* 23 (1982) 51–57.

———. "Psalms." In *Psalms, Proverbs, Ecclesiastes, Song of Songs*, EBC5, edited by F. E. Gaebelein, 1–880. Grand Rapids: Zondervan, 1991.

Van Grol, H. W. M. "Paired Tricola in the Psalms, Isaiah and Jeremiah." *JSOT* 8:25 (1983) 55–73.

Vesco, J.-L. *Le Psautier de David: Traduit et Commenté II*. Paris: Cerf, 2006.

Viviers, H. "The Coherence of the *Ma'alôt* Psalms (Pss 120–134)." *ZAW* 106 (1994) 275–89.

———. "Trust and Lament in the *Ma'alôt* Psalms (120–134)." *OTE* 5 (1992) 64–77.

———. "Why Was the *Ma'alôt* Collection (Ps 120–134) Written?" *HvTSt* 50 (1994) 798–811.

Waltke, B. K., and M. O'Connor. *An Introduction to Biblical Hebrew Syntax*. Winona Lake, IN: Eisenbrauns, 1990.

Watson, W. G. E. *Classical Hebrew Poetry: A Guide to its Techniques*. JSOTSup 26. Sheffield, UK: JSOT, 1984.

———. "Hebrew Poetry." In *Text in Context: Essays by Members of the Society for Old Testament Study*, edited by A. D. H. Mayes, 253–85. Oxford: Oxford University Press, 2000.

———. "Internal or Half-line Parallelism in Classical Hebrew Poetry." *VT* 39 (1989) 44–66.

———. "Problems and Solutions in Hebrew Verse: A Survey of Recent Work." *VT* 43 (1993) 372–84.

———. *Traditional Techniques in Classical Hebrew Verse*. JSOTSup 170. Sheffield, UK: Sheffield Academic, 1994.

Weber, B. "Einige poetologische Überlegungen zur Psalmeninterpretation verbunden mit einer exemplarischen Anwendung an Psalm 130." *OTE* 18 (2005) 891–906.

———. "'Wenn du Vergehen aufbewahrtest . . .' Linguistische, poetologische und theologische Notizen zu Psalm 130." *BN* 107/108 (2001) 146–60.

Weiser, A. *The Psalms.* Old Testament Library. Translated by H. Hartwell. London: SCM, 1962.

Wendland, E. R. *Analyzing the Psalms: With Exercises for Bible Students and Translators.* SIL. Winona Lake, IN: Eisenbrauns, 1998.

———. "Aspects of the Principle of 'Parallelism' in Hebrew Poetry." *JNSL* 33 (2007) 101–24.

———. *Discourse Perspectives on Hebrew Poetry of the Scriptures.* New York: United Bible Societies, 1994.

Willi, T. "Das שיר המעלית : Zion und der Sitz im Leben der <<Aufstiegslieder>> Psalm 120–134." In *Prophetie und Psalmen: Festschrift für Klaus Seybold zum 65. Geburtstag,* AOAT 280, edited by B. Huwyler, 153–62. Münster: Ugarit, 2001.

Willis, J. T. "Alternating (ABA'B') Parallelism in the Old Testament Psalms and Prophetic Literature." In *Directions in Biblical Hebrew Poetry,* JSOTSup 40, edited by E. R. Follis, 49–76. Sheffield, UK: JSOT, 1987.

———. "The Juxtaposition of Synonymous and Chiastic Parallelism in Tricola in Old Testament Hebrew Psalm Poetry." *VT* 29 (1979) 465–80.

Wilson, G. H. *The Editing of the Hebrew Psalter.* SBLDS 76. Chico, CA: Scholars, 1985.

Wyckoff, C. "Poetic and Editorial Closure in the Book of Psalms: A Discourse Analytic Perspective." PhD diss., Brandeis University, Waltham, MA, 2005.

Yaron, R. "The Climactic Tricolon." *JJS* 37:2 (1986) 153–59.

Yeivin, I. *Introduction to the Tiberian Masorah.* SBLMasS 5. Translated and edited by E. J. Revell. Missoula, MT: Scholars, 1980.

Yoder, P. B. "A-B Pairs and Oral Composition in Hebrew Poetry." *VT* 21 (1971) 470–89.

Yoder, J. D. I. *Unexpected This Is: A Study in Ancient Alien Syntax.* Chicago, IL: Lucas, 1979.

Yona, S. "A Type of Expanded Repetition in Biblical Parallelism." *ZAW* 119 (2007) 586–601.

Zenger, E. "Übersetzungstechniken und Interpretationen im Septuagintapsalter: Am Beispiel von Ps 129 [130]." In *Die Septuaginta—Texte, Kontexte, Lebenswelten: Internationale Fachtagung veranstaltet von Septuaginta Deutsch (LXX.D), Wuppertal 20.–23. Juli 2006,* WUNT 219, edited by M. Karrer and W. Kraus, 522–43. Tübingen: Mohr Siebeck, 2008.

Index

Lightning Source UK Ltd.
Milton Keynes UK
UKOW01f1518210917
309635UK00006B/1019/P